Contemporary
Political Thinkers

Contemporary Political Thinkers

BHIKHU PAREKH

MARTIN ROBERTSON · OXFORD

First published in 1982 by
Martin Robertson & Company Ltd,
108 Cowley Road, Oxford OX4 1JF.

**British Library Cataloguing in Publication
Data**
Parekh, B. C.
Contemporary political thinkers.
1. Political science—History
I. Title
320'.09'04   JA83

ISBN 0-85520-337-4
ISBN 0-85520-336-6 Pbk

Typeset by David Green Printers Ltd,
Kettering, Northamptonshire.
Printed and bound in Great Britain by
The Pitman Press, Bath, Avon.

To

RAJ, NITIN *and* PIYU

Contents

Revise :

once

once

once

once

four times

Preface

Political philosophy is a complex discipline. *Qua* political *philosophy* it is concerned to understand and to explain political life and is theoretical in nature. Yet it is also *political* philosophy. Politics is a practical activity which is concerned with how we collectively live together, conduct our affairs, make choices, resolve differences and so on, and it necessarily raises moral issues. Thus it requires a form of theorizing that does not distort or lose sight of its practical nature. A political philosopher cannot be wholly theoretical, as a physicist can be, not wholly practical, as a physician or an engineer can be. Political philosophy is concerned to understand and to explain; it is also concerned to diagnose the malaise of the age, to criticize the trends deemed responsible for it and to propose an alternative. Its two primary concerns are obviously not easy to reconcile; political philosophy therefore contains a tension.

There is a general feeling that contemporary political philosophy has not succeeded in striking the right balance between the two tendencies. For some it is too practical and didactic; for others it is too theoretical, formal, remote and reified. Each group thinks that it has suffered a decline, no doubt, for very different reasons.

My concern in this book is to explore the current state of political philosophy as reflected in the writings of some its ablest practitioners. I am interested in examining their views on the nature and task of political philosophy by considering both what they say they have done and what they have actually done. All chapters, therefore, have a common framework but a different organization. Each begins with a statement of a philosopher's conception of the nature of political philosophy, is then divided into different sections depending on the task he has set himself and ends with a brief critical appreciation.

If it is to do some justice to the rich and complex ideas of the contemporary political philosophers, a book cannot avoid becoming selective. Accordingly, I have selected seven of them for a reasonably careful examination. I excluded some because there is quite a body of literature on them, others because they have left behind a powerful school whose members are better equipped to write about the master than an outsider can hope to, and yet others because I found it extremely difficult to enter into their world of thought.

It is always difficult to write about our contemporaries. One is too near them in time, and sometimes in space, to view their ideas with the required degree of detachment, let alone to appreciate the full force of their original insights. There is an even greater difficulty. In writing about eminent contemporaries one is often tempted not to hurt, not to be too critical, and disposed to follow the easy path of uncritical admiration, even adulation. This tendency has to be avoided. If anything, one must be a little more critical of them than one would wish in order to stimulate, even provoke, them into clarifying their ideas, eliminating misunderstandings, answering criticisms and further developing their thoughts. We often regret that their contemporaries did not ask the great philosophers of the past many a searching question we would like to see answered. It would be a pity if we were not to confront our contemporaries with our own doubts and reservations. As Rawls might say, a commentator is a representative of the future generations and owes them an obligation to do what they would do if they were alive.

In the composition of the book I have incurred many debts. I am deeply grateful to Michael Oakeshott and Brough Macpherson for several long discussions over the years. I am also most grateful to Isaiah Berlin for discussing some of his ideas with me and for clarifying several important points. I must also express my gratitude to Hannah Arendt for a long and stimulating discussion several years ago. I am thankful to Ms Mary McCarthy West for her permission to quote from Arendt's manuscripts, and to the editor of the *British Journal of Political Science* for allowing me to reproduce some parts of my essay on Michael Oakeshott which appeared in the December 1979 issue of that journal. Finally, I am grateful to Mr Michael Hay for bearing with the slow progress of the book with exemplary patience and understanding.

B.P.

July 1981

1

Hannah Arendt

Like Husserl, Heidegger, Jaspers, Sartre and others, Hannah Arendt
contends that the Western tradition of philosophy, as it has
developed since Plato, is inherently ill-equipped to study human
affairs in general and politics in particular. In her view, philosophers
were, from the very beginning, impressed and fascinated by the
simplicity, vastness and regularity of the cosmos and repelled by the
chaos, complexity and superficiality of human affairs. Accordingly,
they took nature rather than man as their primary object of
investigation. They devised appropriate bodies of questions,
categories of thought, modes of reasoning and methods of inquiry
and extended these to the study of man. They viewed man as a
natural being, albeit more complex than, but fundamentally not
very different from, other natural organisms and applied to him
such distinctions as essence and appearance, the subject and the
object, appearance and reality and Being and un-Being, that they
had found useful in their study of nature. They also adopted a
spectatorial approach to men, as if philosophers belonged to an
entirely different species. Arendt argues that a tradition of
philosophy whose entire conceptual framework is designed with
nature in mind is inherently ill-equipped to study the human world,
where many of its questions, distinctions and modes of inquiry
simply do not apply, where man is both the subject and the object of
investigation and cannot adopt a spectatorial and wholly neutral
approach. Her basic concern is to develop a view of philosophy
which does full justice to human affairs and sharply distinguishes it
from other intellectual inquiries, especially science.

1

Men ask all kinds of questions about themselves and the world. In
Arendt's view, most of these fall into two logically distinct
categories.[1] Some represent what she calls the 'pursuit of truth' and

the others a 'quest for meaning'. For convenience I shall call them empirical and hermeneutic questions respectively. The terms are not entirely satisfactory, but no others capture Arendt's intended distinction as well as they do.[2]

The empirical questions seek information about, or explanations for, some aspects of the sensually perceptible world. To ask the name of your neighbour or the capital of Ecuador, if your grandfather is live, the date when Caesar crossed the Rubicon, how a clock, a machine or an atom bomb works, or how cold weather, sexual frigidity, changes in temperature and earthquakes are caused is to ask empirical questions. Arendt argues that although these questions differ in their complexity and in the ease with which they can be answered, they all have several basic features in common.[3] They relate to the sensually perceptible world, are amenable to empirical verification, yield an objective, public and impersonal body of knowledge, have a common origin in intellectual curiosity and a common *telos,* namely, the truth.

Hermeneutic questions are about meaning. Although the concept of meaning is central to her thought, Arendt nowhere clearly defines it, nor does she deal with some of the problems it raises. Sometimes she uses the term in the Hegelian sense of 'reconciliation with the world'; more often, however, she uses it in the Socratic sense of 'significance' or 'worth of things'. Again, sometimes she says that a meaning is conferred by a human agent, but more often that it is discovered by him. For Arendt, then, to ask to know the meaning of an activity, an object, an experience, an institution or a form of life is to ask to know about its significance or worth, that is, whether and why it is valuable and worth doing or supporting.

Arendt argues that, like empirical questions, hermeneutic questions can be asked at different levels and in different contexts.[4] I may inquire into the meaning of a particular experience in my life or that of such organized activities and institutions as the pursuit of knowledge, education, art, the conquest of nature and the state. Going a step further, I may be perplexed about the meaning of a way of life geared to the accumulation of wealth and may wonder if other ways of life are nobler and more worthy of a human being. At the most basic level, I may ask if life itself has any meaning. Like worms and insects, men are born, live out their allotted spans of life and vanish without a trace. I may wonder if my life or human life in general has any point or meaning, whether it has any more worth than that of an insect, why I would be wrong to commit suicide, or why I am justified in killing a wasp but not a waspish neighbour. In Arendt's view, the quest for meaning is ultimately a desire to know what is worth doing or approving, what form of life is worth living, what kind of behaviour is worthy of a human being, and why. It owes its origin to the twofold fact that men cannot avoid making choices and that, as rational beings, they cannot help asking what choices are rational, and why.[5]

Arendt argues that although hermeneutic questions differ greatly in their complexity, they share several basic features. First, they are non-empirical in nature. They do not ask if a thing exists, when it originated, how it works or is caused, but what its significance or worth is. Thus they cannot be answered on the basis of empirical knowledge of the world. No amount of empirical information can tell me why human life has greater worth than that of an insect, nor what behaviour is unworthy of a human being. Second, hermeneutic questions have their origin not in ignorance or curiosity about the world but in existential perplexity. Men undertake activities, undergo sufferings, encounter experiences and choose between forms of life whose point or significance is not obvious to them. As rational beings, they feel the 'need' to 'make sense' of, and give a 'satisfactory account' of, these in order that they can respond to them in an intelligent manner. Third, since hermeneutic questions are non-empirical in nature, the answers to them cannot be verified or falsified but only defended by arguments, and they cannot be judged true or false, only plausible or implausible, insightful or banal.

For Arendt, then to determine the meaning of something is to determine its significance. She is somewhat ambiguous about how its significance should be determined. Her general view seems to be that the significance of a thing is determined by its location within a larger relevant framework, the identification of its place in this framework and an assessment of its contribution. For example, if I wish to determine the meaning of a particular experience of mine, my life constitutes the relevant framework. I need to analyse the experience, relate it to my other experiences, locate it within my pattern of life and elucidate what it tells me about myself and how it affects my life. If I wish to determine the meaning of a particular historical event, I need to locate and analyse it within the context of the history of the nation concerned. If I wish to determine the meanings of culture, art, the pursuit of knowledge, forms of life and life itself, I need to locate them within the widest possible framework available to man. In Arendt's view, human existence constitutes such a framework. Accordingly, she argues that in order to determine the significance of such activities and institutions, one needs to develop a general perspective on human existence and assess their contributions to it.

For Arendt science and philosophy are paradigmatic expressions, respectively, of man's search for truth and meaning.[6] As such, they are 'fundamentally different' modes of inquiry.[7] Science inquires into 'what is', philosophy into 'what it means for it to be'. Science is motivated by a passionate love of truth, philosophy by an equally passionate love of wisdom. The 'basic goal' of science is 'to see and know the world as it is given to the senses'; the basic concern of philosophy is to 'make sense' of it.[8] Science aims to provide a most systematic and comprehensive body of truth about the constitution and inner workings of nature; philosophy aims to provide an equally systematic and comprehensive theory of human existence and to determine in its light the meanings of human activities, institutions and forms of life. Following Kant, Arendt argues that science involves the exercise of *Verstand* (intellect) and philosophy that of *Vernunft* (reason). For her, as for Kant, *Verstand* is an analytical and investigative faculty and *Vernunft* a reflective and speculative one.[9]

In the light of Arendt's views on the nature of philosophy outlined earlier, it is easy to see why she takes a somewhat unusual view of the nature and task of political philosophy. She nowhere clearly states it, but it underlies her entire work and determines both her questions and her manner of dealing with them.

As we have seen, philosophy for Arendt originates in the human search for significance, is sustained by the love of wisdom and aims to answer questions concerning meaning. In order to attain its hermeneutic objectives, philosophy develops an ontology of human existence by elucidating the constitutive and fundamental features of human experiences. To make use of jargon, philosophy is a hermeneutically orientated phenomenological ontology. For Arendt political philosophy is a similar inquiry but on a limited scale. Inspired by the love of political wisdom, it aims to answer hermeneutic questions about political life. And in order to answer them, it develops an ontology of politics by means of a phenomenological analysis of political experiences.[10]

As in other areas of life, men are confronted in politics with such questions as how they should live as a community, choose between different forms of political life and government, respond to political events and institutions, decide whether or not to take an active part in the conduct of public affairs, obey or disobey a particular law, support a particular cause, movement, piece of legislation or government policy, and what objectives they should expect a government to realize. Accordingly, the political philosopher undertakes a phenomenological analysis of political life with a view to developing an ontology of it. He explores and articulates the structure of the political world and points out how its different aspects are internally related and constitute a coherent whole. He identifies and analyses its basic features, the fundamental forms of political relationship, the structures of political experiences, the forms of political consciousness and the modes of knowledge relevant to political life. He examines also the ways in which political actors define themselves, acquire public identity, recognize and respond to one another, the different capacities, aspirations, motivations, passions and emotions that underpin or undermine political life, and so on. Further, he examines the institutions by means of which citizens structure their political world, conduct their common affairs, evolve a collective identity, establish a system of authority and enact and enforce laws. By undertaking a rigorous and comprehensive anslysis of these and other aspects of political life, a political philosopher constructs a coherent ontology of politics, which enables him to determine the 'hermeneutic place' of political institutions and practices on the map of political life.

Having determined the significance of political institutions and practices, the political philosopher goes on to determine the significance of political life itself. He aims to know what contribution it makes to human existence and how this compares with that of other human activities. Accordingly, he undertakes a full-scale ontological analysis of human existence along the lines sketched earlier, identifies the specific conditions of human existence that ontologically sustain political life and determines the character of its contribution.

Arendt argues that the political philosopher is primarily concerned to investigate political experiences rather than political concepts. For her concepts are conceptualizations of experiences, and hence their analysis is neither possible nor necessary, except in relation to the relevant experiences.[11] Such concepts as liberty, equality and community articulate and derive their meanings from the relevant forms of human relationship and experience. They cannot, therefore, be analysed or defined in the abstract; in themselves, and taken in isolation, they are simply words which can be defined as one pleases. They become concepts when used to conceptualize specific experiences which determine their content and meaning. For a philosopher concepts have no intrinsic significance. He is concerned to explore the structure of human experience, and he needs concepts in order to articulate his analysis in systematic, theoretical language. In short, for Arendt political philosophy is concerned primarily not to analyse and define concepts but to decipher and interpret the text of political experience. To be sure, a political philosopher is interested not in the trivial details and infinite varieties but in the structures of political experiences and analyses them not from a psychological but from an ontological perspective.

For Arendt then the political philosopher develops a distinct perspective on human existence. He has a carefully worked out theory of the permanent features of the human condition and of man's basic capacities and needs, and a set of general principles by which to determine the relative worth of human activities, institutions and ways of life. In other words, the political philosopher possesses a measure of wisdom, his unique gift to his fellow men. Furthermore, he is a reflective person, possessing both the disposition and the capacity to examine critically and to assess the significance of the activities of his fellow men. In Arendt's view, the fact that the philosopher both loves and possesses some measure of wisdom and has a capacity for critical reflection enables him to play an important part in political life.

Although she does not herself put it this way, Arendt seems to think that the political philosopher's contribution to political life is fourfold.[12]

First, he offers his fellow citizens the gift of self-knowledge. He provides insights into man's permanent needs as well as a set of general principles by which to determine the worth of human activities, institutions and forms of life. Although he cannot advise men about how to deal with specific situations, he can help them to make intelligent decisions by clarifying the nature, range and the likely consequences of the choices open to them.[13]

Second, the philosopher is a social critic, a 'gadfly' who 'stings' his fellow citizens into critical self-examination.[14] He exposes illusions, false promises and attractive but dangerous doctrines and in general acts as a watchdog for his community. Above all, by offering an example of a courageous thinker who is not afraid to swim against the currents of his time, he nourishes the spirit of dissent in his community and preserves the springs of intellectual criticism and creativity.

Third, Arendt argues that the philosopher is the custodian of the integrity of human existence. Unlike most of his fellow citizens, who are generally preoccupied with their material interests, the philosopher has a clear vision of human capacities and potentialities. He asserts the possibilities of human existence, recalls his contemporaries to their potentialities and awakens in them both guilt at what they are and pride in what they can become.

Finally, Arendt argues that the philosopher stands guard over the public realm and preserves its integrity.[15] For her, political life, like human affairs in general, is a realm of opinion. There are no political truths which a political community can be expected to realize. Differently situated men view the world from their different perspectives and arrive at different opinions. As she puts it, a *doxa* is the 'formulation in speech of that *dokai moi,* what appears to me'. It represents my 'view' of the world from my distinct location in it. If a common and shared public world is to be created, different opinions must engage in a meaningful dialogue. In Arendt's view, the philosopher plays a vital role both in creating the necessary conditions for, and in sustaining, the dialogue. He critically examines conflicting opinions, points out their limitations and prevents them from hardening into dogmas. He elucidates also men's common assumptions, if any, highlights their insights, encourages a dialogue between them and helps them to arrive at a richer view of their common world. He might also demonstrate the restrictive character of the prevailing universe of discourse and help to loosen its constraints. In these and other ways the political philosopher exposes ideological rigidity and blindness, unclogs the channels of communication, increases mutual understanding among his fellow citizens and 'helps establish the common world'.

2

Arendt divides human activities into two broad categories, namely, the theoretical and the practical. Since the former is not relevant to our discussion, we shall ignore it.

For Arendt the world of practice – or what she calls the *vita activa* – consists of three fundamental human activities: labour, work and action. Her reasons for classifying them in this way and her principles of classification are to be found in her general conception of man. For Arendt man is distinguished from the rest of the natural world by his capacity for freedom or transcedence. All objects and organisms in the world have a nature, in the sense that they have a specific set of properties which are inherent in them and determine their behaviour. Hence we call them natural objects, or organisms, and the world they compose a natural world, or simply nature. To say that man has a nature is to imply that he is essentially like a stone or a tree, only more complex. For Arendt such a view reduces the difference between man and nature merely to one of degree and fails to appreciate his *qualitatively* distinct identity.[16]

Man is unique in nature in possessing the capacity for freedom. By freedom Arendt means not a capacity for choice, which animals too possess and exercise, but a capacity to 'transcend' what is given and to 'begin' something new. Unlike other beings, which are constitutionally obliged to behave in specific ways, man is uniquely capable of interrupting natural and social processes and of starting new ones of his own. He is, therefore, the most 'unnatural' member of the natural world and enjoys an 'exceptional' status. No doubt, man has both a body and what Arendt, following Aristotle, calls a soul, or psyche. The human body is like any other natural object, in the sense that it too has a determinate nature and is governed by laws. Similarly, the human psyche, the 'inner life' of moods, passions, emotions and feelings, has its own nature, follows its own rhythm and is largely beyond human control. The moods and passions continually succeed and dissolve into one another and are, like bodily processes, governed by their own laws. Man is, however, not merely a body endowed with a psyche. He is a *human* being, a being endowed with a mind and capable of self-transcendence and freedom. *Qua* human, he not only has no nature but it is of his 'essence' not to have a nature. To the extent that he has a nature, he is not human; and to the extent that he is human, he has no nature. For Arendt the phrase 'human nature' is a contradiction in terms.

Taking nature as her point of reference, Arendt divides human activities into three categories: first, those in which man is lost in nature and indistinguishable from the animal; second, those in which he 'masters' and 'lords over' nature and creates a distinctively human world; and third, those in which he 'transcends' nature altogether and, like Kant's noumenal being, acts as a free and transcendent being. Arendt calls the three activities labour, work and action respectively.

For Arendt labour refers to all those activities whose essential purpose is to attend to life's needs.[17] At the most basic level man must eat, drink, clothe himself, sleep, attend to basic biological functions and so on. He must earn his living, that is, take part in the collective process of material production and secure the means by which to meet his basic wants. He must also preserve the species and undertake such activities as raising children. He is tired at the end of the day's labour and needs relaxation and entertainment. In short, labour covers a wide range of activities which, although different in other respects, have one essential feature in common, namely, they have no other purpose but to serve life by sustaining, preserving, perpetuating or helping it periodically to recuperate its lost energies.

Arendt argues that since labour is required by the needs of the body, which is a natural organism, it has all the phenomenal characteristics of nature. It is necessary and cannot be avoided. It is cyclical and repetitive, in the sense that it follows the circular movement of our bodily functions and recurs with unerring regularity. It produces nothing permanent. Its results are used up by the life process the moment they are produced and must be continually generated afresh. They have no identity and independence of their own but derive their significance from their place in the life process. A loaf of bread, for example, has no other purpose than to assuage hunger. Its existence is entirely one-dimensional. It is made to be eaten, not to last a year, nor to embellish the world, nor to be contemplated with delight. In other words, labour's products are all consumer goods; it produces lasting objects 'only incidentally' and is primarily concerned with the means of its own reproduction. Although necessary, labour is also 'futile', in the sense that the expenditure of human energy involved in it is constantly used up and has nothing lasting to show for it. Its products do not and cannot create an 'objective' world capable of providing men with a permanent home on earth.

For Arendt work is qualitatively different from labour.[18] Like the term 'labour', Arendt uses the term 'work' very widely and subsumes under it all those activities in which man exploits natural material to produce durable objects ranging from ordinary-use objects to everlasting works of art. For her the activities involved in producing chairs, tables, houses, tools and implements, writing a book, composing a poem or a piece of music and painting a picture are all forms of work. To be sure, thinking about what to write or imagining a scene to paint are not in themselves forms of work. Work is involved when a man writes down his thoughts or paints a picture and 'reifies' or gives a 'worldly expression' to his ideas and images.

The products of work constitute what Arendt calls the 'world'. The world is the ordered 'totality of man-made objects so organized that it can resist the consuming process of the people dwelling in it and thus outlast them'. With every durable object man creates a distinctively human world and increases the distance between himself and nature. The world is potentially immortal, and in any case less mortal than man. It stabilizes human existence by imposing a structure on the cyclical rhythm of nature.[19] By creating a physical space between man and nature, it enables him to enclose himself within a man-made world and to acquire a sense of distinctively human identity. Further, the world creates a uniquely human concept of time and replaces nature's cyclical temporality by the distinctively human rectilinear one. Nature knows only the unending cycle of creation and destruction. By contrast, the world enables man to identify the appearance and disappearance of individual entities and makes it possible for him to talk of their birth and death.

Action is one of the most important categories in Arendt's political philosophy, yet the least clearly defined.[20] For Arendt the birth of a human being marks the appearance of a unique being, a being unlike any other in the past, present and future, gifted with the capacity for freedom and self-transcendence. Action refers to that class of activities in which man 'fulfils the promise' inherent in his birth and 'actualizes' his capacity to begin something new. As Arendt puts it, to act 'in its most general sense means to take an initiative, to begin, to set something new into motion', to 'start new and spontaneous processes'. To act is to interrupt what is going on and to begin something new, to introduce an element of unpredictability in the world which can no longer go on as before and must take full account of the action and the agent involved.

Like labour and work, action covers a wide spectrum. In its most elementary form, a man acts when he makes an appearance before others by word or deed. No doubt, men appear to one another because of the very fact that they are embodied and visible beings. However, they remain inert and passive and do not 'count' unless they take the initiative and announce their presence by means of speech or action. By acting a man announces his presence, the presence of a being who is not a 'nobody but a somebody' and must be noticed and reckoned with by others. His presence is now a public event noticed and responded to by others. By making an appearance before others, a human being makes an impact on the world in however small a measure and makes it a 'little better or a little worse'.

For Arendt appearance by means of speech is the minimal form of action and represents one end of the spectrum. At the other end are acts in which an individual is not content to make a fleeting appearance but attempts to change the world, the established social order or specific institutions and practices. Jesus, Napoleon, Lenin, Mao, Gandhi and others acted in this maximal sense. An action can also take a wide variety of forms between the two extremes. Workers challenging the factory management, an academic pleading with his colleagues to change his university's structure and practices, students taking over a university building, civil rights demonstrators, Vietnam draft dodgers, a politician standing up to his bullying constituents and men undertaking acts of civil disobedience are all engaged in action.

Having classified practical activities into three categories, Arendt inquiries where politics belongs. For her it cannot be a form of labour, as it would then have to be seen as a means of attending to the basic needs of life. In such a view, politics is reduced to simple administration; there is no scope for men to take part in the conduct of their common affairs; they are confined to the private realm, denied opportunities to appear in the public arena and to develop relevant capacities and treated not as free subjects but as mere objects of government's actions. Arendt argues that politics cannot be seen as a form of work either, as maintained by Plato, Aristotle, Machiavelli, St Simon, Marx and others, for we would then have to understand it as the activity of imposing a blueprint upon a group of men more or less in the way that a carpenter imposes the form of a table upon the wood. In such a view, men are treated as mere objects, denied the scope for freedom and action and deprived of the opportunity to live a fully human life.

For Arendt politics is best seen as a form of action. It is the activity of conducting the affairs of a community by means of speech. And the *polis,* or a political community, is a group of men united by their common commitment to a political way of life, one that implies that citizens actively participate in the conduct of their common affairs. It is not, however, identical with participation, for citizens may regularly turn up at public meetings and say nothing, or they may participate with a view to promoting their personal or group interests. The political way of life implies not participation *per se* but participation of a kind which springs from a commitment to the public way of being in the world and to all that it entails. Commitment to a public way of life implies that a citizen is concerned about the world, places communal well-being above his own, finds joy and happiness in debating and acting together with his peers, loves freedom, considers his dignity violated when decisions affecting him are made without his participation, takes a sustained interest in his community's affairs, has the courage to act when necessary and so on. Even as monks adopt a religious way of life – that is, make religion the organizing principle of their lives and judge everything in terms of it – citizens in a political community make politics their way of life and so organize other areas that they facilitate and promote the political way of life. Politics is their self-chosen mode of being in the world. Not every community sharing loyalty to a commonly acknowledged authority is a political community. A community owing allegiance to a

common authority is a state; and if the state is governed not by
arbitrary decrees but by laws, it is a legal community. Neither is a
political community, for neither is *politically* constituted. Politics is
not its organizing principle, and its members are not committed to
'living together... in the mode of acting and speaking'.

A political community, then, exists when its citizens are actively
committed to a political way of life. Arendt argues that its existence
is therefore entirely dependent upon what they say and do. Unlike a
state or a legal community, a political community cannot be created
once and for all, nor can its existence be guaranteed by the creation
of a specific set of institutions. For her, representative assemblies,
free elections, free speech, free press and so on are only the
preconditions of politics and cannot by themselves create or sustain a
political community. They do, no doubt, encourage people to
appear in the public realm, exchange opinions, persuade one
another and propose new ideas, but they do not guarantee political
life. At best they can create a stable, 'civil' society characterized by
civil liberties, civil rights, civil conduct and so forth, but not a public
way of life. The latter exists only when most citizens, or at least a
sizeable section of them, cherish public life, prize public matters
more than their private interests and take an active and sustained
part in the conduct of public affairs.

For Arendt the political community is the realm of action *par
excellence*.[21] Men act in all areas of life, but the political community
is explicitly designed to encourage action. It provides a ready
audience; it generally has a long and inspiring tradition of action; it
offers countless occasions for action; and it guarantees 'immortal
fame' for noble words and deeds. Arendt argues that because of all
this the political community inspires and challenges men to 'dare
the extraordinary', to stretch their resources, to 'bring forth what is
great and radiant' and to leave behind inspiring stories. Like Plato's
Ideas, which throw light on the otherwise dark world of the senses,
such shining political deeds 'illuminate' and give meaning to the
'dark' and shadowy world of everyday life and raise the level of
human existence.

3

Arendt argues that in the political community, as she defines it, the
relation between the government and the citizens is radically
different from the way in which it has been generally understood.
The government is often conceived as a body of men ruling over its
subjects and issuing laws or commands which the latter are obliged

to obey. In a political community the government is not an external and superior agency but consists of men whom the people have 'empowered' to exercise the authority on their behalf and whom they are prepared to support.[22] Arendt argues that it is therefore improper to say that the citizens are 'governed' or 'ruled' by the government. No doubt, the government has the final authority to make decisions binding on the community as a whole. However, since its decisions only crystallize and embody the consensus resulting from public discussion, the government's authority ultimately consists in little more than putting a final seal of authoritative approval upon what the vast majority of citizens wish to do anyway.

In Arendt's view, the fact that the government in a political community is not a ruler but an 'initiator' or 'leader' was clearly recognized in Classical Athens and Rome, the two most fully developed political communities known to Western mankind. For the Athenians every political action required the co-operation of other men and had two dimensions. It involved *archein,* meaning 'leading', 'initiating', 'beginning or setting into motion something new', and *prattein,* meaning 'carrying through', 'achieving' or 'finishing'. The Romans too used two separate but related words to describe action. *Agere* meant 'to lead', 'to set into motion'; *gerere* meant 'to bear', 'to carry through'. According to the self-understandings of both communities, a member of a political community initiated new ideas or proposals and persuaded his fellow citizens, upon whose support his initiatives depended, to co-operate with him in bringing them to fruition. An initiative could be made by a citizen or by the government. Like any ordinary citizen, the government proposed new policies, persuaded the citizens that these deserved their support and eventually enacted them as laws. To both the Greeks and the Romans governing meant initiating or leading and necessarily depended upon the support of the citizens. The government's initiative and popular support were two complementary and equally important stages in the single process of governing the country.

When political life in the two communities declined, the link between the two interdependent activities was severed. Initiating was equated with ruling or issuing commands, and popular support with obedience or the execution of commands. This is noticeable, says Arendt, in the ways in which *archein* and *agere* later came to mean 'ruling', and *prattein* and *gerere* to mean 'execution' or 'carrying out'. The interdependence of equals was replaced by a hierarchical structure in which the government, unwilling to 'woo' the support of its citizens, bypassed the process of persuasion and relied exclusively on command. In Arendt's view, Plato was the first to articulate this understanding of the relation between the government and the citizens. For him governing the country is not a public activity in which the government and the people co-operate as equal partners and for whose outcome they remain equally responsible. It is instead an activity in which the government possesses the monopoly of political initiative and *rules* over its passive subjects. For Arendt Plato's view of government as a ruler has had a decisive influence upon the Western tradition of political philosophy; hence it has been her lifelong concern to combat him.

Arendt proposes to revive the 'more accurate' classical conceptualization of the government's relations with its citizens. The conduct of political life requires that someone should take the initiative concerning what the community should do in a given situation and should 'woo' and 'win over' others' support. The initiative may be taken by a citizen or by the government. Since the government is explicitly charged with the conduct of public affairs, it has a greater responsibility to think about them and to propose new ideas. It is *primus inter pares*, and its job is to take the initiative, to guide and lead. It enters the public realm with specific proposals and invites comments and criticisms. After a full public debate, in which it participates as an equal, whatever proposal enjoys popular support is enacted as a law. The government and the people are interdependent. Without their support it is powerless, and without its initiative and guidance they lack a sense of direction. Arendt argues that both together govern the country, and hence the traditional distinction between government and governed or ruler and ruled is false and misleading.

Even as the government is essentially an initiator or leader and not a ruler, the laws are not commands or orders but directives. In Arendt's view, they direct human intercourse even as the rules of chess direct the game of chess and the 'laws' of logic direct thought. Like the latter, positive laws specify what may not be done, not what must be done, and lack the specificity and particularity of a command or an order. Further, although sanctions are attached to laws, they do not constitute their essence. Many ancient legal systems did not provide for sanctions, and even in modern legal systems several laws have no sanctions attached to them. It is possible to conceive a law without sanctions, but not one that does not regulate or direct human conduct. The direction of human behaviour and not the imposition of sanctions is the essence of law. In Arendt's view, laws can best be conceptualized not as commands, nor as descriptive statements of the way people behave, but rather as collective agreements. For example, a law requiring the payment of taxes can best be articulated not as 'Pay taxes', nor as 'Paying taxes is customary here', but rather as 'We have agreed to pay taxes here in this community'. The key word is 'agreed'. It implies that the law in question is no longer a mere proposal but an agreed and therefore authoritative directive; and second, that the citizens have consented to it, are willing parties to it and have given a 'pledge' to observe and to help enforce it.

Since a law is not a command, it cannot be obeyed, only supported. In Arendt's view, the language of obedience and disobedience is derived from the 'age-old notion...that tells us – since Plato and Aristotle – that every body politic is constituted of rulers and ruled, and that the former give commands and the latter obey orders'. Only a child or a slave obeys; a citizen freely decides whether or not a law deserves his support. Further 'obedience' to a law cannot be detached from the general approval or disapproval of a government, for by obeying laws the citizens sustain a government in existence. To obey a law is necessarily to support the government and to help it stay in power. By obeying the laws in the Nazi Germany ordinary law-abiding citizens helped to maintain the totalitarian apparatus of terror. Obedience to a law is, therefore, never mere obedience but a form of support for the government and involves a measure of responsibility for its deeds. As an adult responsible for his actions, a citizen cannot blindly obey a law; he needs to decide if the government deserves his general support and whether he should extend it to the law in question. 'Much would be gained', Arendt argues, 'if we could eliminate this pernicious word "obedience" from our vocabulary or moral and political thought.'

For Arendt, then, a political community is by definition a participatory community.[23] It provides formal and informal forums in which its citizens meet, exchange opinions, persuade one another to action and distinguish themselves. As a participatory community, it is constructed from the bottom upwards rather than from the top downwards, as is the case with all modern states, including the liberal democratic states. In Arendt's view, the political community properly so-called is a 'council state', a 'new power structure' based on a 'federal principle' and composed of 'elementary republics' representing the 'direct regeneration of democracy'.[24] Its basic outlines are broadly similar to those proposed by such other advocates of participatory democracy as Proudhon, Bakunin, Marx and early Lenin. The neighbourhood and ward councils or, where towns are small, town hall meetings constitute its basic units. The councils are not 'local' bodies discussing merely local matters but are concerned with national issues. The citizens meet here not as members of political parties but as individuals expressing their well considered opinions, which they are willing to change in the light of the public debate. The councils elect representatives to meet their counterparts from other wards or towns; these in turn elect representatives to meet their counterparts from other regions, and so on, until the national assembly is constituted. Arendt calls the council state a 'people's Utopia'. She argues that in every revolutionary situation the people involved have spontaneously created and fought for this, although the organized political parties have invariably dismantled it and replaced it by a centralized state. She hopes that although this has been the historical pattern so far, the 'next revolution' will perhaps produce different results.

4

In the previous sections we outlined Arendt's political theory. Parts of it are illuminating; the rest is not persuasive.

Although Arendt's discussion of the *vita activa* contains many useful insights, her trichotomous classification is the source of many of her difficulties. First, the three activities, labour, work and action, do not exhaust the *vita activa,* for many activities, such as making love, humanitarian work and religion, fall outside them. Second, since Arendt defines each activity in terms of the relevant human condition, she is led to define it so broadly that the activities subsumed under it have little in common. For example, as earning one's living serves life, so do eating, sleeping and relaxing. And one can earn one's living in several different ways, such as by working in a factory, teaching in a university and owning a shop. Arendt calls all these activities labour and is unable to specify the characteristics they have in common except the vague and vacuous one of 'serving life'. Third, the three activities are not mutually exclusive. For example, an artist painting a picture to earn his living would seem to be engaged not only in labour but also in work and, if his picture has a political message, action as well. It is not clear how his activity should be categorized. Arendt runs into similar difficulties on many an occasion, and her categorization in each case seems rather arbitrary and dogmatic. She says, for example, that a carpenter making a table is engaged in work, but that if he made many tables in order to earn his living, he would be engaged in labour. Apart from its other obvious difficulties, this form of categorization makes the subjective reason for undertaking an activity, not its objective structure, the locus of its identity, which contradicts Arendt's basic thesis.

As for Arendt's theory of politics, its central insight consists in integrating politics with our general conception of culture. Over the centuries the philosophers have regarded politics as a rather crude and ultimately trivial activity, to be avoided by a man of refined sensibility. In their view a man is deficient if he shows no regard for his fellow men or lacks the ability to appreciate the artistic, literary and other cultural achievements of the human spirit, but not if he lacks active political interest. Arendt questions this view. For her, like morality and culture, politics forms an integral part of human existence. Evan as we expect a man to possess aesthetic, moral and other sensitivities, we must expect him to take active interest in the state of the world at large. Like culture, politics springs from an active interest in, and concern for, the state of the world; hence if a man lacking in cultural interests is incomplete, so is one who is politically apathetic. Similarly, just as morality springs from regard for one's fellow men, so does politics. Politics is the vehicle of morality, for political decisions affect the lives of millions; and therefore a man who is politically apathetic is as blameworthy as one who is amoral. Politics is not a 'brutish' and coercive activity, but a cultural and moral activity which has in its charge the custody of a civilization. Almost like Nietzsche, Arendt argues for the trans-valuation of traditional values. She pleads for nothing less than that we should include among the cardinal human virtues an active concern for the community and the world and should consider it an essential factor in our overall judgement of a man.

Arendt's analysis of the nature of politics is refreshingly original and perceptive. Her view that the government can best be viewed as the initiator and governing as a co-operative activity in which both the government and the citizens participate is novel and provoca-tive. Further, she explores whole new areas of political life that have rarely been discussed – for example, the structures of political experiences, political emotions, virtues and sentiments, political action and the nature of the shared public world. She shows that in addition to the coercive, the political life has heroic, expressivist, inspirational and other dimensions as well, and that it is concerned not merely with the maintenance of order but also with action, the development of character, public freedom, public happiness, the collective assertion of human dignity and the humanization of the world. As she so ably shows, political life calls into play not merely the much discussed human hunger for power but also such noble passions as justice, honour, public recognition, historical immortality and self-revelation. Hardly any political philosopher in history has given as much attention to the phenomenology of political life as she has.

Although Arendt's view of politics is original and offers rich and brilliant insights, it is defective in several crucial respects. She holds two different conceptions of politics and never manages to integrate them. In *Human Condition,* in which she first fully develops her political theory, she advances what she calls an agonal and individualistic view of politics. She argues that politics is an activity in which one strives to excel by doing extraordinary deeds. One is motivated by a 'passionate drive to show one's self in measuring up against others', prove that one is the best of all, become 'apparent' and 'transparent' to others and attain historical immortality. She conceives of political life almost as a sports tournament, a competitive contest in which each tries to break his rivals' or his own previous records. Not surprisingly, Arendt takes as the paradigm of political speech the heroic and defiant polemic rather than persuasion, pays little attention to political institutions and bases political life almost entirely on freely given promises.

In her later writings she takes a more realistic, participatory view of politics. She argues that politics is concerned with the conduct of public affairs and involves co-operation rather than contest, and that a 'politically minded' citizen is motivated by *amor mundi* rather than by a desire to attain glory. She justifies political participation and the political way of life in terms not of glory and historical immortality, but of public freedom and happiness. Not surprisingly, she takes persuasion to be the paradigmatic form of political speech, emphasizes the 'relativity' of opinion, insists on the importance of compromise and consensus and explores new institutions upon which a participatory community could be constructed.

Since Arendt was not aware of the shift in her thought or of the fact that she subscribed to two different conceptions of politics, she capitalized on ambiguity and ascribed to participatory politics a degree of importance attributable only to agonal politics. It makes sense to say that Pericles, de Gaulle, Churchill, Lenin, Gandhi and Mao lived the highest type of active life possible for man and raised the level of human existence. It sounds odd, even false, to say this of an active citizen, a party activist or even a Member of Parliament. Again, it makes perfect sense to say of the great men mentioned above that they left behind inspiring stories and attained historical immortality, but the same cannot be said of active citizens and ordinary Members of Parliament. In other words the type of politics which Arendt glorifies is not a daily occurrence; conversely, ordinary participatory politics does not merit her grandiose description.

Further, Arendt's view of politics is highly spatial and prevents her from giving an adequate account of political life. As she imagines it, the political community consists of unique citizens each of whom occupies a distinct 'location' in the world and forms his own distinct opinions based on his unique 'view' of the world. They have little in common save their concern for the world and common allegiance to the constitution. It is difficult to see how such men can debate and resolve their differences, especially as Arendt insists that no 'common measurement or denominator' can be devised for reconciling the views of differently situated men. She also rules out objective principles and standards and lacks a clearly worked out notion of public interest. *Amor mundi* is too indeterminate to reconcile conflicting views. And since she stresses space and not time as the central category of politics, she is unable to appreciate the importance of traditions in political life. Her citizens exist in a historical vacuum, are not heirs to a common political tradition and do not share an agreed body of values.

Arendt's view of politics contains an area of incoherence and generates a paradox. For her, politics involves great words and deeds. Now great words and deeds require great and noble objectives. One utters inspiring words when one feels passionately about issues involving questions of principle and interest. Since Arendt generally excludes economic, moral and other questions from politics, and since her political epistemology rules out principles and strong convictions, it is not easy to see what issues can inspire men to utter great words. One cannot make a moving speech about the location of a public park or the design of a public monument. Again, it is difficult to see how a man can stake his life on his views and defiantly demand, 'This shall happen or I shall fall for it,' if the issue is not sufficiently noble or if he is firmly convinced that his opinion is necessarily partial and no better than anyone else's. In Arendt's society politics is likely to become a theatrical rather than a dramatic activity, involving a good deal of style, elegant self-presentation and virtuosity but not much clash of powerful passions and principles. Paradoxically the kind of politics she greatly admires is unlikely to occur in her type of society. Her political community is predicated on the assumption that there are no great conflicts of interests, ideologies and moral principles, and that each citizen, not being passionately committed to his beliefs and opinions, disinterestedly canvasses and examines his own and others' opinions and aims to arrive at a generally acceptable consensus. Political discussion here is almost like a leisurely academic seminar. Plato abolished politics; Arendt comes too close to doing so. The reversal of Platonism has the same basic consequences as Platonism itself.

Arendt's phenomenological method is a source of some of her valuable insights. The virtues of her method are obvious. Thanks to it, she focuses her attention on structures rather than on formal features and analyses human activities and experiences as integral wholes. Further, she pays close attention to the differences between activities and appreciates their distinctive character, thereby avoiding positivist reductionism. Again, she does not analyse concepts in the abstract but locates them in their experimential contexts and uncovers the structures of underlying experiences. Despite all their limitations, her analyses of totalitarianism, politics and revolution bring these phenomena to life, uncover the passions and aspirations inspiring and sustaining them and give perceptive accounts of the structures of experiences of those living in a totalitarian society, participating in the conduct of public affairs and engaging in a revolution.

Arendt's phenomenological method is also, however, a source of many of her difficulties. First, like other phenomenologists, she is sensitive to the qualitative diversity of phenomena but not to their relations. She is so concerned to emphasize the autonomous nature of each activity and form of experience that she loses sight of their internal connections. As we saw, her world is a neatly constructed architectonic structure in which each activity is assigned a specific place and required to be conducted in a specific manner. For her labour, work and action are all very different types of activity and totally unrelated. And, similarly, the realms of necessity and freedom, knowing and thinking, truth and meaning are all totally different and entirely unrelated. Her obsession with autonomy prevents her from noticing that economic forces condition political life, that class structure shapes and distorts the language of political discourse, that meaning not based on 'truth' becomes arbitrary, and that action is not 'supernatural' but rooted in, and conditioned by, the natural and social order.

Further, like several other phenomenologists Arendt advocates an untenable form of essentialism and even determinism. Since she treats each activity or form of experience as autonomous and self-contained, she obviously cannot explain its development in terms of its relations with other activities. She has no alternative but to locate its source of movement within itself and to explain it in terms of its own inner logic. Accordingly, she unwittingly equates the structure of an activity with its essence and argues that since an activity has a specific structure, it *must* develop in a specific manner and take specific forms in specific social and historical context. For example, she says that once a totalitarian form of government was introduced into Germany in the 1930s, it had to lead, as a matter of inner necessity, to concentration camps and to plans for global conquest. Once the French launched a revolution to attain economic objectives, it was bound to lead to a reign of terror. Once the activity of labour emerged from the shadowy private realm into the public realm, it had to be subjected to the minute division of labour, for it is in the very nature of the public realm to organize an activity by dividing it into manageable parts. Paradoxically, the method that was intended to enhance our appreciation of diversity and contingency in human affairs leads, in Arendt's hands, to reductionist oversimplification, essentialism and determinism, all of which she so vehemently and rightly criticizes in Hegel and others.[25]

2

Isaiah Berlin

Unlike some other contemporary political philosophers, little work
has been done on Berlin's political thought. Although this is
understandable, for he has not written much on political
philosophy and is generally seen as an historian of ideas, it is
nonetheless a pity. As we shall see, he has challenged many of the
basic assumptions of traditional political philosophy and has
subverted some of its cherished doctrines. His thought, further,
articulates a distinct perspective on political life, which is in many
ways refreshingly original.

1

According to Berlin, men ask all kinds of questions about
themselves and the world. The bulk of them fall into one of two
major categories, namely, the empirical and the formal.[1] Empirical
questions seek invormation about, or explanations for, the world
and are answered by means of direct or indirect observation and
inference from observed data. Questions asked by the natural
sciences, some social sciences and history belong to this category.
Formal questions do not provide information about the world.
They relate to certain axioms and to transformation rules
concerning how to derive one set of propositions from another.
Mathematics, formal logic and other deductive disciplines are
examples of this.

Berlin argues that although formal and empirical questions
differ in significant respects, they have several features in
common. They are identifiable with relative ease, in the sense that
we can tell whether a question is formal or empirical in nature.
And once we have identified its nature, we know how to go about
answering it. We may not know the answer, but we know where to
look for one. Further, the concepts in terms of which the two types
of question are formulated, the methods of answering them and

the procedures for checking the answers are all fairly clear, easily identifiable and widely agreed among the practitioners of the relevant disciplines.

According to Berlin, philosophical questions fall into neither of these two well organized compartments. While we generally know how they *cannot* be answered, we do not always know how they *can* be. As Berlin puts it, 'We do not feel sure how to set about clearing our minds, finding out the truth, accepting or rejecting earlier answers to these questions.' For him the absence of any clear conception of how to look for the answer to a nagging inquiry is the hallmark of a philosophical question.[2] He does not wish to suggest that lack of clarity about the way to answer a question is enough to make it philosophical, for, as he himself acknowledges, this is also the case with many non-philosophical questions. Berlin does not specify what further characteristics distinguish philosophical questions. His reason seems to be that they are of many different types and do not have any single feature in common. Thus they cannot be defined, although they can be identified. In his view, questions about the grounds of human beliefs, the nature, structure, basic categories and assumptions of human activities, forms of inquiry and ways of life, and the permanent features of man and the world are all philosophical questions. Berlin's point would become clear if we took a few examples.

Every human activity is based on certain concepts, rests on specific assumptions, has specific aims and employs various models as aids to self-understanding. Physicists freely use such concepts as light, mass, energy, gravity, measurement and time, and lawyers use such concepts as guilt, innocence, justice and responsibility. Both generally regard their respective concepts as unproblematic. And consequently they think *in terms of* them but not *about* them. The philosopher is concerned to think *about* these concepts and to elucidate their nature and meaning. He asks what exactly we mean by light, energy, guilt or innocence, under what conditions the concepts become applicable, what exactly we are doing when we measure something or pronounce someone guilty, and so on. The concepts, further, rest on certain assumptions which inform and shape their meanings. Such concepts as guilt, innocence and responsibility make sense only if certain assumptions are made about the nature and capacities of man. Lawyers do not notice the assumptions because they take the concepts for granted. And since the assumptions go undetected, they 'get smuggled into our conclusions'. The philosopher interrogates the concepts and elucidates and criticizes their underlying assumptions.

Berlin argues that we think in terms not only of concepts but also of what he calls paradigms or models.[3] The latter constitute the 'hidden structure of our thought' and inform the way in which we think about specific activities and forms of inquiry. For example, ordinary men and even natural and social scientists tend to think of society, the universe or the human body as a machine, an organism, a process and so on. These models generate their own language, concepts, images and ideas, and shape our attitudes and beliefs in all sorts of ways of which we are never fully aware.[4] In Berlin's view, we cannot dispense with the models altogether, for it is almost impossible to 'think at all' without them. To think is to impose a measure of order on our experience. Since several areas of our experience are opaque or relatively unfamiliar to us, we make sense of them only by 'consciously or unconsciously' imposing on them models based on those that are familiar and congenial. This is as true of ordinary men as of philosophers, almost all of whom have sought to conceptualize their subject matter in terms of specific models. Indeed, says Berlin, the history of philosophy is largely the history of changing models.[5] Now, while the models illuminate some areas of experience, they distort others. Unless we articulate them, we cannot understand why people think and argue in a certain way or find persuasive certain types of argument about society, the state or the world. Although not himself wholly free from them, the philosopher is uniquely equipped to articulate and criticize the models underlying and informing our thoughts.

Berlin argues that man, the natural world, forms of human experiences and thought and so on have several permanent or historically more or less invariant features.[6] Human beings are characterized by such features as self-determination, rationality, a sense of values, the capacity to distinguish between good and bad and an awareness of themselves as somehow different from the non-human world. And the external world is distinguished by such universal features as materiality, the three-dimensionality of space, casuality and the irreversibility of time. The degree of permanence of the features varies. The basic features of the external world are the most permanent of all. Those of human beings are less stable and universal. Men are historical beings and change over time. However, changes in their basic features occur extremely slowly and, for most practical purposes, can be regarded as relatively permanent. The basic features of moral and political life are even less stable. However, they too are comparatively invariant. Berlin argues that such comparatively permanent features are 'simply given'. They are 'brute facts' and inhere in man and the world as we know them. This is not to say that they are *a priori* truths or logically necessary, for it is 'not absurd to suppose that things could have been otherwise'. Rather, we simply cannot think about morality, human beings or the natural world without taking into account their relevant features and using appropriate concepts.

The philosopher is concerned to elucidate the permanent features of his subject matter. In this respect his inquiry differs decisively from all others. Since he investigates permanent features, his mode of inquiry is not purely formal. And since permanent features are not open to empirical investigation but require critical analysis and reflection, his mode of inquiry is not empirical either. An empirical inquiry into a particular subject matter (say, man) begins, and cannot but begin, by taking his permanent features for granted, for the simple and obvious reason that they are 'presupposed in the very language in which we formulate empirical experience'. An economist, for example, studies how men maximize their satisfactions and, in so doing, takes for granted the ideas of choice, purpose, rationality and so on. These ideas are 'not matters of induction or hypothesis' but 'intrinsic to the way in which we think and evidently...cannot but think' about men. Thus they are amenable only to philosophical investigation.[7]

Since permanent and basic features are qualitatively different from transient and derivative ones, the concepts used to articulate them are logically different from those used to articulate the latter. Accordingly, Berlin suggests that they 'deserve to be distinguished by the name of categories'.[8] We could therefore say that philosophy differs from other forms of inquiry in that it is concerned with categories, that is, those concepts in terms of which we cannot but think about the relevant subject matter. In Berlin's view, Kant put the point well when he distinguished between the content of experience and the categories in terms of which it is conceived and structured. The categories lie so deeply buried in the way in which we articulate and talk about our experiences that we do not even notice their presence. To uncover and analyse them is the task of philosophy.

In the light of Berlin's view of philosophy, it is easy to understand his view of political philosophy. For him political philosophy aims to ask and answer the most basic questions about political life, which are necessarily beyond the reach of empirical inquiries. It elucidates the relatively permanent features of political life and develops the categories in terms of which we 'cannot but think' about it. It analyses the concepts taken for granted by ordinary men and by empirical students of politics. It uncovers the hidden models or structures in terms of which both ordinary men and philosophers have thought or think about political life, demonstrates their limitations and attempts to construct a less misleading model. It analyses the basic assumptions underlying the forms of argument characteristic of political life. And it attempts to answer such 'fundamental' questions of political life as why anyone should obey anyone else, what ends a government should pursue, in what areas men should remain more or less undisputed masters, and how equally ultimate and conflicting moral and political values should be balanced.

Berlin argues that in order to give an adequate account of political life, the political philosopher needs to develop a general conception of man, by which he means a conception of the characteristics which distinguish men from the other organisms, are relatively invariant and are fundamental to the way they perceive, interpret and order their experiences. As we have seen, he lists as examples of these permanent features man's capacity to choose, to formulate his purposes, to regulate his life, to give and demand reasons, to distinguish between good and bad and between fact and theory and to change himself and his environment. In Berlin's view, it is only because all men share these features that they are able to understand, communicate with and share 'a common world' with their counterparts in different cultures and historical epochs. As he puts it, the 'modes of thought of cultures remote from our own are comprehensible to us only to the degree to which we share some, at any rate of their basic categories'.[9]

For Berlin every political philosophy is underpinned and informed by a specific conception of man. Political activity is undertaken by human beings and cannot be understood without some conception of their nature. As he puts it, the 'ideas of every philosopher concerned with human affairs in the end rest on his conception of what man is and can be'.[10] He goes further and observes that a philosopher's political ideas 'depend *logically* and *directly* on what man's nature is taken to be'.[11] Hobbes, for example, took a particular view of man – of his purposes, ends, aspirations, goals, capacities, values, personality, and so on – and arrived at a particular view of politics. Rousseau took a very different view of man and found Hobbes's view of political life totally inadequate.[12] In Berlin's view, the fundamental disagreements between political philosophers spring not from their disagreements about certain empirical facts about man and society, nor from their divergent forms of reasoning or modes of argument, but from their conflicting accounts of man. When Rousseau rejected Hobbes's account of political obligation, he did not claim that Hobbes had not observed certain empirical facts about men but rather his general account of the nature of man was 'in conflict with what…we all know men to be'. In his view Hobbes's very model of man was 'inadequate in principle', and it was inadequate 'because it was based on a failure to understand what we mean by motive, purpose, value, personality, and the like'.[13] Hobbes had, in Rousseau's view, utterly failed to appreciate, among other things, man's capacities for freedom and social co-operation and his aspirations for personal integrity, fullness of existence and collective self-determination. Berlin argues that this is also why Kant disagreed with the naturalists, Marx with Bentham and Tolstoy with Marx. They were not attacking their targets on grounds of 'empirical ignorance, poor logic, insufficient experimental evidence or internal incoherence' but for 'blindness…to those constant characteristics…that they regard as fundamental to the notion of man as such'. In their view, the philosophers they criticized gave distorted accounts of man and therefore of moral and political life.

Berlin argues that since political philosophy is an analytical and critical inquiry, it has an inescapable normative dimension. A political philosopher analyses and evaluates the arguments for and against, and the assumptions underlying, different systems of moral and political beliefs. In so doing he shows which of them are incoherent, vague, misconceived or at odds with man's permanent features and therefore deserve to be rejected.[14] He also places specific moral and political goals in a larger moral context, draws out their probable consequences and relevant implications, explores alternatives, weighs up the arguments for and against the alternatives and shows what the pursuit of them commits one to in future. In these and other ways the political philosopher demonstrates the impossibility of some goals, casts doubt on some others, recommends yet others and proposes certain ways of seeking them. He injects also a dose of healthy and much needed scepticism into political life, prevents beliefs from becoming dogmas and sustains the spirit of criticism. He cannot obviously 'guide people in their lives', nor can he solve particular problems of conduct, but he can certainly clarify their choices, alert them to what is at stake, indicate the implications of certain types of action, relate their goals and problems to the values embodied in their way of life and so on. In Berlin's view although he cannot tell them what to do, he can say 'a very great deal' that is practically relevant.

Berlin argues that since political philosophers deal with the relatively permanent features of political life, man and the world and aim to develop the categories in terms of which we cannot avoid thinking about them, their theories have a permanent value. Their subject matter is never out-dated; it preserves 'a considerable degree of continuity and similarity from one age and culture to another'.[15] Their categories too are never out-dated and can be deployed in different historical epochs and societies. And since the problems they discuss arise out of the relatively permanent features of man, the philosopher's formulations, analyses and solutions have a perennial value and interest. The permanent and abiding characteristics of men create among them a common identity, a common world, a common set of concerns, a common general interest. And it is these that engage the attention of political philosophers. This does not mean that all political philosophers are equally persuasive and interesting. Some who do not probe deeply enough, or ignore man's permanent attributes, or offer superficial analyses of them are deservedly forgotten. The more gifted, however, survive and will retain their appeal until man and his conditions of existence radically alter or some 'new empirical knowledge' revolutionizes our conception of him.[16]

According to Berlin, then, we are entitled to expect of a political philosopher, first, a general conception of man and, second, a comprehensive analysis of the nature, structure, basic concepts, assumptions and ends of political life.

2

Berlin's conception of man can be best understood against the background of his critique of what he calls the 'deepest assumptions of Western political thought'. In his view, the political philosophers from Plato onwards have been bewitched by a combination of rationalism, monism and moral objectivism and have constructed their political theories on the basis of a highly dubious conception of man.

First, much of Western political thought rests on what Berlin calls a 'great despotic vision' of man and the world.[17] Although they have used different idioms to articulate it and have justified it in different ways, most philosophers from Plato onwards have assumed that the universe is a rational and intelligible whole and is informed by a single principle which they have called by such names as Natural Law, the divine Logos, Immutable Reason, Ideas and Dame Nature. Animals follow the principle by instinct. Being rational, men follow it consciously. The answers to questions concerning how men should live and what form of life is best for them are logically deducible from knowledge of the structure and purpose of the universe and man's place in it. Only that type of action or form of life is rational which fulfils the objectively given cosmic purposes and harmonizes with the cosmic structure. Man's purpose, and hence his true perfection, consists in understanding and living up to the requirements of his place in the cosmos. In Berlin's view, this cosmic vision of man, first articulated by Plato and advanced by such philosophers as Aristotle, the Stoics, Acquinas, Spinoza and Leibnitz, was later historicized by Marx and other nineteenth-century thinkers. They conceived of history as a process with a purpose and took man's true end and destiny to lie in fulfilling that purpose.

Berlin rejects the 'despotic vision' on several grounds.[18] He finds 'something absurd in the very asking' of such a general question as the meaning and purpose of life, history or the universe. He cannot see what the question can possibly mean, since meanings are not inherent in things but are given by man. Further, the question assumes that everything has a purpose. In Berlin's view, such an assertion can make sense only on the assumption of a belief in God, and the foundation for such a belief is not rationally demonstrable.[19] He argues, further, that it is difficult to see what could possibly count as evidence for or against such an assertion. Indeed, the statement that everything has a purpose does not even make sense. We know what blue is by comparing it with something that is coloured but not blue. If *everything* has a purpose, we have no means of contrasting purposiveness with non-purposiveness and cannot therefore give any clear meaning to the concept of purpose.

Berlin also questions the view that the universe is an integrated whole, capable of being studied by a single method, articulated in a single system of concepts or explained by a single system of principles. For him the universe is plural. It consists of different types of phenomenon and being which need to be studied by different methods and about which we possess different types of knowledge. Above all, there is a fundamental distinction between man and the non-human world.[20] In Berlin's view, Vico was one of the first to have demonstrated conclusively that the natural and human world require two radically different methods of inquiry, namely *scienza* and *coscienza,* and call for radically diferent sets of concepts. Any attempt to assimilate the two leads to gross distortion and denies what we know to be true about men.

According to Berlin, the second basic assumption of Western

political thought consists in the belief that the good is, and must be, a coherent and frictionless whole. At the heart of Western moral and political thought lies the 'optimistic' belief that even as no true propositions conflict, so no moral values, principles, capacities and ideals can conflict.[21] In Berlin's view, some philosophers have gone even further and have argued not only that all good things are compatible but also that they necessarily entail one another. And if they are seen to conflict, that can be only because men are ignorant or insufficiently rational or because their society is not rationally organized.[22] In Berlin's view, the belief appears in one form or another in the works of most political philosophers. It is strikingly evident in the fact that hardly any major philosopher has systematically discussed the nature of the conflict between human capacities and values and the problems arising from it. According to Berlin, the belief also underlies the 'radical patter' that true liberties never conflict, and that if others are not free, I am not free either.[23] It underlies also the widespread view that if two values or ideals conflict, one of them is not 'true', or is improperly defined, or is not a value at all. Many a philosopher has argued that only a life lived according to reason is truly free. When it is pointed out to them that some or most men may freely decide otherwise, their standard rejoinder has been that this freedom so to choose is not 'true' or 'real' freedom, and that freedom 'properly so called' never contradicts reason.

Berlin rejects this view on several grounds. For him the conflicts between values, principles, human capacities and so on are the fundamental and inescapable features of human life and cannot in principle be eliminated.[24] In his view, Machiavelli's great contribution lay in highlighting this fact.[25] Machiavelli distinguished two systems of morality: the morality of the pagan world, stressing such values as courage, vigour, valour, honour, self-assertion and public achievement, and Christian morality, with its emphasis on such values as charity, mercy, self-abnegation, anonymity, sacrifice, forgiveness and contempt for worldly goods and honours. For Machiavelli, according to Berlin, the two systems are both 'ultimate'. These are 'not two "autonomous" regions, one of "ethics", another of "politics", but two (for him) exhaustive alternatives between two conflicting systems of value'. If a man chooses one, he must give up all hope of living by the other. And he cannot make the choice on the basis of certain allegedly higher principles.[26]

Berlin argues that even as values conflict, so do human capacities and aspirations.[27] For example, rationalists have argued that knowledge is always a good thing, and indeed that it is the *sine qua non* of freedom. Berlin argues that while this is true in some cases, it is not so in others. A singer may lose his capacity to sing if he becomes acutely self-conscious or is persuaded that his songs or his wish to sing have ugly psychological roots. Scientific knowledge of the natural and human world may destroy the myths and illusions that sustain a poet's poetry and may dry up his sources of inspiration. At a different level the attempts required to develop one set of capacities may render a man incapable of developing others.[28] To be a good scientist may involve despairing of ever being a good poet, or a philosopher, or an athlete. And the attempt to develop to the highest degree the capacity for abstract thinking may mean losing the capacities for personal affection or aesthetic and moral enjoyment.

According to Berlin, the third fundamental assumption of Western political thought is related to the second and consists in the belief that it is possible to form, and even to realize, a conception of a perfect man or a perfect society. For Berlin this belief is 'one of the oldest and most deeply persuasive elements in Western thought' and has given rise to images of the Golden Age, the Garden of Eden, the rational society and the classless communist society, which are all imagined either to have once existed or to be capable of being achieved in the future. Berlin argues that from Plato onwards moral and political philosophers have devoted considerable energy to inquiring into the best form of personal or social life. And even historically minded philosophers who have appreciated the diversity of forms of life have assumed that they were all moving, each in its own way, towards the same destination.

In Berlin's view, the concepts of a perfect man and a perfect society are incoherent and absurd.[29] As we have seen, human capacities, aspirations and values conflict, and they do so necessarily. As Berlin puts it, the great qualities of Achilles cannot, by their very nature, be combined with those of the Buddha or Spinoza. Further, men can live morally in several different and incompatible ways, and they must choose one among them. It is logically impossible to combine them all into a harmonious whole; hence the concept of a perfect man is incoherent. Berlin argues that the concept of a perfect society is equally incoherent. Different societies develop different human capacities and pursue different goals and values. Human capacities cannot be developed in the abstract. They presuppose, and can only grow within, appropriate patterns of social relations. Each culture or social structure provides a soil conducive to the growth of some but not other human capacities, values and forms of human excellence. For Berlin each has its own centre of gravity, represents a uniquely wonderful exfoliation of the human spirit and is valuable in itself and not as a step towards an allegedly higher form of life. Each is 'self-validating' and realizes an 'ideal of indefeasible validity'. Since each is self-contained, they cannot all be combined into a frictionless whole. If we choose to emulate the Greeks, we cannot also emulate the Hebrews or the Florentines of the Renaissance. Further, since each form of life is an integrated whole, their components cannot be abstracted and sewn together into a seamless garment. Berlin concludes that for these and other reasons the notion of a perfect society in which men can realize all their potentialities is 'not merely utopian but incoherent' and 'literally absurd'.[30]

According to Berlin, the fourth fundamental assumption of Western thought is its moral monism. Philosophers from Plato onwards have believed that moral and political values can be hierarchically graded, and that it is both possible and necessary to classify and grade different forms of life. In their view, all values are reducible to one, which sums up their essence and is embodied in them in different degrees. Moral monism may take obvious or invidious forms. It is easily recognizable in Plato, the Christian philosophers and Marx, who respectively emphasized the absolute supremacy of the life of reason, the vision of God and the classless society. It is less easily recognizable but nonetheless present in the liberal writers who have stressed the absolute value of liberty and have either rejected or welcomed equality, social justice and so on as hostile or essential to it. For them these values are not autonomous and independent but derive their importance from their relation to liberty. The egalitarians make the same monistic assumption when they welcome such values as liberty, justice, solidarity, community and friendship as essential to the fullest realization of the principle of equality. For them too these are not all independent values but necessary means to, or conditions of, equality, with which allegedly they can never conflict.

Berlin finds moral monism an untenable doctrine. In his view, there is no single value or principle to which all others can be reduced. Such obvious candidates as reason, utility, happiness and self-realization are so vague that they cannot specify what kind of life or conduct incarnates them. As we try to make them specific, we need to resort to other values.[31] A happy life can be a life of freedom or of servitude and may be devoted to the pursuit of knowledge or wisdom, or to counting the blades of grass in a garden, or to making a nuisance of oneself. By itself the principle of happiness cannot tell us how to choose among these. Further, Berlin cannot see how all the different values can be reduced to any one of them. Each refers to a distinct human experience or relationship and has a distinct nature and distinct requirements. Liberty refers to the opportunity to make unhindered choices, equality to the relationship between a group of men, community to their collective ethos and spirit, and so on. They are all different, even disparate and discrete, and cannot possibly be reduced to a single value.

It is against the background of Berlin's criticisms of some of the central assumptions of Western political thought that his conception of man can best be understood. Like most other philosophers, he defines man in terms of his essence and defines the latter in terms of the characteristics that distinguish man from the non-human world. For Berlin man is distinguished by his capacity for 'autonomy' or 'self-determination'. He is unique in being able to choose ahd pursue his purposes and regulate his life. He is not a 'natural object', played upon and determined by external factors, but a being capable of directing and determining his own actions. As Berlin puts it, the 'essence of men is that they are autonomous beings', and freedom is their unique and 'principal characteristic'. Man is most himself in choosing rather than being chosen for and realizes and develops himself in the course of making free choices.[32] Berlin uses the terms 'autonomy', 'self-determination' and 'choice' interchangeably and seems to think that the capacity for self-determination is somehow inherent in man.

For Berlin, then, man is an autonomous being. Since he is autonomous and capable of formulating his own ends, he is an end in himself. As Berlin says, it is their capacity for autonomy 'which makes men and their values ultimate'.[33] Men, and not natural objects or animals, have dignity because they differ in significant respects. Berlin observes:[34]

> If I am told not to treat something as a chair, the reason for this may be the fact that the object in question possesses some attribute which ordinary chairs do not, or has some special association for me or others which distinguishes it from ordinary chairs, a characteristic which might be overlooked or denied. Unless men are held to possess some attribute over and above those which they have in common with other natural objects - animals, plants, things, etc. - (whether this difference is itself called natural or not), the moral command not to treat men as animals or things has no rational foundation.

Since man is capable of choice and will, to block his choice is 'to sin against the truth that he is a man, a being with a life of his own to live'.[35] To coerce men to pursue goals they have not themselves chosen or whose point they do not see is 'to deny their human essence', to treat them as 'objects without wills of their own and therefore to degrade them'.[36] To use them as means, even for their own benefit, is to treat them as subhuman, which is 'a contradiction' of what we know men to be. Berlin, then, seems to take a rather extreme view of autonomy and comes close to Sartre. For him man is the highest being in the world, an end in himself. As such he is the only locus of value.

His freely chosen purposes are his choices and therefore possess the value that is inherent in him. As Berlin says, there is 'no principle or value higher than the ends of the individual'. This seems to imply that nothing is a value in itself; it only becomes so when accepted as such by men. Berlin lends support to this view when he observes that men are 'the sole authors of all principles and all values', and that all moral values 'are made so by the free acts of man, and called values only so far as they are his'. Since there is nothing higher than the purposes of the individual, Berlin maintains that there is no principle in the name of which men can be treated as means and their dignity violated.

Berlin argues that as autonomous beings, men choose their purposes and values. Since for Berin nothing is a value prior to and independently of human choice, it is difficult to see what he means by choosing values. He must be taken to mean that certain things are values in themselves, independently of human choice. For Berlin some values that men choose are means to other values; the latter, however, are ultimate. The ultimate values are all 'equally ultimate and sacred'.[37] There is no higher standard by which they can be assessed, no absolute value to which they can be all reduced, no common moral currency in terms of which their conflicts can be expressed and resolved. Since they are 'incommensurable', a choice between them must be made 'for no better reason than that each value is what it is'. The considerations of 'rationality and calculation' can be applied to means and subordinate ends but 'never' to ultimate ends. Equality or liberty, for example, is 'neither more nor less rational than any other ultimate principle; indeed, it is difficult to see what is meant by considering it either rational or non-rational.' An ultimate value needs 'neither explanation nor justification, being itself that which explains other rules or ethical principles'. We choose some values rather than others because in the last analysis we 'find that we are unprepared to live in any other way'.[38]

Berlin argues, further, that the ultimate values are often

'incompatible' and 'irreconcilable'. Some can be realized only at the expense of others. They conflict 'intrinsically' and not because of human ignorance, or some deficiency in the structure of society, or the human condition. Thus to choose some is to reject others, and almost every gain involves a loss. As Berlin puts it, the need to 'sacrifice some ultimate values to others' is a 'permanent characteristic of the human predicament'.[39] It is not only Utopian but conceptually incoherent to believe that there could ever be a condition of life in which collisions of values were for ever forestalled and painful choices permanently avoided.

For Berlin, then, there are several permanent truths about human existence. Men are autonomous and self-determining beings who can, and wish to, choose their purposes and values. As such, they have dignity. There is nothing higher than them to which they can be seen as means; they determine their own ends and in that sense are ends in themselves. As autonomous beings, they cannot avoid choosing what values they wish to live by. There are many such irreducible, ultimate, absolute and sacred values.[40] They are incommensurable, often incompatible and involved in 'perpetual rivalry with one another'. Since they conflict, men cannot avoid making choices between values. All choices involve loss and are painful. Men must learn to live with this tragic knowledge and must at all costs avoid the 'self-deceit or deliberate hypocrisy' involved in pretending that we may one day eliminate the moral necessity to choose between uncomfortable alternatives. Berlin argues that since pluralism is grounded in the full recognition of these permanent truths, it is 'truer and more humane' than monism.[41] It is truer because it acknowledges the permanent truths about men and their conditions of existence, and it is more humane because it does not deprive men of their freedom and dignity in the name of some objective and impersonal ideal.

3

Given Berlin's views of the basic features of the human condition, it is easy to see why the concept of liberty occupies a central place in his thought. Accordingly, it offers the most fruitful point of entry into his political thought.

Berlin notes that the term 'liberty', which he uses synonymously with 'freedom', has been employed in scores of different senses.[42] He thinks that two of them have been the most influential and aims to determine which is the 'truer' sense.

Berlin's concept of positive liberty is rather ambiguous and encompasses several different senses of the term, which ought to be distinguished.[43] We cannot here disengage and discuss all of these, but we shall concentrate on what seems to be the central idea of the term. As Berlin himself says, what he calls positive liberty is logically connected with the type of rationalism discussed above.[44] For the rationalist freedom and reason are man's distinctive characteristics. Since he believes that all human capacities, especially those unique to men, form a coherent whole, he identifies freedom and reason and argues that freedom consists in acting and living according to reason. The rationalist draws a neat distinction between reason and passion or, what comes to the same thing, between the higher and the lower, the spiritual and the natural, or the real and the phenomenal self. For him reason constitutes man's essence, and hence to live according to it is to follow one's true nature, to be autonomous and self-determining, to be free. By contrast, the passions represent the alien element in the human self, and hence to be guided and governed by them is to be heteronomous, to be a mere plaything of the causal influences of natural forces. For the rationalist only a rational man, a man who lives according to the principles discovered and laid down by reason, is truly free.

As we have seen, the rationalist philosophers disagree about how human reason arrives at these principles and argue that it deduces them from the structure of the universe, or from some transcendental reality lying 'above', 'outside' or 'beyond' the world of appearances, or from the essence of man, or from the laws of history, and so on. Whatever their sources, the principles are considered to be objective, demonstrable, universally valid and rationally necessary. If someone is unable to discover and live according to them, he may be 'guided' or coerced by those privileged enough to know and to live according to them. Such 'guidance' or coercion promotes not only his good but also his freedom. It liberates him from the 'tyranny' of his passions or the lower self and helps him become a truly free and autonomous being. Freedom in the rationalist sense is not only compatible with but also identical with authority, and men can legitimately be forced to be free. As Berlin says, the idea of 'liberation by reason' lies at the heart of positive liberty.[45]

According to Berlin, the concept of positive liberty rests on, and derives its plausibility from, several basic assumptions.[46] First, it rests on the theory of the two selves. Second, it assumes that reason is an objective principle rather than a human faculty. Third, it equates 'what X would choose if he were something he is not . . . with what X actually seeks and chooses'. Fourth, it assumes that the true ends of man can be determined independently of human choices. Fifth, it assumes that there is one and only one true way living a good life. And, finally, it assumes that there are men who can claim expertise in moral and political matters. Berlin skilfully demonstrates the falsity of these assumptions. Since we have already considered most of his arguments, we need not go over them again and should turn instead to his discussion of negative liberty.

As we have seen, the concept of choice is central to Berlin's political thought for at least two important reasons. First, men have dignity and are ends in themselves because they are capable of choosing their own purposes and ends. Second, since they are inescapably confronted with incompatible and equally ultimate values, they cannot avoid making choices: 'Indeed, it is because this is their situation that men place such immense value upon the freedom to choose.'[47] If values never conflicted, 'the necessity and agony of choice would disappear, and with it the central importance of the freedom to choose.' The freedom to make choices, then, is both an expression of man's dignity and a moral necessity inherent in the human condition. Accordingly, Berlin calls it a 'fundamental human need', a demand of human nature or essence.

Berlin uses the term 'negative liberty' to refer to the ability to make choices without external interference.[48] As he says, negative liberty refers to 'a field without obstacles, a vacuum in which nothing obstructs me'. It signifies the 'absence of obstacles to the freedom of choice', the 'absence of obstructions on roads along which a man can decide to walk'.[49] Liberty so defined is obviously a matter of degree. The fewer the obstacles to a man's actual and possible choices, the greater is his liberty. Berlin, of course, appreciates that obstacles cannot be defined independently of human choices and insists that we must take into account not only how many doors are open to an individual but also how open they are, where they lead, their relative importance in his pattern of life, the ease with which they can be opened and so on.[50] The two concepts of obstacle and choice are central to Berlin's concept of negative liberty and deserve a brief discussion.

The obstacles to an individual's choices can be of many kinds, of which we may note the four most important. They may be natural or human. In the case of the latter, they may be placed by others, or may arise out the lack of means needed to execute the choice, or, finally, may arise out of an 'internal' or psychological incapacity or inhibition. For example, I may wish to fly to America like a bird but cannot, or I may wish to travel by plane but cannot because I am held a prisoner or a hostage, or lack the money to buy the ticket, or have a morbid fear of falling out of the plane. The question therefore arises of whether all or only some of these limitations are to count as obstacles to liberty.

Berlin argues that naturally imposed limitations do not constitute restrictions of liberty. They are rooted in man's physical organization and are unalterable and inescapable.[51] In Berlin's view, liberty is affected when the obstacles in a man's way are placed by other men, that is, when they involve deliberate interference or coercion by others. For him this is a paradigmatic case of the restriction of liberty. As he says, the 'fundamental sense of freedom is freedom from chains, from imprisonment, from enslavement by others'. And again, freedom is 'coterminous with the absence of bullying or domination'.[52] It is possible, however, that others may interfere with me not directly but indirectly by making arrangements which obstruct my choices. Berlin thinks that this could justifiably be called a form of coercion and a restriction of liberty, if one could show that the arrangements in question were made and could be unmade by men. Thus the question of whether or not a man's poverty, which does interfere with his choices, is a restriction of his liberty or not depends upon his 'particular social and economic theory' about its causes.[53] It is not enough that he personally believes it to be man-made; he must show this to be the case by means of well considered arguments. Given that all such arguments are inherently inconclusive, Berlin's view seems to imply that there can be no general agreement in any society on what counts as a restriction of liberty.

A man may be unable to achieve his objective for lack of the necessary means; for example, I cannot fly to America because I do not have the money to buy the ticket. Berlin contends that this does not constitute a restriction of my liberty. The absence of means affects the *value* but not the *essence* of liberty, for the means relate to the exercise and not to the possession of liberty. If a man is too poor or too ignorant to make use of the liberty available to him, the latter is not thereby annihilated. The door is still open to him, even though he is unable to walk through it. Berlin argues that to equate liberty and its conditions is to be required to say that to create the latter *is* to create the former, and we know from the examples of communist societies that this is simply not true. It is not clear what Berlin would say if an individual thought that his lack of means was the result of social arrangements and therefore amounted to an interference by other men.

The question of internal obstacles seems to give Berlin some difficulty. He admits that a man may be unable to realize his chosen goals because of the obstacles created by his fears, complexes, illusions, compulsions, neuroses and so on. He admits also that these 'internal' obstacles are 'most formidable and insidious', and that their importance has not been 'understood adequately'.[54] Berlin is unclear, however, about what to make of them. He says that they imply the absence or restriction of 'moral' or 'spiritual' but not political liberty. However, if we were able to show that they are products of social arrangements, they would amount to deliberate interference by other men and would constitute the absence of political liberty as well.

Berlin is ambiguous at another level too. Sometimes he says that internal obstacles affect the value, but not the essence, of political liberty. Even if a man were too neurotic to take advantage of an opportunity, the latter would still in principle be available to him. On other occasions he suggests that internal obstacles may be just as much an obstacle to what an individual chooses to do as the chains imposed by other human beings, and that therefore they restrict liberty itself. This may perhaps explain why Berlin sometimes says that self-discipline, inner harmony, rational self-control and so on are both 'forms' or 'species' and the 'conditions' of freedom.[55] Despite this ambiguity, it is obvious that Berlin fully appreciates the importance of the relationship between psychological and moral qualities on the one hand and negative liberty on the other. In so doing he begins to bridge the chasm he opened up earlier. Some of Berlin's discussion of liberty since the publication of his *Two Concepts* represents an attempt to explore the complex links between the two concepts of liberty.

Having briefly discussed Berlin's concept of obstacle, we may now examine his concept of choice. For him liberty consists in the absence of obstacles to actual or potential choices. Choice, however, cannot be unlimited, since otherwise every man would be free to interfere with every other. Further, liberty is not the only moral and political value. Other values, such as equality and social justice, are equally ultimate, and their claims cannot be ignored. In any political community a proper balance needs to be struck between their claims and those of liberty. Berlin does not discuss the principles regulating such a balance, since in his view that would depend on the moral values of the community involved. His main concern is that, however the balance is struck and whatever limits are imposed upon human choices, there must remain a 'minimum area' of liberty which should be accepted as inviolate and should be preserved at all costs. As Berlin puts it, there is 'a minimum level of opportunity for choice – not of rational or virtuous choice alone –

below which human activity ceases to be free in any meaningful sense'.[56] If it were to be overstepped, the individual would be unable 'to pursue, and even to conceive, the various ends which a man canot give up without offending against the essence of his human nature'.

Like J. S. Mill, then, Berlin thinks that negative liberty requires a fairly clear demarcation of an 'area', a 'frontier' or a 'portion of existence' generally accepted as 'absolute' and 'inviolable'.[57] Unlike Mill, however, Berlin demarcates it on the basis not of those whom an individual's action primarily affects but of a conception of man. For him the area of inviolability is necessary because otherwise man's dignity is violated, and he cannot be fully human, and its extent should be determined by what is necessary for him to preserve his dignity and to develop his basic human capacities. While this is a fascinating argument, it raises several difficulties to which Berin pays insufficient attention.

The conception of man is too vague to act as a principle of demarcation and must be made more specific. Berlin's remarks on this point are somewhat ambiguous. He says that the area of inviolability should be wide enough to allow the 'minimum development of [man's] natural faculties' but does not indicate what he means by natural faculties or what their minimum development requires.[58] He says also that the area must be broad enough to allow an individual to 'conceive' and 'pursue' the ends he holds sacred, but he is silent on what this means.[59] He says, again, that the area should be demarcated 'solely with a view to preventing collisions between human purposes' but does not throw much light on the application of this complex and essentially Millian principle.[60] On other occasions Berlin refers to such rules as the absence of retrospective laws, not punishing the innocent, not requiring the children to inform on their parents or the friends to betray one another and barring soldiers from using barbaric methods. These rules, however, lay down what the government may not do but do not specify the area of individual *choice*.

4

According to Berlin, every philosophical system is informed by a particular vision of reality. This is especially true of his own thought. Berlin is struck by what he calls the 'vague and rich texture' and the irreducibly plural nature of reality. On every subject upon which he has written he has brought to bear the full force of this profound insight.

Over the centuries philosophers have argued that philosophy is a homogeneous form of inquiry with a fairly clear objective, and that its aim is to develop a comprehensive and coherent conceptual framework in which the categories needed to conceptualize the world are all logically interrelated. Berlin questions both assumptions. He argues that philosophy is not a single but a plural inquiry. It asks a number of interrelated but distinct questions, which cannot all be reduced to anyone of them. It analyses the basic concepts, forms of reasoning and types of argument characteristic of different forms of inquiry, life or activity. It elucidates their basic assumptions and the conditions under which they are possible. It examines their ends and inquires if they are coherent, legitimate and worth pursuing. It also critically examines the grounds of moral and political beliefs, the moral propriety of specific human goals and so on. Since philosophy is a family of inquiries, Berlin insists that any attempt to schematize it or to construct a neat definition of it is bound to mean that some types of question that do not easily fit into the scheme will be neglected, undervalued, distorted or defined out of existence.

Berlin also questions the traditional preoccupation with system building. Although, unlike the linguistic and analytical philosophers, he is not hostile to the enterprise, he asks if the attempt to link basic concepts and categories in a tightly knit system does not involve ignoring or distorting whole areas of human experience. In order that they can be logically linked in a single system these concepts must be sharply defined and distinguished from each other, de-concretized, denuded of much empirical content and rendered highly abstract. Berlin argues that the world of human experience which the concepts attempt to comprehend and explain is too rich, vague and varied to satisfy any of these conditions, and that therefore every philosophical system necessarily distorts its subject matter in the very process of comprehending it. Berlin, of course, recognizes that every form of systematic thinking culminates in a comprehensive system, and that such systems are necessary if we are to give coherent accounts of human experience. His point, however, is threefold. First, since no philosophical system can capture the whole of reality in all its richness, each is inherently inadequate. Second, the pursuit of logical coherence conflicts with the attempt to give a faithful account of complex reality. The philosopher must appreciate that his two ultimate ideals are not necessarily in harmony and involve painful choices. Third, although Berlin does not himself put the point this way, he seems to think that the philosopher need not regard system building as the only worthy goal. Since reality is rich and complex, the philosopher may explore and illuminate different areas of experience without necessarily systematizing his philosophical insights. For Berlin the philosopher is principally a thinker, not a theorist. He thinks about a set of problems and returns to them again and again until he has probed them from all available directions and grasped them in their full complexity. What he offers is a cluster of illuminating insights, which cannot all be systematized into a neat theoretical structure.

The pluralist vision also informs Berlin's conception of man. Although he exaggerates the rationalism, monism and moral objectivism of the Western philosophical tradition, he skilfully highlights and criticizes some of its basic assumptions. His discussion of the ways in which various forms of life differently define and realize human excellence, and of why they cannot all be reduced to or measured in terms of a single transcendental or ahistorical principle, is most illuminating and makes many telling points. He subjects the concepts of perfect man and perfect society to a devastating critique and demonstrates that moral and political plurality is a tribute to man's creativity, something to be cherished and celebrated rather than regretted.

Berlin's discussion of liberty is informed by his pluralist vision and contains many valuable insights. As we have seen, he grounds his discussion of it in a wider analysis of the human condition. He shows that the need to make choices and take decisions is inherent in the human condition. It is not something for which only some men or some societies have developed a taste; nor does it owe its origin to an eliminable and contingent condition of human life, or even to such relatively permanent features of human existence as the scarcity of material resources, time or human energy. As he demonstrates, the need to choose is inherent in the very nature and predicament of man, and therefore liberty is a moral and ontological necessity. To be denied it is tantamount to being denied one's humanity.

Although Berlin's concept of positive liberty is rather ambiguous and he takes on more than he needs to, his analysis of it is well taken. In its rationalist version it is not yet defunct, as Marcuse's political thought shows. The rationalist conception of freedom mistakenly reduces the whole man to but one of his faculties, namely, reason. And it equally mistakenly defines reason not as a human faculty, the way men actually reason, but as an objective principle and argues that man is rational only to the extent that he embodies it. When so defined, reason comes to consist in conforming to the real nature or essence of a thing and is identified with truth or necessity. As Berlin shows, the rationalist argument leads to the paradoxical conclusion that since reason consists in acting according to truth or necessity, and since freedom consists in living in accordance with reason, freedom equals necessity! Berlin is right to expose this whole chain of argument and the assumptions from which it derives its plausibility.

As for Berlin's concept of negative liberty, it is, as we shall see, open to several objections. However, his three basic theses are valid. He is right to insist that whatever else political liberty involves, it must include the absence of coercion by other men. He is also right to argue that the concept of liberty involves a fairly clear demarcation of an area of relative inviolability in which an individual is free to choose his purposes and plan his life as he wishes. Finally although Berlin's principle of demarcation is not clearly formulated, he rightly insists that it must be based on what, in a given historical epoch, has come to be accepted as a normal conception of man.

Most of Berlin's difficulties arise from the fact that in the course of reacting against monism, he swings to the opposite extreme and embraces an equally extreme form of pluralism. Since the extremes are tarred by the same brush, his pluralism turns out to be as problematic as the monism he rejects. The monists reduce all values to one. Berlin rightly rejects this. However, he does not accept the view that no value can ever be absolute. Instead he talks about several absolute, incommensurable, ultimate and irreducible values. Berlin therefore does little more than replace monistic absolutism with pluralist absolutism. The monistic philosophy is dominated by one absolute; Berlin's is dominated by several absolutes. The logical distance between the two is short. Berlin's critique of monism is not searching enough or critical enough to allow him to transcend the absolutist framework of thought altogether. As a result, his pluralism lacks openness, does not allow a dialogue between competing values and is not really pluralism but plural monism. His moral and political world remains neatly broken up into several closed and monadic islands, each dominated by its own appropriate absolute.

Berlin's pluralistic absolutism creates insuperable difficulties and subverts some of his important insights.[61] He says that human beings commit themselves to different incommensurable and equally sacred and ultimate values. This would seem to suggest that we cannot sit in judgement on others' ultimate values, however outrageous they may seem. If a man were to commit himself to the value of killing every human being on the ground that the shorter their lives, the fewer the sins they will commit, Berlin's pluralism would imply that we should not only not judge him but also respect him. This cannot be right, for, as he himself recognizes, a minimum morality is inherent in our conception of man. If a man saw no difference between hammering a nail into a wall and into a child's head, we would think that he lacked one of the basic moral capacities we expect in a human being. To think of someone as a human being is to expect him to behave in at least a minimally moral manner. This means that all values, however different they might otherwise be, must conform to, and be judged by, those we regard as minimally human. Radical pluralism conflicts with Berlin's own conception of man and is an untenable doctrine.

It is also untenable for another reason. To say that there are several ultimate and equally sacred values is to imply that we possess a universal and objective standard by which to decide that some values are sacred, and as sacred as some others. Radical pluralism cannot allow such a criterion, and yet it cannot make sense without one. It is therefore self-contradictory. We can press the point further. To say that such things as liberty, equality, friendship, compassion, justice and patriotism are all values, and that murdering, maiming and rape are not, is to imply that each group has something in common and that there is a principle by which we can decide what is or is not a value. Radical pluralism asserts the incommensurability of values and yet requires a general principle in order to define and identify values. It is an incoherent doctrine.

Further Berlin is ambiguous about the nature of value and seems to oscillate between the extremes of objectivism and subjectivism. Sometimes he argues that men 'choose', 'accept' or 'commit themselves to' certain values, implying that the values exist independently of human choice. This is Platonism in a pluralist disguise. Like Plato's Ideas, the ultimate values occupy a realm of their own and inspire men to commit themselves to any one of them. On other occasions Berlin takes the opposite view. As we have seen, he says that there is 'no principle or value higher than the ends of the individual' and that all values 'are made so by the free acts of man'. It is difficult to see how such a view can be sustained.[62] To say that whatever an individual chooses is a value, and that all such values are ultimate, is to imply that the purposes men follow and the choices they make are beyond moral evaluation, and that is simply not true. We do evaluate human purposes, and would not allow a Hitler to claim that his purposes were sacred, ultimate and beyond criticism. Further while it makes sense to say that *men* are the sole authors of values, in the sense that systems of values do not grow on trees but are products of human decisions, it does not follow, and is in any case empirically false to say, that *every man* is the sole author of his values. Since Berlin slides from man in the collective to man in the singular sense, he does not notice that what can plausibly be said about men in plural becomes false when said of each individually.

As for Berlin's discussion of liberty, it has been widely commented upon, and hence a few general points should suffice. A systematic discussion of liberty requires many important distinctions to be drawn, and Berlin does not always draw them. The liberty of an individual, of a group within a state and of the state itself raise very different questions. Berlin generally concentrates on the individual. So far as the individual liberty is concerned, it is of various kinds. Such different types of freedom as the moral, the spiritual, the social, the economic and the political are all logically distinct, raise different sorts of problems and are achieved in very different ways. For example, spiritual freedom, meaning the liberation of the spirit from the temptations of the 'flesh' so as to offer a 'pure soul' in the service of God, not only is not restricted by, but positively calls for, an authoritarian environment, as training for the priesthood and the monastic life show. Moral freedom, meaning the ability to discipline oneself, regulate one's desires and emotions and free oneself from envy, competitiveness, aggressiveness, spitefulness or whatever else one disapproves of, is not always attained by leaving an individual alone and may not suffer from external interference. Economic freedom, meaning, among other things, the freedom to earn one's living and to choose an appropriate occupation, necessarily involves dependence upon others and cannot, by its very nature, be negative. In short, freedom, understood in the negative sense, hardly applies outside political life.[63]

Even as an account of political liberty, however, Berlin's negative liberty is inadequate. Political liberty encompasses a number of things, such as the freedom to choose a government, influence its conduct of public affairs, protest against its policies, debate and discuss public affairs with one's fellow citizens, enjoy easy access to the press, the radio and the media in general, acquire the relevant information about the government's activities, form one's opinions and so on. The liberty to do what one likes within a demarcated area is only one of them. Indeed, it is strictly speaking, a civil and not a political liberty. Political life is inherently public and communal. It involves acting, talking and thinking *with* others, and therefore the liberty it requires is the liberty to act, talk, argue and think *with* them. Political liberty can only be enjoyed together with and in the company of others, not away from them. To emphasize negative liberty at the expense of the other liberties is to give an imbalanced account of political liberty.

Berlin's view of liberty seems to be underpinned by an unarticulated conception of the natural or pre-social man characteristic of the Contractualist thinkers. Like them, he assumes that men somehow come to possess the liberty to do everything they like. Since the organization of society on such a basis is not possible, he asks how much of their liberty they should give up. As he says, social life involves 'giving up some of our liberty to preserve the rest'.[64] This is a strange view of liberty. It implies that an individual enters society already possessed of liberty, that his liberty is infinite, that it can be broken into bits, and that men in civil society are like traders investing in the common political pool portions of their liberty that are as small as they can get away with in order better to preserve the remainder. Like the Contractualists, Berlin assumes that men derive their liberty from nature, not from society, but does not ask if the assumption is valid. If we were to make the opposite assumption, the whole question would appear differently. We would argue that an individual is not a natural but a social being and derives his liberties from society. We would ask not what 'portion' of his pre-existing and pre-social liberty he should be asked to give up, but rather what liberties he should enjoy. We would not talk of *liberty*, for that implies a homogeneous and undifferentiated mass capable of being broken up into bits, but of *liberties*, implying that each of them is specific, distinguishable and related to a determinate area. And, again, we would not say that social life or law implies a *restriction of* liberty, since that implies that liberty predates society, but rather that it implies *restricted* liberties.

Once we formulate the problem of liberty in this way, much of what Berlin says about the loss of liberty appears unpersuasive. He argues that when a man is prevented from doing something, he suffers a loss of liberty. For Berlin to prevent a man from raping a woman or murdering a child is to *deprive* him of his liberty, to cause him to *suffer* a *loss* of liberty.[65] Berlin's argument rests on two dubious assumptions. First, it assumes that the rapist and the murderer have somehow acquired and enjoy the liberty to rape and murder. Since society has not given it to them, they can only have acquired it from nature. (As we have seen, the ideas of natural man and natural liberty are questionable.) Second, Berlin assumes that liberty is *in general* a good thing and that whenever it is 'restricted', a loss is suffered, even though the loss may be compensated by an overall gain. To call something a loss is to imply that the thing lost is desirable. Now, to take our examples, rape and murder are obviously not desirable. And therefore the only desirable thing that the rapist or the murderer has lost is the *liberty* to rape or murder. It is not clear how Berlin can show that although specific liberties may be undesirable, liberty in general is a good thing. Like man in general or equality in general, liberty in general is a myth. There are only specific liberties, and each is judged on its own merit. What is more, liberty in general cannot be a good thing, for nothing can be good or bad in the abstract and outside all context.

3

C. B. Macpherson

Unlike many contemporary political philosophers, Macpherson is a radical political thinker. In an age when radicalism is almost automatically equated with Marxism, many have called him a Marxist, only to be told by the Marxists that he is really a liberal! Almost along among his contemporaries, he has devoted the bulk of his work to one particular tradition of thought, namely, Liberalism, with which he has developed a fascinating and ambiguous relationship. In this chapter we shall analyse the nature of this relationship after a brief discussion of his conception of the nature of political theory.

1

According to Macpherson, political theory is a two-dimensional inquiry. It is both explanatory and normative. We shall take each dimension in turn.[1]

For Macpherson every political theory aims to explain political life. To explain something is to show how it is constituted, how its various parts are related and why they behave in a certain manner. In so far as it has an explanatory intention, political theory analyses the nature of the prevailing political system, the way its various parts are held together, the patterns of causal and other relations between them and so on. A political system does not exist in a vacuum, however. It is an integral part of, and is profoundly shaped by, wider society. Accordingly, a political theorist examines the nature of wider society, its major social groups, the distribution of wealth and power among them, its institution of property, its direction of development and so on and explores the relations between its economic, legal, political and other institutions.

Political theory is also normative, prescriptive, justificatory or advocatory. Macpherson uses these terms interchangeably. Every political theory recommends and justifies a particular type of society, which may coincide with one that already exists or may offer an alternative. For Macpherson to justify a social order 'is to find a moral basis' for it. To find a moral basis for it is to show that it is grounded in, and can be 'derived from', the 'nature' or 'essence' of man.[2] The essence of man consists in those basic capacities and needs which are peculiar to him and distinguish him from the animal. In Macpherson's view, a normative political theorist is therefore led, by the very nature of his enterprise, to develop a 'concept of man's essence'. As he puts it, the 'great question political theorists seek to answer may be put [thus]...What sort of state is most congruous with the nature of man, most in conformity with man's needs and capacities?'[3] In his view, the 'adequacy' of a political theory is to be assessed by, among other things, the 'penetration of its analysis of human nature'.[4]

Macpherson argues that no political theory is ever exclusively explanatory or normative. It cannot be entirely normative because, unless its view of man is grounded in an historical analysis of human capacities and needs and of the nature and structure of social and political institutions, its normative content remains abstract and Utopian. A political theory cannot remain entirely explanatory either, for one cannot explain political life without some conception of what men are like, what they consider worth doing and what values inform their conduct. Macpherson argues, further, that in the course of explaining social and political life, a political theorist cannot wholly avoid making critical judgements. And even if, *per impossibile*, he could, Macpherson cannot see why he should.

Macpherson maintains that although a political theory is *necessarily* both explanatory and normative, it may be *primarily* one or the other. So-called empirical or scientific political theory is primarily explanatory, and its normative content is limited, implicit and inadequately analysed.[5] By contrast, traditional or 'grand' political theory, which Macpherson sometimes calls political philosophy, is primarily normative, and its explanatory content is limited and insufficiently developed. The difference between the two types of theory is one not of kind but of orientation and emphasis. In Macpherson's view, a well considered political theory must pay adequate attention to both explanation and justification. He regrets the 'increasingly sharp division of labour' between the two types of theory on the ground that it impoverishes them and prevents them from giving adequate accounts of political life.[6]

For Macpherson every political theory is inescapably historical in nature. This is so for two reasons. First, unlike a historian of ideas, a political theorist is primarily concerned to understand his own society and historical epoch. The normative and explanatory content of his theory is therefore designed to apply to them. As we have seen, his view of man remains unrealistic and Utopian unless it is grounded in the capacities and needs that men have already developed or are in the process of developing. And his theory can hardly explain contemporary society if it is not based on a full knowledge of its nature and structure. Second, a political theorist does not exist in an historical vacuum. He is a member of, and is shaped by, a specific society at a specific stage of its development.[7] Thus many of the basic features of contemporary man and society appear self-evident to him, and he therefore takes them for granted. They structure and inform his thought and often lie too deep to be amenable to critical self-consciousness.

According to Macpherson, then, every political theory is a product of its age and has a 'time-bound quality'.[8] Since its basic premises and assumptions are 'drawn from' and 'apt for' a particular kind of society, its 'value...is relative' to that kind of society. When men and society change, its premises no longer apply to them, and it turns out to be 'no longer as accurate it was'.[9] If at a later stage a social order were to come into existence resembling the one within which the political theory was conceived, it would once again become relevant. For example, the fundamental premises upon which Hobbes's political theory was constructed were those of a society in transition to mercantilism. After 1688 European societies underwent profound changes, making his picture of man and society less accurate than it once was. With the advent of nineteenth-century imperialism and twentieth-century mercantilism, his theoretical insights once again became relevant. For Macpherson the so-called permanent significance of a theory 'is usually only a recurrent significance'.[10]

Macpherson argues that political theorists have not generally appreciated the historicity of political thought and have claimed 'a wider validity for [their] conclusions than they can have'.[11] As a result, theorists have ended up universalizing the basic features of contemporary man and society and turning 'an historically valid relationship into a necessary and universal principle'. In so doing they have committed two fallacies. First, they have been guilty of historical anachronism. They have applied to past societies the categories of thought that only make sense with respect to the present and have wholly misunderstood them as a consequence. Second, by claiming universal validity for their historically derived views of man and society, they have presented the latter as if they were natural and unalterable. In so doing they have idealized prevailing types of man and society and have placed them above all criticism. Macpherson argues that the danger of universalizing present society becomes more accute the more abstract and general the level at which a philosopher operates. Hobbes, for example, read market relationships into the very nature of man and abstracted away the reality of class structure, whereas Harrington, who stuck close to his contemporary society, avoided the error.[12]

For Macpherson, then, a work of political theory is time-bound and a product of its age. In his view, this has four important implications.

First, the basic problems of a political theory are set by its age. Different historical epochs throw up different problems, which set the agenda for the political theorist. For example, the Greek political theorists lived and wrote in a society which was relatively simple and not market-orientated. This is reflected in their views of man and society. They placed a low value on economic activity, confined it to the private realm, attempted to restrain the influence of economic motives, formulated the ends of the *polis* in terms of the good life and defined the central problems of political theory in moral terms. With the emergence of the market society, economic relations became extremely important. Further, released from all traditional restraints, men sought to maximize their gains and displayed restlessness and aggressiveness in their relations with each other. Macpherson argues that in response to these and other changes, the character of political theory underwent important changes. Its basic problems were now no longer moral but economic, and it aimed to explore not what kind of life was best for men but how to cope with economic conflicts. Moreover, it came to be heavily preoccupied with the problems of order, stability and power. Again, since modern man defined himself in economic terms, the political theorist found it necessary to justify the political order in economic terms and gave such concepts as freedom, equality, rationality and obligation an economic content. As Macpherson says, the unprecedented 'economic penetration' of political theory in the modern age completely changed the latter's character and structure.[13]

Second, every political theory rests on several unarticulated assumptions which constitute the limits of its thought. Its assumptions shape its questions, methods of analysis, basic concepts and answers. The most effective way to criticize it, therefore, is to articulate and scrutinize its basic assumptions. One need not even criticize them. Simply to articulate them is enough, since this exercise demonstrates the 'limits of its vision' and deflates its claim to universal validity. This is how Macpherson analyses Hobbes, Locke, Bentham, James Mill, J. S. Mill and others. Of course, it is not easy to identify the assumptions of a thinker, especially when he belongs to a type of society of which one is oneself a part, as is the case with most of the thinkers whom Macpherson discusses. There is also the further danger that the commentator may attribute to a theorist assumptions which he may not, in fact, have made. Macpherson is aware of these and other dangers and suggests various ways of guarding against them.[14]

Third, in Macpherson's view, the most satisfactory way to understand a tradition of political thought is to understand it in terms of the changing fortunes of its basic assumptions.[15] A tradition of political thought rests upon certain assumptions about man and society. When it is first articulated the assumptions correspond to reality and have 'substantial validity'. As the social structure changes, the assumptions no longer apply. The problems that the new social structure throws up cannot be adequately solved within the framework of thought dictated by the old assumptions, which therefore require revision. As they are revised, they generate a new body of political thought capable of illuminating social reality. Over time the social structure begins to change again, and the assumptions about man and society have to be revised yet again. In Macpherson's view, a tradition of thought can best be studied in terms of how different writers see, or fail to see, the need to revise their assumptions, of how they may only partially revise them, juxtapose old and the new assumptions, and so on. (Macpherson's work on liberalism, to be discussed below, best exemplifies his approach.)

Fourth, Macpherson argues that the 'strength' of a political theory consists in its ability to penetrate and articulate the basic features of its age. The deeper it penetrates into the innermost structure of its age, the greater is its power to explain it and the more persuasive are its prescriptions. For Macpherson, Hobbes was a greater thinker than Harrington, the Levellers and Locke because he articulated with unsurpassed clarity some of the most basic features of man and society in the seventeenth century. Since, in Macpherson's view, every political theory is historically grounded, he advances the interesting thesis that a philosophically satisfactory political theory is one that best articulates its age, and that there is no conflict between its historical and its philosophical character. Its philosophical ambition cannot consist in articulating universal truths about man and society in general, for man and society in general are ahistorical abstractions and there are no universal truths to be articulated about them. Rather, it can only aspire to lay bare the innermost structure of its age. Its historicity, therefore, does not impugn its philosophical integrity. On the contrary, a political theory that aims to transcend its own historical epoch in search of non-existent universal truths will turn out to be neither historically nor philosophically illuminating. For Macpherson the truer a theory is to its age (that is, the more historically accurate and penetrating it is), the more philosophically satisfactory it is likely to be.

Given Macpherson's view of political theory, the task he sets himself is obvious. He is concerned to construct not a universally valid theory but one that is specific to the modern age. Such a historically based theory has two objectives: first, to develop a historically relevant theory of man's capacities and needs; and, second, to explain the character of the modern state and society and to explore how they can be so structured as to realize human capacities and needs.[16]

2

For Macpherson to determine the essence of man is to ascertain 'what it is that distinguishes human beings from the rest of the animal universe'. In his view, man differs from animals in that he has several distinctive capacities. Of these, the capacity for 'self-direction' is the most important.[17] By 'self-direction' Macpherson means the capacity to choose one's purposes and to undertake activities capable of realizing them. Man is unique in the world in having both the capacity for choice and will. Thus he is an end in himself and should not be used as a means by another. 'With all its difficulties this is at bottom simply the assertion of the dignity of man.' As a being capable of freedom, his activity is human 'only in so far as it is directed by his own design' and not undertaken 'at the dictate of another'. When his actions are dictated by another, his freedom is compromised and his dignity violated.

Macpherson argues that in addition to the fundamental capacity for freedom or self-direction, man has various other 'uniquely human capacities' as well – for example, rational understanding, moral judgement and action, aesthetic creation and contemplation, friendship, love, religious experience, materially productive labour, co-operation, wonder and curiosity.[18] Macpherson acknowledges that man also possesses such other distinctive capacities as the capacities to cheat, lie, exploit and manipulate his fellow men, but he insists that they are not 'essential' to man and therefore not 'human'. It is not entirely clear how he proposes to distinguish between those capacities which belong to man's essence and those which do not. Sometimes he says that only those capacities which are necessary in order for man to be fully human can be regarded as pertaining to his essence. This argument is circular, however, for it defines what is essential to man in terms of what he needs to be human and the latter, in turn, in terms of what is essential to him! On other occasions Macpherson suggests that only those capacities can be considered essential which inhere in man and are not socially derived or developed under pathological conditions. For example, he says that men are not greedy 'by nature' but are 'only made so by the market society'. Although plausible, the distinction between the natural and the socially derived runs into obvious difficulties. Musical, artistic and other capacities are all socially derived, yet Macpherson calls them essential to man. Besides, the market society develops several other capacities as well, which Macpherson welcomes. As for the concept of pathological social conditions, it requires a standard which can only be derived from an independently formulated concept of human essence.

For the most part, Macpherson seems to think that those capacities are to be considered essential to man which can be harmoniously developed by all. The capacities that harm others or can be developed by some only by preventing others from realizing theirs are not 'morally justifiable' and cannot be essential to fully human development. For Macpherson, then, the harmonious development of a capacity by all men is the criterion by which to decide whether or not it is essential to man. This implies that in order to be fully human, a man needs only those capacities that are not 'destructively contentious' and, conversely, that essentially human capacities are fundamentally harmonious. Macpherson admits that the latter is a 'staggering' assumption but insists that it is a necessary assumption of a democratic society. He observes:[19]

> the case for a democratic *society* fails without the assumption of potential substantial harmony. For what would be the use of trying to provide that everyone should be able to make the most of himself, which is the idea of a democratic society, if that were bound to lead to more destructive contention?

For Macpherson, then, men have several distinctive and essentially human capacities. A capacity, by its very nature, can be developed only by being exercised or exerted, and that involves action or activity. Macpherson argues, therefore, that man is by nature an active being, not a passive consumer of utilities; he is an active 'exerter', 'developer' and 'enjoyer' of his capacities, a being who finds his deepest satisfaction in exercising his capacities. Macpherson does not wish to say that all men, in fact, strive to develop and exercise their essentially human capacities but rather that many do and that others have the potentiality to and should be encouraged to do so.

Macpherson argues that since the capacities listed above are essential to his humanity, man has a right to develop and exercise them. To describe a capacity as human is to say that man has a right to develop it and others have an obligation to help him to do so. Macpherson thinks that this is so because 'the very structure of our thought and language puts an evaluative content into our descriptive statements about "man".'[20] His argument appears less implausible when interpreted to mean that since man is an end in himself and has dignity, his essential capacities too are ends in themselves and sources of moral claims. Macpherson argues that since the right to develop and exercise human capacities can be 'deduced from the nature (that is, the needs and capacities) of man as such, whether of men as they now are or of men as they are thought capable of becoming', it is a 'species of natural right'.[21]

For Macpherson, then, every man has a natural right to develop and exercise his essential capacities. A society in which this is accepted as a central ethical principle he calls a democracy. For him democracy is not just a form of government, but a type of society. As he says, it is a 'kind of society – a whole complex of relations between individuals rather than simply a system of government'. It is based on the principle not only of 'one man, one vote' but also of 'one man, one equally effective right to live as fully humanly as one may wish'.[22] In Macpherson's hands a democracy becomes synonymous with a fully human society. This explains such apparently strange remarks as that democracy 'requires', or does not allow, a particular conception of human essence, or of human right, or of power. According to Macpherson, the 'democratic quality' of a society is to be judged by ascertaining whether or not it allows the 'maximum' development of human beings possible under the currently available technological resources.[23] The more a society maxzimizes its members' development, the more democratic it is.

Macpherson argues that in order to develop his capacities, man needs what he calls 'power'. In his earlier writings he had used the term 'power' widely to cover capacity as well. In his later writings he distinguishes the two and puts the distinction to an interesting use.

For Macpherson power refers to 'the actual ability to exercise one's capacities' or, what comes to the same thing, 'access to the means of using one's capacities'.[24] If a man can do something but lacks the necessary means, he has the capacity but not the power to do it. According to Macpherson, a man's power is at a maximum when there are no impediments in the way of the exercise of his capacities. The quantity of his power varies with the extent of the impediments. As Macpherson says, 'a man's power...is to be measured in terms of the absence of impediments to his using his human capacities.'

The impediments are of two types. They may be natural, such as the force of gravity and man's physical inability to do certain things, or they may be 'socially variable'. Macpherson rightly disregards the former. Social impediments fall into three categories. First, the lack of adequate means of life: by this Macpherson means both the means of material sustenance and the general level of material confort needed to enable an individual to take full part in the cultural life of his community. Second, the lack of access to the means of labour. Since the exercise of a human capacity requires materials to work on or with, it requires access to them. Macpherson uses the term labour in the broadest sense, that of the exertion of human energy. Third, the lack of protection against invasion by others: if a man is to exercise his capacities freely, he should obviously be left alone by others.

In Macpherson's view, the third impediment is removed when the law guarantees the protection of life, liberty and property. He argues that while this is generally secured in a liberal capitalist society, very little is done to remove the other two kinds of impediment. In a capitalist society the means of production are privately owned, and the vast majority of men therefore have to depend upon a few for their livelihood. Macpherson argues that this has several important consequences. First, during the contracted period the worker's activities are no longer under his control. Since freedom or self-direction is the chief ingredient in man's humanity, the worker suffers a 'diminution of human essence'. Second, the worker transfers to the capitalist his ability to use his capacities. During the time contracted for, the use of the workers' capacities, and whatever value they produce, belong to the capitalist. He receives back a small part of the value of his product in the form of wages; the rest of it constitutes the capitalist's profit.[25] Third, since the worker's activity is controlled by the employer and undertaken under monotonous, mindless and degrading conditions, he finds no satisfaction in it. As a result, he builds up frustrations and resentment, has little zest and enthusiasm left at the end of the day and tends to develop the attitude of a passive and mindless consumer, with little interest in developing his essential human capacities. Macpherson argues that capitalist society involves not only a transfer but also a good deal of unnecessary wastage of the worker's powers.

For Macpherson, then, there are two types of power: first, the power to develop and use one's capacities and, second, the power to use and derive benefit from others' capacities. He calls the first 'developmental' power and the second 'extractive' power. In a capitalist society the vast majority have no extractive and 'negligible' developmental power, whereas a few have both kinds of power. There is therefore a vast inequality of power. Macpherson thinks that this inequality can be quantified and measured. If, say, 10 per cent of the people in a community owned all the capital, each of the owners would possess, on average, extractive power equivalent to virtually all the powers of nine other men. Since inequality of power implies the unequal development of capacities and inequality in the degree of self-direction, Macpherson suggests that it ultimately implies inequality in men's humanity. In capitalist society some men are human, while the rest are 'reduced to a commodity'.[26]

On the basis of his analysis of the nature of power, Macpherson argues that private ownership of the means of production is the expression of a power relationship. It represents not only control over material things but also a form of power over other men. That includes the power to decide who will enjoy access to the means of production and therefore to his means of sustenance, the power to regulate a man's conduct in the first instance during the contracted period of time and ultimately during his leisure time as well, the power to appropriate his capacities and influence the general tenor of his existence, and so on. To say that private property is the basis or bastion of freedom is therefore to utter a half-truth, for the relationship to the means of production is also a 'coercive' relationship. While it appears to the owner, no doubt, as an expression and exercise of his freedom, it appears in quite the opposite light to his workers.

Macpherson contends that private property symbolizes not only a power relationship but also a political relationship. An individual has a right to ownership of the means of production because the law has given it to him. The institution of private property, therefore, ultimately depends upon the government for its existence. It is not a direct relationship between two private individuals but is politically mediated and occurs within a framework created and maintained by the government. Macpherson argues that a system of government is ultimately nothing but a system of power exercised by the governors over the governed. In a civilized society private violence is forbidden, and 'violence, the power to compel by physical force or constraint, [is] a monopoly of the government.'[27] Thus all relations of power in any society 'fall within the jurisdiction of the state'. Power needs superior power to enforce it. This is no less true of the power relation embodied in the institution of private property. The laws enacted by the government distribute rights and obligations. They determine who owns what, how much, within what limits, whether or not he can exclude others, dispose of his property at will and so on, and they place the government's monopoly of coercive power at the disposal of the owners of property. In Macpherson's view, it is wholly wrong to say that the government has nothing to distribute. It distributes some of the most important things in life, namely, rights, obligations and the full weight of its coercive power. The important question to ask about it, therefore, is not *whether* but *how,* on what principles, it can and should distribute these things. Macpherson argues that the state in a capitalist society 'cannot be a neutral uncle: it must serve the interests of capital.'[28] It is naïve to think that the distribution of rights and obligations is dictated solely by considerations of public interest.

3

Since the institution of private property in a capitalist society frustrates the development of the vast majority of men, Macpherson asks how it came into being and whether there is an alternative to it. In his view, the concept of property embodied in a capitalist economy goes no further back than the seventeenth century. He detects four important differences between pre-modern and modern concepts of property.[29]

First, until the seventeenth century the term 'property' was used in a broad sense to include life, limbs, liberties, capacities, rights, and so on. Property was both material and non-material in nature, and the ownership of non-material objects was considered more important than that of material objects and revenues. In Macpherson's view, this broad meaning of property was lost 'in the measure that modern societies became full market societies' and the term property came to be confined to *material* property. He thinks that this was so because in a bourgeois society an individual's ability to develop his capacities depended almost entirely upon the amount of material property owned by him. His capacities, liberties and so on had no meaning unless he had the material means to develop them. Furthermore, his ownership of these material means gave him control over the capacities and liberties of others. For these and other reasons, material property acquired decisive importance.

Second, until the seventeenth century ownership of property entailed two kinds of right: first, the right to exclude others from the use or enjoyment of a thing and, second, the right not to be excluded from the use and enjoyment of such things as common land, parks and roads that had been declared to be for common use. Men enjoyed both these rights, which constituted their property. From the seventeenth ceentury onwards only the first kind of right came to be regarded as part of their property, and the term 'property' came to be defined in *exclusive* terms. In Macpherson's view, this was so because a bourgeois society required the universal marketability of goods and services. And since only the first kind of right could be alienated, it came to be considered the essence of property.

Third – and this is really a consequence of the second – in a bourgeois society the right to dispose of a thing came to be considered a crucial component of the right to ownership of property. It was not enough that one was able to use and enjoy something; one had to be able to sell it, destroy it and do with it whatever one liked.

Finally, until the seventeenth century property largely meant the right to a revenue rather than to a thing. The great bulk of property was in the form of land, and, at least in the case of substantial estates, the owner was not free to sell it. His property consisted in the revenues accruing from his land. Another large segment of individual property consisted in the right to a revenue from such generally non-saleable things as corporate charters, monopolies and various political and ecclesiastical offices. In a bourgeois society the bulk of individual property was in the form of freehold land, saleable leases, physical plant and money. Property, therefore, came to be defined as a right *to* things rather than a right *in* things, as is evident in such everyday expressions as 'properties for sale' and 'property to let'. Macpherson argues that as a result of these and other changes, the right to property came to imply a more or less absolute and exclusive right to own, use and alienate material things. The new concept of property justified the private ownership of the means of production and the appropriation of the products of the workers who, having nothing to sell but their labour, offered themselves for hire. This new concept, in turn, was justified on the ground that the conditions of scarcity created by the hiatus between low productivity and infinite desires could not be conquered without giving the individual an absolute and exclusive right of ownership.

Macpherson argues that the situation today is very different. Thanks to the enormous development of productivity, scarcity is no longer the inescapable human predicament it once was. And thanks to the increasingly democratic temper of our age, our moral values have undergone important changes, and we now believe that every human being has an equal right to the conditions necessary for his fullest self-development. As a result of both these developments, the concept of property is undergoing significant revision. The developed capitalist economy is being regulated by the state, and the exclusive and absolute right to property is being questioned. The increasingly unbearable pollution of the environment (of air, water and so on) has meant that these are now being thought of as common property, and a right to them is coming to be regarded as a form of property from which nobody should be excluded. The recognition of an individual's right to a job, a pension or a guaranteed annual income has meant that property is increasingly being defined as a right to a revenue rather than to a thing. Macpherson welcomes these and other attempts to break out of and, indeed, reverse the 'narrowings' suffered by the concept of property from the seventeenth century onwards and suggests that our revisions of it should proceed along the following lines 'if they are to be consistent with the needs' of a fully democratic society.

First, we must 'recapture' the older concept of property and define it broadly to include ownership not only of things or revenues but also of 'life and liberty...the use and development and enjoyment of human capacities'. We saw earlier Macpherson's reasons for saying that every man has a natural right to a 'good' or 'full' life. Macpherson goes further and argues that rather than seeing it as a human right, we should see it as a property right. His 'compelling reason' for this is that since the institution of property enjoys enormous prestige and sanctity in our society, a right is likely to be respected and enforced only if it is seen as a part of property. According to Macpherson life, liberty, a guaranteed income, access to the means of production and even the right to political participation should all be seen as forms of property. By defining property so widely and turning every right into a property right, Macpherson seems to fall victim to the bourgeois virus of possessive individualism that he so strongly attacks. He does not transcend the basic categories of bourgeois society; he merely universalizes them and invests them with a new content that they seem hardly capable of accommodating.

Second, Macpherson proposes that a clear distinction should be drawn between ownership of the means of life and ownership of the means of producing the means of life, that is, between ownership of the means of consumption (or life) and that of the means of production (or labour). In his view, the two are not only very different in nature but also incompatible. Every man 'needs' ownership of the means of consumption, for otherwise he cannot develop his capacities and satisfy his needs. By contrast, he does not 'need' ownership of the means of production, since that is in no way necessary for the development of his capacities. What is more, such property reduces the vast majority of men to subhuman existence and prevents them from developing their capacities. Macpherson argues that since ownership of the means of consumption is obviously justifiable and that of the means of production so obviously unjustifiable, the advocates of bourgeois society have systematically confused the two. Locke is the most striking example. He begins by justifying ownership of the means of consumption and illicitly concludes that he has also justified ownership of the means of production. Macpherson insists that the two forms of property should be clearly separated and the rights to them sharply distinguished. Every man should enjoy the right to exclusive ownership of the means of life and the right not to be excluded from access to the means of production. Although Macpherson does not explicitly say so, his proposal implies that the means of production should be collectively owned.

4

Macpherson's political theory, outlined above, offers the most useful vantage point for an examination of his well-known critique of liberalism and liberal democracy. Macpherson's analysis of liberalism is rather ambiguous. He uses the term in three related but distinct senses.

In its first sense he equates it with individualism. As he understands it, liberalism takes the individual to be the ultimate moral and political unit and makes his freedom, defined as free choice, the organizing principle of social and political life. As he puts it, the 'principle of freedom of choice' is the 'central ethical principal of liberalism'.[30] Liberalism insists upon each individual's right to choose his own purposes, beliefs, religion, mariage partner, way of life, occupation, form of government and so on, as well as his right to think, speak and write without undue restraint.

In its second sense Macpherson uses liberalism to mean possessive individualism, that is, not individualism *per se* but a specific form of it.[31] As he understands it, possessive individualism advances the following seven theses. First, a man's humanity is constituted by his freedom from dependence on the wills of others. Second, freedom from dependence on others implies that an individual has no obligations save those he has voluntarily incurred in his own interests. Third, the individual is the proprietor of his person and capacities, which are his by nature and for which he owes nothing to society. Fourth, although he cannot alienate the whole of his ownership of his own person, he may alienate his specific capacities. Fifth, human society consists of a series of market relations. Sixth, each individual's freedom can rightfully be limited only by such obligations and rules as are necessary to secure the same freedom for others. And, finally, a political society is a human contrivance for the protection of property and the maintenance of orderly relations of exchange between individuals.

The third sense of liberalism is closely connected with, but distinct from, the second.[32] As Macpherson defines it, liberalism in this sense maintains that man is essentially a passive being, has limitless desires and is primarily interested in consuming utilities. He acknowledges that these are not all logically connected, for one can define man as a passive consumer without maintaining that his passion for consumption is limitless. However, Macpherson insists that they are all historically connected and grew up together. The postulate of infinite desire was introduced to justify capitalist society, of which man, as the consumer, was the necessary basis.

The three senses of liberalism outlined above are not necessarily interrelated. It is possible to stress the value of individual freedom without holding that man is the proprietor of his capacities or that a human society is nothing more than a series of market relations. Similarly, one can subscribe to the possessive, individualist view of man without holding that he is essentially passive and/or infinitely desirous. Sometimes Macpherson appreciates that the three senses of liberalism are not necessarily related. He then says that he wishes to retain liberalism in the first sense and to reject it in the other two. And he also says that liberalism in the second sense was articulated by Hobbes and Locke at a time when market society was just beginning to acquire dominance, and in the third sense by Bentham when capitalism had more or less fully developed. On other occasions Macpherson treats the three senses as if they were the same. Like Marx, he then treats liberalism as basically an ideology or a justificatory theory of capitalism. It is this ambiguity that at least partly explains why he says both that he is and that he is not a liberal, and why he sometimes traces liberalism to Hobbes and sometimes to Locke.[33]

These and other ambiguities do not affect Macpherson's central thesis, that liberalism stands for the supremacy of individual choice. When liberalism first appeared it insisted that men were rational and free beings who must be allowed to make their choices without external interference. In economic life liberalism expressed itself in the form of the competitive market economy whose 'fully developed form' was capitalism. In political life it insisted on a form of government based on individual choices, as articulated through periodic elections and freedom of association and speech and charged with the task of maintaining and promoting a liberal society. As Macpherson puts it, 'the liberal state was the politics of choice in the service of a society of choices.' He argues that although initially the liberal state was not democratic and rested on a limited franchise, its very nature generated, in due course, a demand for democracy. Those without the vote had no political weight and therefore no purchasing power within the political market. If all men were to compete freely in the political market, it followed that they must all have equal political purchasing power. It was unfair to exclude some from a market which claimed to be competitive. As Macpherson puts it, the universal franchise was the 'logical completion of the capitalist market society'; democracy 'was something the competitive society logically needed'.

Macpherson argues that although the liberal state accepted democratic demands, its structure and basic assumptions could allow it to accommodate them only up to a point. If democracy had been accepted in its full sense of political and economic equality, it would have subverted the very foundations of liberal society and the state. Democracy, therefore, had to be 'liberalized' in order that liberal society and the state could accommodate it. Accordingly, democracy, which had originally and for long meant class rule, came to be individualized and to mean little more than equality of individual rights. Further, equality of rights was taken to mean not an equal right to full personal development but an equal right to compete with others in liberal society and the state. The newly enfranchised sections of the population were required to accept the competitive market society as inviolate and to take their full and fair competitive places in it. As Macpherson puts it: 'The liberal state fulfilled its own logic. In so doing, it neither destroyed nor weakened itself; it strengthened both itself and the market society. It liberalized democracy while democratizing liberalism.'[34]

The marriage between liberalism and democracy took place in the early nineteenth century, and a new form of government called 'liberal democracy' came into existence. As the new form of government was consolidated, it threw up interesting theoretical problems, especially those relating to its nature and justification. In the course of grappling with these, political theorists developed new theories or 'models'. In Macpherson's view, these fall into four distinct categories, namely, the protective, developmental, equilibrium and participatory theories of liberal democracy.

Even as Hobbes and Locke were the first to theorize about market-orientated liberalism, Bentham and James Mill were the first to articulate the basic principles of liberal democracy.[35] For both, men were self-centred maximizers of utilities or pleasures and concerned to obtain the largest possible amount of wealth. Most men were unlikely ever to rise above the level of bare subsistence and were held in check only by the fear of starvation. According to Macpherson, neither Bentham nor James Mill had great moral enthusiasm for democracy. They attempted to limit it in various ways and saw it largely as a mechanism for restraining the government and for ensuring fair competition in the political market.

Moved by the inhuman conditions of the working classes and the danger they posed to property, J. S. Mill developed the developmental view of democracy.[36] He defined man as a developer and enjoyer of his powers and energies and articulated the vision of a truly human society. He did not, however, appreciate that his democratic ideal of the equal development of all conflicted with the capitalist relations of production and rather naïvely imagined that class inequalities were 'accidental and remediable'. For Macpherson Mill's idealistic view of man represented an advance over that of Bentham and his own father. However, his view of society marked a 'decline in realism'. Unlike them, he did not fully appreciate the reality of class conflict and postulated a universal harmony of interests. Mill's theory of man was subverted by his theory of society. Macpherson argues that this was also true of such 'neo-idealist' pluralists as Hobhouse, Barker, Lindsay and Dewey, all of whom naïvely attempted to combine the developmental model of democracy with the class inequalities of capitalist society.

Macpherson argues that in the middle decades of the twentieth century a new 'equilibrium' model of democracy was developed by Schumpeter, Dahl, Almond Verba and others.[37] For them democracy is a form of government, not a form of society, and politics is about achieving an equilibrium between the supply of, and the demand for, political goods. In their view, the masses are apathetic, incapable of taking an effective and intelligent part in the conduct of public affairs. And hence the only viable form of democracy is one in which voters freely choose between competing elites, whose main job is to forge from a mass of chaotic popular opinions a coherent set of political goals and policies.

Macpherson criticizes all three and supports the participatory theory of democracy.[38] For him democracy is 'a pyramidal system', with direct self-government at the base and indirect self-government at every level above that. Delegates are mandated and subject to recall. Macpherson appreciates that any system of government in modern industrialized society requires political parties, but he is worried lest these should acquire a monopoly of political initiative and power. He attempts to combine the two by introducing pyramidal organizations within the structures of the political parties themselves. He acknowledges that participatory democracy cannot be sustained unless the citizens see themselves primarily as exerters of capacities and unless prevailing social and economic inequalities are drastically reduced. He argues that a change is already under way in the direction of the former and that this should, over time, create a fully participatory form of government committed to achieving the latter.

We have so far outlined Machpherson's analysis of liberal democracy. He argues that, contrary to widespread belief in the Western world, democracy should not be equated with liberal democracy, which is only one of its several forms. In the contemporary world he finds two 'non-liberal variants' of democracy, namely, the communist variant and that of the Third World, both of which have a 'genuine historical claim to the title democracy'.[39]

According to Macpherson, communist society aims at the fullest self-realization of all its members.[40] If the term 'democracy' is defined in its 'broader sense' and is used to refer to a type of society, then a communist society 'may be called democratic', at least 'so long as it remains true to its purpose'. If, however, it is used in its 'narrow or strict sense', as a form of government, then a communist state may be called democratic only if there is full internal democracy within the ruling party, and if its membership, thrown open to all, does not require a greater degree of political involvement than can reasonably be expected of an average citizen. In Macpherson's view, communist societies are democratic but communist states are not. As societies, they have a 'moral advantage' over their liberal counterparts;, as states they suffer from a 'moral disadvantage'.

The 'underdeveloped variant' of non-liberal democracy is 'neither communist nor capitalist' but is based on a rejection of both the possessive individualism of the liberals and the class analysis of the communists. It goes back to the 'pre-industrial' and 'pre-liberal' model of democracy, draws its inspiration from Rousseau, sees no intrinsic value in accumulating wealth and stresses the ideals of equality and community. Its members are all agreed on their collective ends, and the resulting general will is articulated and enforced by the dominant political party. In Macpherson's view, the underdeveloped countries are democratic in the wider sense and, when the three conditions listed above are met, also in the narrow sense. Their claim to be called 'democratic' in the narrow sense is 'somewhat better' and, in the wider sense, perhaps 'a little better' than that of communist societies.[41]

For Macpherson, then, 'three concepts of democracy [are] actively at work in the world today.'[42] One indicates a 'political and economic market' in which people make free choices; the second implies 'rule by and for the proletariat'; and the third suggests 'rule by the general will'. Macpherson asks if it is proper to call all such systems of government democracies and answers in the affirmative. First, they are so called by those involved, and Macpherson accepts their claims. Second, all three can lay claim to the original usage of the term and have immaculate pedigrees in the writings of the liberal thinkers, Marx and Rousseau respectively. Third, although their means are diferent, 'their ultimate goal is the same' - namely, to provide the 'conditions for the full and free development of the essential human capacities of all the members' of the society. Since every government, however autocratic, claims to pursue this ideal, it is difficult to see if there is any to which Macpherson would deny the coveted description 'democratic'.

5

I have offered above a brief outline of Macpherson's political thought. Much of it stimulating and worth saying. Some of Macpherson's basic theses about the nature and task of political theory are well taken. He is right to insist that since political life is profoundly shaped by, and cannot be understood without reference to, the wider social structure, political theory must somehow be closely linked with wider social theory. No political theorist can hope to give a satisfactory account of his subject matter unless he has a carefully worked out theory of the nature of society and the relations between its major institutions. Macpherson is equally right to argue that political theory is not a transcendental activity operating in a historical vacuum. It is undertaken by socially situated men at a specific time, in a specific society, about a specific subject matter to which they stand in a specific relationship. The political theorist is profoundly influenced by his society, from which he derives many of his basic ideas and assumptions about man and society. His subject matter consists of man and society as they are in specific historical periods. And his relation to his subject matter is socially and historically mediated and varies from one historical epoch to another.

Again, Macpherson is right to insist that a political theorist cannot rise above the political and ideological battles of his society. Although he operates at a highly general level, he remains rooted in his society and is profoundly influenced by its controversies. He intervenes in them, takes sides, affiliates himself to some groups, is opposed to others and so on. He may not do so directly, and he may name no names. However, as Macpherson argues, the conflicts of his society find a powerful echo in his thought and can be uncovered by means of a careful analysis of it.

Since political theory has, for Macpherson, these and other ineradicable features, he proposes a novel way of reading past political thinkers. He argues that we should locate them in their historical and social contexts, look for their basic assumptions about man and society, relate them to the political and ideological battles of their times and inquire into the general political problems which their ages set for them and which they could not avoid discussing. With all their limitations, Macpherson's studies of Hobbes, Locke and others have been widely acknowledged to have produced worthwhile results. It is not generally appreciated that his *Political Theory of Possessive Individualism* represents not only a novel approach to the history of political ideas but also a novel way of treating political theory. To acknowledge that his analyses of Hobbes and Locke illuminate their ideas in a fresh way is implicitly to acknowledge the value not only of his historical methodology but also of his conception of the nature of political theory.

This is not to say that Macpherson's view of political theory is wholly free of difficulties. As we shall see below, he is mistaken in his view that political theory is wholly historical or 'time-bound' and lacks a universal dimension. Further, when he stresses the explanatory task of political theory, he defines explanation almost entirely in empirical terms. He fails to notice that although the so-called grand political theory and empirical political theory are both explanatory, they offer different *types* of explanation, the former being interested in the philosophical and the latter in the scientific explanation. Again, while he is right to stress the justificatory dimension of political theory, he fails to appreciate that it is subordinate and derivative, and that philosophical justification is much more subtle and complex than mere advocacy of a specific social order. Further, as we saw, Macpherson does not adequately analyse the complex logical relationship between explanation and justification and suggests that the two somehow lie side by side in a theoretical system. Again, his view of political theory implies that the thought of a thinker (or an age) rests on an unambiguous and easily identifiable body of social assumptions which can be neatly classified as bourgeois, feudal, working-class and so on. This leads him to ignore nuances of thought and to subsume thinkers and theories within problematic categories, as Berlin, John Dunn, Keith Thomas and Quentin Skinner have shown. Despite these and other limitations, some of which are not inherent in his approach but incidental to his pioneering application of it, much of what he says offers a stimulating perspective on the nature and history of political thought.

At the substantive level, there is little doubt that Macpherson's work breaks new ground and opens up several interesting areas of inquiry. One of his abiding concerns has been to develop a social and political theory integrating the fruitful insights of both liberalism and Marxism.[43] Even if Macpherson were to be mistaken in what he takes to be the essential insights of liberalism and Marxism and/or to have failed to integrate them into a harmonious conceptual whole, his project would still have considerable theoretical interest. Only a fanatical partisan would deny that each of the two major traditions of thought contains illuminating insights into the nature of man and society and benefits from its dialogue with the other. Furthermore, it is one of the political philosopher's important tasks to loosen ideological rigidity, to explore common ground and both to stimulate and to monitor a dialogue between different political doctrines. J. S. Mill put the point well when he observed that since Bentham and Coleridge represented opposing views of philosophy and society, 'whoever could master the premises and combine the methods of both would possess the entire English philosophy of his age.' Macpherson's contribution lies in insisting that no social and political theory can deal adequately with the problems of our age unless it elucidates and incorporates the central insights of liberalism and Marxism.

Macpherson's concern to integrate liberalism and Marxism has two important consequences. First, he elucidates both the strengths and the limitations of liberalism. He shows that its great contribution lies in its emphasis on the supreme value of the individual, the importance of critical reason, the moral dimension of social and political life, civil liberties and responsible government. He also points to its crucual limitations, such as its beliefs in the self-sufficiency of the individual, the possessive nature of man, private property as the basis of a free society, the neglect of the reality of the economic classes and a disregard for the structural constraints on individual choices. As he shows, although some liberal theorists were able to break away from the narrowly individualistic view of man, they remained unable to build on their insights largely because of their rather naïve theories of society.

Second, Macpherson identifies both the strengths and the limitations of Marxism. He appreciates the importance of its emphasis on the classes, the partisan nature of the government, common ownership and the inescapability of the structural constraints on individual choices inherent in the capitalist economy. At the same time he also highlights some of its basic limitations. He questions its traditional antipathy to morality. While recognizing the incoherence of abstract and ahistorical morality, he is right to insist that the alternative lies not in rejecting morality or reducing it to an epiphenomenon of historical determinism but in exploring a form of moral thought that is socially and historically grounded. Further, he rightly challenges the facile equation between capitalism and civil liberties current among some Marxists. The defenders of capitalist society have tended to equate the two and have argued that civil liberties are historically and conceptually linked with, and cannot exist outside, a capitalist economy. Many a Marxist has accepted the ideologically biased equation and has rejected the institutions of civil liberties and liberal democracy as the vehicles of capitalism. Macpherson challenges this view. Although his own view is ambiguous and raises several intricate problems, he is right to insist that liberalism and capitalism, civil and political liberties and capitalist relations of production can be conceptually separated, and that a socialist or a Marxist need not feel uneasy about, or encounter any theoretical difficulty in, appropriating the vocabulary of human rights and civil liberties. They are as much a part of his historical heritage as they are that of the liberal. This is an extremely important point.

Despite these and other important insights, Macpherson's thought is open to several criticisms. We shall briefly consider the most important. Although the concept of human essence is central to his social and political theory, Macpherson's analysis of it is inadequate and raises several questions. He is ambiguous about whether or not man has an historically invariant nature. Sometimes he answers in the affirmative.[44] Sometimes he says that man has 'no permanent, unchanging nature' and that he 'changes his nature by changing his relation to other men and the material environment'.[45] On yet other occasions he draws an interesting distinction. Although he is not entirely clear Macpherson seems to think that when we talk about human nature, we mean one of two things. First, we may refer to such highly formal capacities as reason, sense perception, imagination and memory, or, secondly, we may refer to the substantive content of human desires and motives.[46] He seems to suggest that the former are historically invariant and characterize the 'human animal as such', whereas the latter are subject to historical change. Macpherson does not develop the distinction, nor does he explain how we can decide which human characteristics belong to which category and whether they can be so neatly separated.

Macpherson pays scant attention to the nature and development of human capacities. He does not notice that the capacities he lists are too general to have unequivocal meanings or to indicate how they can be exercised. It is difficult to see, for example, what is meant by the development of rational understanding, moral judgement and love. Since human capacities conflict, the development of one may frustrate the development of others. What is more, human capacities are disparate, not easily measurable and not translatable into a common currency or gradeable on a single scale. It is therefore difficult to see what the maximization of human capacities and powers means, and one may even wonder if the concept of maximizing human development is logically coherent. The ghost of Bentham haunts even the shrewdest critic of liberalism.

Macpherson does not explore how human capacities can be developed or what sorts of factor hinder their realization. He remains imprisoned within the liberal individualist belief that if only an individual had the necessary material resources, he would develop and exercise his capacities and satisfy his needs. Accordingly, Macpherson concentrates on the economic obstacles to the development of human capacities. He does not examine how such capacities as rational understanding, friendship, religious experience, love, curiosity and moral judgement are hindered by the lack of material means or by the transfer of powers. Further, in linking the development of human capacities so closely with material resources, Macpherson accords to the latter far greater importance than they merit and neglects other equally, if not more, important obstacles, especially the quality of social relations. Like many a liberal, he sees self-development as essentially an individual process and is preoccupied with material means rather than the quality of both the relations of production and other social relations. This partly explains why he lays so much stress on material scarcity in his explanation of the development of capitalism and sets so much store by its abolition in his account of the conditions of full human development.

Human capacities cannot be developed and exercised by an individual in isolation. They are located within, and sustained by, the framework of social relations and are developed when the latter make them both possible and necessary.[47] Men develop greed, aggressiveness and the desire and ability to manipulate others when their social relations are so constituted that they cannot otherwise survive or attain their goals. When social relations are based on mutual exploitation, each individual is compelled to cultivate the capacities necessary to exploit, and avoid being exploited by, others. The same is true of such very different capacities as social co-operation, trust, intellectual and aesthetic interests, mutual respect and concern. A social theorist, therefore, needs to ask what kinds of social relation stimulate and nourish the exercise of these and other capacities which Macpherson rightly values.

Since Macpherson does not undertake such an inquiry he is unable to specify the forms of life that obstruct or promote human development, and his critique of capitalism lacks depth. He does not give us any reason to believe that if the transfer of powers were to be eliminated, men would want to develop, and help others to develop, their capacities rather than remain, and encourage others to remain, passive consumers of utilities. Within the framework of his individualistic account of human development, Macpherson is unable fully to appreciate that human development is a co-operative process, that men grow together, that the excellence achieved by one does not diminish but raises others, that men complete one another, and that it is therefore in the interest of each to help others grow and flourish. To be sure, he is not wholly unaware of this profound insight of Marx. However, he does not explore its full implications or make it the basis of his social and political theory.

Despite his penetrating criticisms of liberal individualism, Macpherson fails to transcend its basic assumptions and is unable to lay the foundation of an alternative theory of man. Notwithstanding his claim to the contrary, he too conceives of the individual as the proprietor of his capacities. Each individual is the master of himself and aims to develop his capacities as he 'freely chooses'. He needs liberty not in order to co-operate with others in developing a common way of life but to 'live in accordance with [his] own conscious purposes...and decide for [himself] rather than to be acted upon and decided for by others'.[48] This is an exclusivist definition of liberty, precisely the criticism Macpherson makes of the liberal theory of property. Unlike the liberals, Macpherson rightly stresses the development of non-contentious and socially orientated human capacities. However, the form and content of their development remain individualistic. Instead of accumulating material objects or wealth, an individual may maximize his aesthetic, emotional and other pleasures. It is not clear why such an individual is necessarily more social and co-operative or even less possessive. Further, as we have seen, Macpherson even outbids liberalism and views liberty, political participation, the quality of life and so on as possessions to which an individual has a proprietary right. No doubt he does so in order to secure recognition of the individual's right to the conditions of his development. However, to deploy the vocabulary of possessive individualism, even for such a defensible purpose, is to be infected by the very disease one is determined to combat.

Macpherson retains not only the individualism and some of the possessivist ethos but also several other important features of liberalism. Like the liberals, he seems to think that the essence of man mutely inheres in each individual rather than in the ensemble of social relations. And, like them, he views reason as an essentially instrumental and maximizing capacity, as is evident from his preoccupation with the 'maximization of capacities' and the 'maximization of aggregate powers'. Bourgeois man aims to maximize his aggregate utilities; Macpherson's socialist man aims to maximize his aggregate powers. The two differ in their objectives but share the same basic view of life in general and of reason in particular. Not surprisingly, Macpherson's thought reveals the weighty influence of liberal utilitarianism. Again, like some liberals, especially Mill, Macpherson is much more worried about the injustice of exploitation and the unfair transfer of powers in capitalist society than the atomization of man and the distortion and corruption of human potential. All this is not to say that Macpherson is not concerned to synthesize the fundamental insights of Marx and Mill, rather that Marx's influence is largely limited to his analysis of society and does not extend to his conception of man. As a result, Macpherson seems to wish to create a *socialist* society in order to realize *liberal* man. He himself says that his basic concern is to 'retrieve' the ethical values of liberalism, and that it is largely because they cannot be realized in capitalist society that he wishes to replace it with a socialist one. Macpherson is primarily committed to liberalism and absorbs as much of Marxism as his liberal assumptions permit. As a result, he liberalizes Marxism but does not Marxianize liberalism. His fascinating synthesis remains imbalanced and fails to transcend, or provide an alternative to, the liberal framework of thought.

4

Herbert Marcuse

Alone among contemporary philosophers, Marcuse had the unusual distinction of being declared the father of a once powerful radical movement and being catapulted into the political realm. His social and political ideas were chartered in the service of dubious causes and were interpreted in a manner that showed scant regard for their subtlety and nuances. Even the Pope in Rome condemned him as a prophet of sexual perversity. All this was a pity, for Marcuse was an audacious and original thinker, some of whose ideas about the nature and task of political philosophy were genuinely novel.

1

Marcuse argues that despite their differences, almost all Western philosophers have held several basic and interrelated beliefs in common. Of these the most important are, first, the distinction between essence and appearance; second, reason as man's highest capacity; third, reason as the basis of human freedom; and fourth, reason as an essentially negative and critical faculty. Although they have defended them on different grounds and have drawn from them divergent conclusions, almost all philosophers have subscribed to them in one form or another.

According to Marcuse, the distinction between essence and appearance was first clearly formulated in Plato's theory of Ideas and has since remained the basic principle of Western philosophy.[1] It is fundamentally a distinction between two levels, or forms, of reality. Sensually perceptible objects display a wide variety of forms, undergo changes, enter into different relations with each other and create a complex and confusing world of appearances. In their attempts to understand the phenomenal world, Western philosophers have introduced the concept of essence, which they have sometimes called nature, being or inner structure. For them sensually perceptible objects have an essence, a set of dispositions and potentialities, which shape their behaviour and relations with each other and preserve their identity amid a diversity of forms. Although their essence is realized in their phenomenal forms, it is rarely realized fully, and hence they do not always appear as they might. According to Marcuse, the belief that phenomenal forms can never be understood in their own terms but only by reference to their *edios, essentia* or nature runs like a red thread through the history of Western philosophy.[2]

For Marcuse reason refers to man's capacity to grasp the essence, or essential nature of an object. It abstracts away diversity of forms, distinguishes between what necessarily belongs to an object and what is merely an accidental and adventitious feature and elucidates its essential characteristics. Reason grasps the essence of an object and expresses it in the form of a concept.[3] For Marcuse the concept of an object is a theoretical articulation of its essence. To develop the concepts of man, the state, philosophy, beauty, art and so on is to claim to comprehend and to articulate the essential nature of the relevant objects. According to Marcuse, to think rationally is to think in terms of concepts and hence to think in terms of the distinction between essence and appearance. The distinction between essence and appearance is the ontological basis and necessary precondition of the human capacity for conceptual or abstract thought.

Marcuse argues that it is only because man is able to grasp the essence or, what comes to the same thing, formulate the concept of a thing that he is able to transcend and confront it as a free subject. Thanks to his capacity for conceptual or mediated thought, he is able to interpose a space between himself and his object of perception, to protect himself against being overwhelmed by it, to perceive himself as a subject and it as an object and to confront and interrogate it freely. In other words, the capacity for conceptual thinking is the basis of the human capacity for freedom and autonomy. It is also the basis of the human capacity to evaluate critically and to change the object. Man can 'measure' or judge it on the basis of its potentialities and can evaluate its various forms as adequate or inadequate realizations. His knowledge of its essence enables him to change it in the light of his interests and needs.[4]

For Marcuse, then, reason represents man's capacity to grasp the essence of the phenomenal world and is the source of his freedom as well as his ability to criticize and change the world. As such, it is the source of man's humanity and is his highest capacity. Marcuse argues that from the very beginning Western philosophy grasped the unity of the concepts of essence, reason, freedom and criticism. This is its great 'heritage', which almost all philosophers have cherished, the only exception being the empiricists, who denied the decisive distinction between essence and appearance upon which Western philosophy was founded. As a result, they were unable to effect the 'critical transcendence toward essence' or to find an adequate basis for rationality. They could not explain the human capacity to form concepts except in terms of externally determined associations of ideas and ended up reducing reason to habit and custom. Further, since they were unable to transcend appearances, they could not explore the untapped potentialities of objects and hence, obviously, could not criticize them. Not surprisingly, empiricism succumbed to 'helpless relativism'. What is worse, it could not even remain philosophical and fell an easy prey to positivism and to science.[5]

Marcuse contends that although Western philosophy grasped the importance of the four beliefs outlined above, it was long unable to capitalize on its profound insights because of its idealist ontology or, rather, onto-theology. It assumed that the universe was a harmonious whole governed and sustained by reason. For Western philosophy there was no radical and qualitative difference between man and the natural world, both of which reflected the same basic 'substance', namely, reason. Further, it understood reason as essentially divine in nature and thought that its basic task consisted in demonstrating the rationality of the natural and social order. Thanks to its idealism and its assumption of the 'identity of subject and object', it was unable to understand reason as a critical faculty.

In Marcuse's view, Kant was the first to challenge this view.[6] Kant denied the 'identity of subject and object' and neatly separated man from the world. Moreover, he saw reason as a property of the human subject rather than of the universe and understood it in the form of 'rational subjectivity' rather than substance. The rational subject judged the world in terms of *his* reason and was not content to demonstrate the assumed rationality of the universe. In Marcuse's view, Kant was the first Western philosopher to establish reason 'as a critical tribunal' and rightly called his a *critical* philosophy.

According to Marcuse, Kant's concept of critical reason suffered from several limitations. Kant was an idealist and although he denied the idealist philosophy of identity, he retained its dualism. For him reason was a transcendental faculty. Its home was not in the world of everyday experience. Theoretical reason freely excogitated its principles and imposed them upon the world, and practical reason realized itself not in the world of social relations but in good will. This meant that, for Kant, men 'could become rational and

free within the established order.... Reason and freedom become
tasks that the individual is to fulfil within himself, and he can do so
regardless of external conditions.' Kant appreciated the critical but
not the social and historical nature of reason. Since his view of man
was ahistorical and asocial, his concept of critical reason remained
abstract, transcendental and powerless to become an active force in
the world.

In Marcuse's view, Hegel transcended Kant's dualism but within
the framework of the idealist onto-theology. He stressed the
dialectical unity of essence and appearance and insisted that essence
acquired actuality or existence only through its appearances, and
that appearance was real only as a manifestation of essence. He
stressed also the historical nature of essence and understood it as a
process of gradual realization. And, like Kant, he emphasized its
critical character and role. However, he conceived of the realization
of essence as a process occurring only in thought. For Hegel the
world, not man, was the locus of reason, and man was considered
rational to the extent that he grasped and participated in the world's
rationality. This meant that critical reason achieved reconciliation
with the world not by changing it but by coming to terms with it. It
did not subject the real world to its demands; instead it 'submitted'
itself to the world as it was. Marcuse observes: 'Hegel's conception of
essence already contains all the elements of a dynamic historical
theory of essence, but in a dimension where they cannot be
effective.... Hegel's theory of essence remains transcendental.'[7]

According to Marcuse, Marx took the decisive step. He turned his
back on idealism and developed historical materialism. For him
there was no reality other than the world of human relationships;
hence he insisted on realizing reason in this world rather than in an
allegedly transcendental world. He argued, further, that reason
derived its goals neither from itself nor from a trans-historical
source, as Kant and Hegel respectively had argued, but from a
historical study of the social world. It analysed the potentialities of
the social order, explored the most effective ways of realizing them
and identified the revolutionary social agent capable of acting as the
'locus of reason'. In Marcuse's view, Marx realized that in order to
do this one must move away from the abstract and ahistorical study
of ideas characteristic of traditional philosophy and undertake
instead an empirical and historically orientated investigation into
the nature of contemporary society. Marx, therefore, felt it necessary
to go beyond 'philosophy's boundaries' and to replace philosophy
with social theory as the paradigm of critical reason.[8] To be sure,
Marx's critical social theory does not reject philosophy's heritage as

outlined above; rather, it gives it a more adequate 'new form'. Even as Kant's critical philosophy represented a further development of traditional philosophy, whose fundamental insights it preserved and developed, Marx's critical social theory marked a further development of Kant's critical philosophy. According to Marcuse, Marx saw that Kant's and Hegel's critical intentions were frustrated by their philosophical forms of thought, and that neither could become fully critical as long as he remained a philosopher. In his attempt fully to develop the critical potential of reason, Marx felt it necessary to replace philosophy by critical social theory.

Along with the other members of the Frankfurt School, Marcuse takes over Marx's concept of critical social theory and suitably modifies it.[9] For him critical theory views reason as 'the highest potentiality of man and of existence' and understands it as 'the power of the negative', as an inherently critical faculty which 'contradicts' or 'negates' the given and 'projects' the alternative. Critical theory preserves the philosophical heritage but goes beyond philosophy; that is, it preserves its content but rejects its 'form'. Like philosophy, it is analytical, critical, speculative and committed to preserving 'obstinacy as a genuine quality of philosophical thought'. Unlike philosophy, it rejects the distinction between formal and empirical inquiry, studies the world of social relations and derives its goals 'only from the present tendencies of the social process'. Critical theory is theoretical rather than philosophical in orientation, in the sense that its analytical, critical and speculative investigation is not abstract and ahistorical but socially and historically grounded. Further, like the critical philosophy of Kant and Hegel, critical theory places man at the 'centre' of theory; unlike it, however, critical theory understands him not as an ahistorical abstraction but as an historically and socially situated being. It regards him as the highest being on earth and is committed to his worldly well-being. As Marcuse puts it, 'the judgement that human life is worth living, or rather can and ought to be made worth living... underlies all intellectual effort'; it is 'the *a priori* of social theory, and its rejection (which is perfectly logical) rejects theory itself'.[10] In other words, critical theory is motivated by an emancipatory interest and aims to explore the form of life worthy of man and ways of attaining it.[11]

For reasons discussed above, its critical and emancipatory interest requires critical social theory to make the 'essence of man' its 'object of inquiry'. Marcuse objects to what he calls the 'idealist' view of essence, according to which the essence of anything, especially man, is eternally fixed, fully formed from the beginning, transcendental and capable of being grasped only by means of intellectual intuition. Despite some confusion, Marcuse seems to think that the essence of man is historically acquired; it 'can be defined in *history* and *only* in history'. Marcuse is very vague about how he proposes to discover and to 'validate' his view of it.[12] By and large, he seems to think that it is arrived at and validated in three ways: first, through a careful analysis of past and present historical struggles and what these reveal about man; second, through an assessment of past and present conceptions of the good life; and third, with the aid of theoretical knowledge about man as developed by philosophical and scientific inquiries.

In the light of his theory of the essence of man, the critical theorist analyses contemporary society.[13] He assesses its technical, productive, intellectual and other resources and determines the extent to which they are capable of realizing man's essence. He works out the 'optimal development' of the individual possible under the 'optimal utilization' of the available resources and formulates a conception of what his society can and ought to be but is not. He points out the nature and extent of the 'arrested possibilities', articulates the alternative social order capable of realizing them and identifies the social groups which can be expected to struggle for it.

Marcuse contends that this way of judging the social order is not subjective or based on personal preferences but objective and capable of rational demonstration. And it is grounded not in abstract and universal criteria but in those derived from, and applicable to, a specific social order. The 'ought' that the critical theorist invokes is not a dream or a fantasy but another level of 'is'. It represents a possible reality, a realistic account of the possible truth, a realistically possible 'is', a 'different order' of 'is'. The 'ought' ultimately refers to nothing other than 'the futuristic mode in which the truth exists'. As Marcuse puts it, the 'twofold meaning of "is" would express the two-dimensional structure of the one world'.[14] The 'is' separated from the 'ought' becomes 'reified' and prevents free and critical thought; the 'ought' separated from the 'is' becomes subjective and politically irrelevant.

For Marcuse the political judgement the critical theorist makes on a given social order is necessarily comparative. He rejects a social order not merely because it arrests certain possibilities but also because he can show that another social order capable of realizing them is on the historical horizon. He demonstrates that the new social order, which he calls a 'transcendent project', is not only desirable but also both possible and necessary. Marcuse formulates the comparative criteria of historical rationality as follows:[15]

(1) The transcendent project must be in accordance with the real possibilities open at the attained level of the material and intellectual culture.

(2) The transcendent project, in order to falsify the established totality, must demonstrate its own *higher* rationality in the threefold sense that

   (a) it offers the prospect of preserving and improving the productive achievements of civilization;

   (b) it defines the established totality in its very structure, basic tendencies, and relations;

   (c) its realization offers a greater chance for the pacification of existence, within the framework of institutions which offer a greater chance for the free development of human needs and faculties.

For Marcuse critical social theory replaces political philosophy, as it has been hitherto understood. In his view, traditional political philosophy is open to two forms of criticism. First, it is a philosophy, and, as we have seen, Marcuse proposes to replace philosophy by (social) theory. Second, political philosophy is centred on politics and assumes that politics is an independent and autonomous area of inquiry. Although he does not share the naïve epiphenomenalism of some Marxists, Marcuse believes that politics represents the mode in which the deeper reality of class domination is articulated and enforced. It refers to the world of authority through which the world of power legitimizes itself. It cannot, therefore, be understood except in the context of the social whole. In short, Marcuse replaces philosophy by critical theory, the study of politics by that of the social structure and political philosophy by critically orientated social theory.

As Marcuse understands it, critical social theory is grounded in materialist ontology, is humanist in its inspiration, historical in its orientation and at once explanatory, critical and Utopian in nature.[16] It studies the social whole, for the 'truth lies in the whole', and analyses its component institutions and practices in terms of its structural dialectic. Its central concern is threefold: first, to develop a concept of man; second, to analyse contemporary society and identify its arrested possibilities; and third, to project, and point out the path to, the alternative. As Marcuse puts it, his intention as a critical theorist is 'to develop a critical theory of *contemporary* society, a theory which analyses society in the light of its used and *unused* capabilities for *improving* the human condition'.[17]

2

Marcuse's conception of man is rather complex and ambiguously formulated. On the basis of a perfunctory examination of past political struggles and conceptions of the good life and of a careful but imbalanced analysis of Freud, he concludes that reason, freedom and happiness are the three fundamental concepts in terms of which an adequate theory of man must be formulated. As he says, 'That man is a rational being, that this being requires freedom, and that happiness is his highest good are all universal propositions.'[18] Since we have already considered his concept of reason, we shall briefly discuss the other two.

As Marcuse understands it, freedom has three components or dimensions. First, as a rational being capable of conceptual and mediated thought, man is free in the sense that he is able to create a space between himself and the world, to distance or detach himself from the immediacy of the given and to decide freely his response to it. Freedom in this sense is the basis of freedom in the second sense, namely, the capacity for 'autonomy' or 'self-determination'. By this Marcuse means that man has the capacity to formulate his purposes, opinions, thoughts and beliefs and to realize his freely chosen way of life. Third, man is capable of 'being free with the others'; that is, he is capable of co-operating with them, participating in the conduct of their common affairs and arriving at, and abiding by, collective decisions.[19] Of the three, the first is inherent in the human capacity for rationality and therefore natural to man. Since we have already discussed it, we shall concentrate on the other components of freedom, namely, personal and collective self-determination.

Marcuse uses the term 'self-determination' in the strong sense of 'being in full command of one's life'. For him it implies a number of things. It implies that an individual's existence is not at the whim and mercy of anyone but entirely under his own control. For Marcuse a slave whose existence depends upon the good will of his master and a worker whose livelihood depends upon whether or not someone employs him do not satisfy the minimal condition of self-determination. Self-determination implies, further, that an individual freely formulates his purposes, directs his activities, determines the use of his capacities and forms his own thoughts, beliefs and feelings. It means, finally, that his identity is self-defined in the sense that he freely decides how to structure his way of life in harmony with his ideals and aspirations rather than conforming to others' expectations of him or to the role they may have decided for him. His centre of gravity, or his frame of reference, lies within and not outside him.[20]

For Marcuse domination is the opposite of freedom. As he puts it, domination occurs when 'the individual's goals and purposes and the means of striving for and attaining them are prescribed to him and performed by him as something prescribed.'[21] An individual is said to be dominated when he is subject to others' wills and realizes not his own but their purposes. For Marcuse domination can take many forms. To require an individual to do something by physical force is to dominate him. To coerce him by threats of disagreeable consequences is also to dominate him. To condition his psyche by subjecting him to systematic propaganda, indoctrination or socialization, so that he makes his choices within the framework of a 'preformed mentality', is also a form of domination. To plant certain desires in him by subliminal advertising and such other means is also to dominate him, since the wants are externally induced and do not express his free and autonomous decision. 'Unfreedom' is already built into the 'structure of his wants', and therefore his decision to satisfy them is not free.

For Marcuse domination implies that some men use others for their own purposes. This occurs when two conditions obtain: first, when the social structure is so constituted that the interests of some can be served only at the expense of others; second, when some have the power to use others, and the latter lack the power to resist and counter them. The two conditions are met in a class society. In a class society a large number of men are dependent upon a few for their livelihood; hence their existence, no longer under their own control, has a disturbing air of contingency. Further, their capacities, activities and products are not under their own control. Others decide how they should use their capacities and what is to be done with their products. Again, since the dominant class feels constantly threatened by the workers, it must win over their allegiance and control their thoughts and feelings by means of ideological indoctrination. A class society is based on material domination and necessarily calls for ideological domination. Marcuse, therefore, regards its elimination as the primary condition of human self-determination. He acknowledges that men may dominate each other for the non-economic reasons as well but insists that such forms of domination are all comparatively trivial and ultimately derive their strength from the more basic fact of class domination.

About collective self-determination, the third component of freedom, Marcuse has little new to say. He agrees that every organized society requires a commonly acknowledged structure of authority. In his view, the concept of authority contains a dialectical tension.[22] As distinct from coercion and force, A cannot have authority over B unless B freely accepts and acknowledges it. At the same time, for A to have authority over B means that B accepts A's will and judgement as his own. The *form* of authority is grounded in, and presupposes, B's freedom; the *exercise* of authority, however, involves B's surrender of his judgement and will and acceptance of those of A. Marcuse argues that B is therefore 'simultaneously free and unfree, autonomous and heteronomous'. Freedom and 'unfreedom' are thus 'yoked' in the concept of authority. Men must be free subjects in order that they may create a relation of authority. However, once authority is instituted, the bulk of them are reduced to the status of 'unfree' objects.

Marcuse argues that no political philosopher has successfully resolved the tension inherent in the concept of authority.[23] Most have not even noticed it. Some who have considered it have thought it enough if an individual freely acknowledges the authority to which he is bound. In their view, it is not a necessary part of his freedom that he should participate in the exercise of authority or even judge what authority requires of him. For Marcuse such a 'solution' avoids the question. The relationship of authority cannot come into being unless those subject to it are free. All authority presupposes freedom. To say that men remain free to acknowledge authority is therefore to utter a tautology. The real problem is not whether men are free to acknowledge authority, for this is inherent in the very concept of authority, but how to ensure that free individuals do not forfeit their freedom once they have created authority. In Marcuse's view, the form of authority is always grounded in freedom; the question is to how to bring its content or purpose within the ambit of freedom. Although Marcuse states the problem well, his solution, such as it is, consists in arguing, with Rousseau and Marx, that freedom and authority are reconciled when free citizens participate in the conduct of public affairs, formulate their collective purposes and require the government to realize them.[24]

Marcuse's concept of happiness is not easy to define.[25] It is articulated differently in different writings and contains several disparate and not easily reconcilable ideas. Basically, it is an unhappy combination of Schiller's concept of playfulness, Nietzsche's concept of joy and Freud's concept of pleasure.

Following Freud, Marcuse argues that the human psyche is characterized by the two 'antagonistic instincts' of *eros* and *thanatos* fulfilling themselves in 'fundamentally different modes'.[26] In his view, the difference between them is 'tantamount to that of sustaining and destroying life'. *Thanatos* represents the principle of destruction, strives to return to the quiescence of the inorganic world and is at work in such impulses and acts as aggressiveness, brutality, cruelty and the destruction of life, be it one's own or that of others. By contrast, *eros* represents the affirmation of life and is expressed in such impulses and acts as the creation, preservation and enjoyment of life, tenderness, love of oneself or of others and the pursuit of a joyful, expansive and playful mode of existence. For Marcuse the two instincts compete for available psychic energy, and the power of one can only be combated by increasing that of the other. Their interplay constitutes the 'dialectic' of civilization'.

Contrary to what some critics (including the Pope) have said, Marcuse does not equate *eros* with sex, and his plea for its development is not a plea for unrestrained sexuality. For him *eros* represents the search for pleasure and joy as attained through the affirmation of life, and sexuality is one of its many manifestations. As Marcuse says, the 'sex instincts are *life* instincts' and the 'impulse to preserve and enrich life by mastering nature...is originally an erotic impulse'. The desire to conquer disease and decay, to abolish the toil and drudgery of work, to eliminate noise and pollution, to produce pleasing objects, to create beauty, order, harmony, peace and calm in one's environment, and so on, are all expressions of the erotic impulse.[27] He goes even further and says that 'spiritual "procreation" is just as much the work of *eros* as is corporeal precreation, and the right and true order of the *polis* is just as much an erotic one as is the right and true order of love.' Marcuse inflates the meaning of *eros* to cover everything, ranging from the love of simple physical pleasures to that of truth, beauty and goodness.

For Marcuse happiness consists in the affirmation of *eros,* that is, in the exercise of libidinal energy in the activities one loves and finds pleasurable. So understood, the pursuit of happiness implies a number of things.[28] It implies that human existence should not be haunted by contingency and continual anxiety about one's present and future livelihood and requires material security. Ideally, it calls for the abolition of the class society and of scarcity. It implies also that the work men do, and the conditions under which they do it, should be pleasant and enjoyable. It also implies the elimination of the competitive struggle for existence which pits men against one another, brutalizes them and turns them into tough, suspicious, cynical and aggressive beings who give away their lives to prove their superiority to others. It also implies the creation of an aesthetically pleasurable natural and social environment characterized by beautiful buildings, parks, gardens, areas of calm withdrawal rather than noisy centres of organized fun, and relaxed social relationships. The pursuit of happiness involves also what Marcuse calls the 'eroticization of the entire personality'. As we shall see, this rather complex notion means basically that the erotic impulse should not remain confined to the genitals, as is the case today, but should be decentralized and polymorphously 'spread' over the entire body, so that the body and the environment become erotogenic zones. In short, for Marcuse the pursuit of happiness involves the creation of an 'erotic' or 'libidinal civilization'.

Marcuse's philosophical anthropology can best be seen as an attempt to construct a conception of man in which the two principles of *logos* and *eros* are integrated, and 'reason and happiness converge'.[29] He argues that the Western philosophical tradition has rarely appreciated the importance of *eros*. From Plato onwards philosophers have been increasingly suspicious of *eros* and, as a means of countering its influence, have insisted on the 'supremacy of the *logos*'. They have given reason the monopoly of cognition, have dismissed imagination and fantasy as important sources of knowledge and have viewed reason as a repressive faculty devoted to commanding, directing and mastering the 'lower' erotic desires.[30] In general, they have defined *logos* as the 'logic of domination' and have denigrated man's sensuous and aesthetic faculties and impulses.

Marcuse is concerned to establish and assert the 'ontological link' between *logos* and *eros*.[31] For him the senses are not confused and chaotic but play an active and 'constitutive' role in the perceptual process; they synthesize the primary data of experience and provide the 'basis for the epistemological constitution of reality'. Further, reason is not the sole, or even the most important, source of knowledge. Fantasy and imagination too play a crucial role.[32] They preserve against the realism and positivism of reason men's dreams of, and aspirations for, a life of joy and integral fulfilment. Marcuse insists, further, that *logos* is not self-moving but is inspired and sustained by the *eros*. It is because men love knowledge and truth that they suffer the agonies, hardship and toil involved in their pursuits. He argues, again, that it is only because man's search for happiness and unity with his environment and fellow men is constantly suppressed that the repressive, rationalistic morality of the super-ego becomes the only way to ensure civilized behaviour. In his view, when *eros* is weakened, *thanatos* gains the upper hand and *logos* is called upon to play a fiercely repressive and punitive role. In combating *thanatos*, *logos* acquires a good deal of its enemy's aggressiveness and suffers corruption. Marcuse argues that rather than rely solely upon *logos* to ensure moral conduct, as Western man has done during most of his history, we should aim to strengthen *eros* by creating a society in which the natural and social environment encourages tenderness, trust, gentleness, mutual concern, love of peace, beauty and harmony and so on and so shapes men that they become biologically or instinctively incapable of cruelty, aggressiveness and destruction. In other words, Marcuse's conception of man is designed to integrate *logos* and *eros*.[33] It aims to secure a 'union of the new sensibility with a new rationality' and to develop both a 'sensuous' conception of rationality and a 'rational' conception of sensuousness.[34]

3

For, Marcuse, then men are rational beings who find their highest fulfilment in the maximum possible realization of freedom and happiness. Since there is no being higher than man and there are no human values higher than freedom and happiness, there is no higher principle to which the pursuits of freedom and happiness can be subordinated. Accordingly, Marcuse argues that man has a 'self-evident' and natural right to a free and happy life, and that human societies exist to make it a worldly reality. A free and rational man cannot blindly offer his allegiance and support to his community. He must ask, 'What is this community like to which I am to obligate myself? Can it sustain human happiness and dignity?'[35] He has an obligation to support it 'only if the community...secures him the possibility of a fulfilled existence worthy of man, or if the community can be directed toward such an end'. Marcuse argues that every social institution and practice must be judged by the 'principle of sufficient reason, the authentic and basic principle of rationalism'.[36] Not everything that exists has a right to exist; its existence is only 'legitimate' if it accords with reason. Not 'pure existence' but essence is the source of right, and reason is its sole judge and custodian.

According to Marcuse, the 'rationality' of a social order, the 'legitimacy' of a form of government and the 'lawfulness' of a law must be judged in terms of their ability to promote the 'greatest possible' freedom and happiness.[37] In his view, the authority of a government cannot lie in its formal origin but only in the content of its substantive purposes.[38] For him the trend towards 'formalization' and 'reification' evident in post-Kantian philosophers' attempts to locate the authority of a government wholly in the office and the formal rules that constitute it rests upon fundamentally false assumptions. It implies that one is free to acknowledge the existence, but not to question the purposes, of authority, that the form and content of a law can be neatly separated, that what is universal in form is also necessarily universal in content, that the freedom of an individual is located in the subject's will and not in the real world of social relationship, and so on – all of which Marcuse rejects largely along the lines of Marx's criticism of Hegel's *Philosophy of Right*. In his view the question of the 'ends of government' is the most basic question in political theory and has rightly occupied the attention of all great political philosophers. He regrets that, under the influence of amoral positivism, political theorists today have ignored the question and have concentrated on analysing the nature, and justifying the existence, of the established authority.

For Marcuse, then, men are entitled to expect that their society will use all available resources to maximize human freedom and happiness. When it does not do so, but instead remains content to sustain the prevailing pattern of domination, it forfeits its claim to the allegiance of its members. A revolutionary situation arises when a new society capable of creating a much greater amount of freedom and happiness than could the established social order becomes a realizable possibility. It is a 'tragic' situation, in the sense that two 'historical societies' confront each other, one refusing to give way and the other demanding to be realized, each supported by powerful social groups. The established society is not wholly irrational and therefore not wholly devoid of a moral claim. However, since its rationality is vastly inferior to that of the new society, its moral right to exist is 'overridden' by the higher moral right of its superior rival. In this conflict of 'right against right', of the claims of the positive against those of the negative, a citizen is 'guilty' no matter what he does.[39] However, the alternatives confronting him are not morally equal, and his line of action is clear, namely, to respond to the superior moral claim of the new social order.

If the established society were to give way voluntarily, or if it were capable of being replaced by democratic means, the revolution would be peaceful. However, since no society ever abdicates voluntarily, the overthrow of one society by another always involves violence. Marcuse argues that in absolute ethical terms – that is to say, in terms of 'suprahistorical validity' – violence is inherently evil, and no one is ever justified in taking even a single life.[40] In his view, however, this kind of abstract reasoning is inapplicable to politics. First, although violence is evil, it is not the only evil. Exploiting, starving and oppressing fellow human beings are also evil, and violence may be the only way to eradicate them. One needs to work out a 'calculus of violence', therefore, to decide where the balance of evil lies. The second (and, in Marcuse's view, far more important) reason why violence cannot be rejected *a priori* is that politics is an historical activity and can only be judged by historical standards, as opposed to 'suprahistorical' and absolute ones. If there were to be a complete embargo on violence, the political community itself would become impossible, for there is no society which does not resort to war, or use the police and prisons to maintain the established institutions, or threaten potential law breakers with physical punishment. The government, further, is responsible not only for the violence it uses itself but also for that which it authorizes, connives at, exports or is unwilling to prevent. Marcuse argues that to invoke the principle of the sanctity of life against the revolutionary use of violence but to remain silent about the violence of the established society is hypocrisy: 'one cannot start becoming moral and ethical at an arbitrary but expedient point of cut off: the point of revolution.' In Marcuse's view, the abstract and *a priori* rejection of violence is meaningless, since the choice in any historical context is always between one form of violence and another, between the violence of the established society and that of the revolutionary. One has therefore no alternative but to work out 'the inhuman arithmetic' of 'immoral history' and decide which form of violence is more progressive and economical. Marcuse is convinced that the violence used to close the 'tragic' and 'unnecessary' gap between 'real possibility and actuality, between the rational and the real' is fully justified. Since the term 'justification' carries 'a moral connotation and has an air of subjectivity', Marcuse prefers to say that violence is 'rational' when it can be shown to be historically progressive.

4

Marcuse's political theory is obviously uneven. It contains both brilliant, profound insights and also some extremely naïve and untenable ideas. The latter are often only the result of his misinterpretation of his insights or his keenness to put them to a questionable use. Accordingly, we shall take them together.

Marcuse's theory of man, upon which his social and political theory rests, is open to several fundamental objections. He freely talks about human essence as if it were an unproblematic concept. As Kierkegaard, Marx, Heidegger, Jaspers, Sartre and others have argued, the concepts of human nature and human essence raise some very difficult philosophical problems and may even turn out to be incoherent. Marcuse makes no attempt to counter their arguments, or to show why the concept is necessary or whether man can know his own essence in the same way as he can know that of the non-human world. Further, he is ambiguous about the nature of human essence. Sometimes he says that man is an historical being – all his needs are 'historically determined and historically mutable' – and that human essence is historical in nature. On other occasions he insists that man has an historically invariant essence. He claims to lay bare the 'structure and tendencies of the psyche prior to its organization by the reality' and freely attributes to man such 'instincts' as *thanatos* and *eros*. On yet other occasions he says that man has an historically invariant essence but its content is subject to historical variation. He never explains what possible universal properties can inhere in human essence when its content is wholly historical.

As we have seen, Marcuse claims to advance 'essential theoretical truths' about man but does not explain how he arrives at them. He claims that they are based on analyses of past and present political struggles and visions of the good life but nowhere undertakes such an analysis. He claims, further, that his statements about human essence are 'ultimately verified' by historical struggles, but he does not justify this claim, nor does he explain how historical struggles can validate universal truths.[41] Sometimes he says also that the statements are verified 'only *post festum*', in the sense that men make them come true by acting on them. He evidently does not notice the difficulties of historical pragmatism, nor the fact that historical praxis can make even otherwise false beliefs come true. In short, Marcuse lacks the epistemology needed to sustain his onto-logical assertions about man. As a result, they remain statements of personal preferences, and his claim to provide the objective criteria of moral and political judgement turn out to be suspect.

This is not to say that Marcuse's view of man does not contain important insights. Much of what he says about the epistemological role of the senses in the construction of reality, the ontological link between *logos* and *eros*, the erotic basis of morality and so on is fascinating and persuasive. And his criticisms of many of the neat disjunctions characteristic of much of traditional philosophy are perceptive. The point, however, is that he replaces the disjunctions by arbitrary and undifferentiated fusions, and this is wholly unsatis-factory. For example, he is right to criticize the post-Cartesian dualism between *logos* and *eros*. However, rather than sensitively exploring the complex connections between the two and relating them without destroying their autonomy, he fuses the two. He talks of 'sensuous' rationality and 'rational' sensousness without explaining what these concepts mean or showing that they are even coherent. A dualism is not overcome merely by juxtaposing the conflicting concepts in an evocative but ambiguous linguistic formula.

Again, Marcuse is right to insist upon the inner connections between apparently diverse human desires and aspirations. However, rather than analysing and examining their nature and relations, he indiscriminately reduces them all to an abstract drive for erotic gratification, of which the human search for identity, integrity, self-respect, truth, beauty and so on are supposed to be so many different forms. On the basis of an extremely tenuous and unargued assumption that beauty is always 'one and the same', no matter what its forms, he asserts that the love of one's body generates the love of other bodies, and that the love of corporeal beauty generates the love of intellectual and spiritual beauty. He evidently does not realize that physical beauty is a different *type* of beauty from intellectual beauty, that the expression 'intellectual beauty' is at best a metaphor, and that there is no obvious reason why the love of flowers or of women should necessarily generate the love of ideas or of knowledge. He makes a similar mistake in believing that sexual love is basically the same as, for example, intellectual love and that the pleasures of sexual intercourse are not qualitatively different from those of writing a book, contemplating the beauty of nature or making a good speech in Parliament. Once it is recognized that *eros* is not a simple homogeneous principle and that therefore there is no 'unbroken ascent in erotic fulfilment' of the type Marcuse imagines, the entire basis of his theory of man turns out to be questionable.

Marcuse's theory of man, and also therefore his social and political theory, is articulated in terms of such concepts as autonomy, self-determination, happiness and natural right, none of which he carefully analyses. Take, for example, his concept of autonomy or freedom. It would seem that since for Marcuse autonomy is inherent in rationality, every rational man is autonomous. Marcuse, however, is not content to say this. As with other concepts, he advances the maximalist definition of autonomy. He contends that only a man who fully and freely determines his needs, desires, thoughts, feelings and purposes is autonomous, and that anyone falling short of this is 'dominated'. Marcuse's radical version of Mill's similar view is highly dubious.

First, it is not clear why autonomy should be defined in such extreme terms. Second, the definition rests on an untenable dualist view of the self. It implies that the human self occupies a transcendental realm and 'descends' from time to time to the world of everyday experience to choose between various desires, feelings and needs. The incoherence of this Kantian view of the self has been amply demonstrated by the philosophers from Hegel onwards. Third, when defined in the strong sense, autonomy becomes an impossible ideal. To say that autonomy requires freedom from all influences other than those originating from the individual agent's own consciousness is to imply that the self can somehow transcend all social and historical influences, a view that Marcuse himself rejects. As a social being who necessarily acquires his self-consciousness and sense of identity within the framework of a specific way of life, no man can every be fully aware of, let alone freely determine, all his innermost feelings, forms of thought, basic assumptions and so on. Fourth, as Marcuse defines autonomy, we have no means of knowing whether or not a man is autonomous, for any coincidence between his views and those of his society arouses the suspicion that he may not have arrived at them autonomously but may have imbibed them from his environment. As Marcuse's antinomian and manicheist ethic shows, his view of autonomy has a tendency to encourage an intense desire to be different, even destructuve, for there can be no better proof of one's autonomy than the courage to reject and 'contest' established institutions.[42] This is hardly autonomy, however, for it is parasitic upon, and perpetualy defines itself in terms of, what it rejects.

There is yet another difficulty. Even if a man were persuaded that he had acted autonomously, Marcuse would not call him autonomous if his desires, needs and views did not serve his 'true' interests. For Marcuse only a rational man is autonomous; a rational man follows the objective dictates of human essence, and therefore only a man whose needs and thoughts conform to human essence is truly autonomous or free. This raises the obvious question of who defines human essence. Step by step Marcuse is led to the predictable conclusion that only the man whose thoughts and needs correspond to his definition of human essence is autonomous. Like most rationalists, Marcuse defines autonomy in terms of its content rather than its form and cannot avoid measuring it against the allegedly objective principle of reason.

Marcuse's view of reason is a source of many of the inadequacies of his political and social theory. He rightly views reason as one of man's highest capacities and stresses its negative and critical nature. However, his own view of it remains largely uncritical. He argues that reason is the source of man's capacity for autonomy, and that the autonomous men freely formulate their own goals. It is strange, therefore, that he takes freedom and happiness as unproblematic human goals and never asks if men may not violently disagree about their nature and importance or, indeed, if some of them may not prefer other goals. It is even more strange that in his ideal society, in which men are at last fully autonomous, they are not supposed to disagree about the nature of the individual and collective purposes, the ordering of their priorities and the allocation of their resources. It is not at all clear why the more autonomous men become, the less they should disagree. In any case Marcuse does not seem to notice that the negative reason he so rightly cherishes as man's highest capacity more or less withers away in his ideal society.

Further, although Marcuse emphasizes the negativity of reason, he does not grasp its full implications. He judges a social order principally on the basis of the good it prevents rather than the evil it inflicts, and he anchors reason in the possible future rather than the real present. This way of defining the negative reason creates obvious difficulties. While the evil a social order generates is real and identifiable, the good it prevents is hypothetical, indeterminate and not amenable to rational discussion. Marcuse's negative reason can therefore hardly avoid becoming indeterminate and vague, recommending ill-defined and elusive goals and making vague and abstract criticisms. Moreover, since the good that critical reason pursues is not grounded in an historical analysis of the frustrations and aspirations of specific groups of men, Marcuse is confronted by the rather absurd problem of looking around for men and women who will accept and die for his conception of their good. He works out an abstract, 'rational' ideal and wonders how it can be realized. He turns to the proletariat, which he has considered his ideal constituency, for which he has designed this ideal. When it declines, he frantically looks around for less unwilling groups, such as the poor, the unprivileged, ethnic minorities, the Third World, students and Hippies. When they too refuse to be the agents of social change, Marcuse mumbles curses and despairs. He never pauses to inquire if the alleged hiatus between reason and reality does not spring from the fact that he has defined reason independently of reality. The hiatus would have been reduced to a manageable gap if he had fixed his gaze on a burgeoning and immanent actuality rather than a 'transcendental project' summoned from on high, like Plato's Ideas.

As we have already observed, Marcuse understands practical reason almost wholly in instrumental terms. Once theoretical reason has formulated man's true ends, his sole concern is to realize them to the highest possible degree. Marcuse takes freedom and happiness to be the true ends of man and judges the rationality of an action, institution or social order in terms of their ability to attain an objectively identifiable maximum of freedom and happiness. This means that for Marcuse a rational action has three character-istics. First, its rationality is located in its consequences; second, it aims to maximize whatever is considered to be good, so that to be content with a lesser amount of this than is objectively possible is to be irrational, or at least not fully rational; and third, the model of a rational action can be objectively worked out and used as a standard by which to assess the rationality of the specific actions chosen by human agents. In short, Marcuse takes a consequentialist, maximalist and objectivist view of reason.

Marcuse's view of reason is strikingly similar to that of Bentham. Just as Bentham argues that since pleasure alone is good, only that society capable of promoting the maximum possible amount of it is fully rational, Marcuse argues that since freedom and happiness alone are good, only the social order capable of maximizing them is rational. For Marcuse reason is the pursuit of the maximum. And hence it is not enough to improve society; society has to be made as good as objectively possible. Whatever good *can* be achieved *ought* to be achieved. As he puts it, 'Something is true if it is what it can be, fulfilling all its objective possibilities.'[43]

Marcuse's utilitarian view is open to many of the criticisms generally directed against Bentham. He assumes that human beings are abstract maximizers of whatever they consider to be their good. This is surely a false account of human conduct, as Mill pointed out in his critique of Bentham. Further, Marcuse treats freedom and happiness in the same way that Bentham treats pleasure and pain, that is, as abstract and homogeneous entities capable of being quantified and pursued independently of the capacities and needs of the human beings involved. Even as he reduces the different types of reason to *logos,* the different types of love to *eros* and the different types of social control to domination, Marcuse treats the different types of freedom and happiness as if they were all capable of being reduced to one common denominator. Freedom and happiness are not self-subsistent entities which can be considered in isolation. Freedom, minimally, is the ability to choose one's purposes. It cannot therefore be maximized in the abstract but only in relation to the wishes, desires and aspirations of the members of a given society. What is true of freedom is even more true of happiness. Whatever else happiness may mean, it must involve the satisfaction of desires. And since desires conflict and need to be integrated into a coherent pattern of life suited to one's temperament, aspirations and so on, happiness must necessarily be defined in terms of human agents. It is they alone who can ultimately decide where they can find their happiness, how they can pursue and promote it and how they can integrate their various pursuits into a coherent whole. In short, the very idea of maximizing freedom and happiness *in general* is logically incoherent.

Since Marcuse ignores the centrality of the human agent and defines freedom and happiness in the abstract, his essentially instrumental and utilitarian view of reason borders on the technological, precisely the charge he levels at the dominant conception of reason in modern society. For Marcuse a social order is irrational and deserves to be overthrown if it does not achieve all that its technological resources could enable it to achieve. And a transcendent or alternative society deserves to be realized if it is technologically possible. Certainly, he also introduces the concept of intellectual resources among his criteria of political evaluation. However, he uses the term to mean little more than a body of organizational skills and revolutionary ideas. Marcuse's is a highly technological approach to politics, and is therefore, open to obvious objections. A society may be technically but not intellectually or morally possible, in the sense that the intellectual and moral preconditions for its institution (such as moral disillusionment with the established order, a profound sense of outrage at the suffering inflicted by it and the intellectual and moral capacities needed to sustain a better society) may not, in fact, exist. A society's technical resources cannot be abstracted from the capacities, needs and character of its members and used as an independent criterion of evaluation. When Marcuse says that a differently constituted society is possible but that men, alas, do not feel the need for it, he is drawing a false distinction. If men do not need it and are not prepared to fight for it, the new society is simply not possible. Its possibility cannot be defined independently of a human capacity and desire to achieve it. To put the point differently, the intellectual, moral and political preconditions of a new society must be built into the very definition of what is historically possible. Inasmuch as Marcuse's technologically orientated theory of political rationality does not and cannot take account of this, it is incoherent and cannot provide a viable alternative to the currently dominant conception of rationality.

Marcuse's instrumental view of reason prevents him from giving an adequate account of some of the crucial aspects of political life, especially the nature of law, authority and the state. For him a law should be observed and a government should be obeyed if they are rational, and they are rational if they promote human freedom and happiness. He defines legality and legitimacy in wholly instrumental terms. The limitations of this view are obvious. A law is not merely a means of realizing certain ends; it is also a *law*, an authoritative enactment binding upon all the members of a community, including those who disapprove of its purposes. And a government is not any group of men pursuing certain objectives; it has the legitimately acquired authority to take collectively binding decisions and is entitled to the allegiance of its subjects. Marcuse completely ignores the formal character of a law and a government. Since he does not comprehend a law *qua* law and a government *qua* government, he obviously cannot account for them. In general, Marcuse's essentially end-orientated and instrumental approach to social and political life is inherently ill-equipped to account for those relations and institutions which are not wholly or primarily instrumental. Since the relation of authority is one of these, Marcuse's conceptual framework is incapable of providing a coherent theory of authority. He can articulate the purposes of an authority. However, since it is not its purposes that make an authority what it is, Marcuse cannot account for authority *qua* authority. This is evident in his discussion of political obligation. Unlike Rawls, he does not recognize that a law is *prima facie* binding, although one's obligation to it may be overridden if its objectives are thoroughly unjust. Since Marcuse judges a law wholly in terms of its content or purposes, the obligation to obey it, which is entailed by its form, never enters into his calculations. He reduces a law to a mere piece of advice, and ignores its authoritative form. Besides, he advances the fallacious argument that a law of whose *content* one disapproves does not have the *form* of the law either. A law is necessarily two-dimensional; it has the form of a law, and it pursues a specific purpose. In order to judge it, one must take both into account. Further, Marcuse's argument implies that any man may at any time refuse to observe a law on the ground that he disapproves of its objectives. Marcuse is naturally very unhappy with this conclusion, especially because it enables Fascists and other right-wing groups to subvert liveral society. However, he has no answer to them except to invoke an inherently indeterminate and inconclusive distinction between progressive and reactionary uses of violence.

5

Michael Oakeshott

Michael Oakeshott is one of the very few contemporary political philosophers to have given systematic consideration to the nature and task of political philosophy. He has developed not only a distinct style of philosophizing about politics but also an almost entirely new language. He is unhappy with the term 'political philosophy' and would like to replace it with 'civil philosophy'. Almost alone among his contemporaries, he has attempted to replace the concept of reason with intelligence or reflective self-understanding and man with the agent. In many ways he is a philosophical revolutionary whose works have not been read with the care they merit. In this chapter we shall attempt to highlight some of his important insights.

1

Michael Oakeshott first systematically outlined his conception of philosophy in *Experience and its Modes*. Like other Idealist philosophers, he rejects the traditional empiricist dichotomy between the mind and the external world. Objects in the 'external' world become a subject for discussion, and reality can be attributed to them when they form part of human experience, that is, when they are sensed, judged and mediated by thought. And, conversely, all experience is experience of the world. As Oakeshott puts it, 'Subject and object...when separated from one another degenerate into abstractions.... There is...no object apart from a subject; no subject independent of an object'.[1] Such questions as how we know that the external world exists and how it is related to the mind are 'not merely misleading but, to me, nonsensical'. Experience, the 'concrete unity' of the experiencing subject and the experienced object, is the only reality. It is a 'single whole', of which the mind and the 'external' world are one-sided and arbitrary abstractions.

Reality is not 'out there', nor 'in the mind' but is an achievement of thought; it is what experience 'obliges' us to think.[2]

Since experience is the only reality, Oakeshott argues, all intellectual inquiries are concerned with it in one form or another. They differ in the kind of knowledge they seek and offer. Philosophy is distinguished by its concern to offer a 'definitive' understanding of experience. Since experience and understanding are not different it would be more accurate (though perhaps clumsier) to say that philosophy attempts to give an unconditional and absolutely coherent experience. This does not mean that philosophy is concerned with some 'inscrutable Absolute' beyond conception and outside the world of experience'. It aims to offer absolutely coherent experience, not experience or knowledge of the Absolute. Thus it has two basic objectives: first, to understand the 'whole of experience' and, secondly, to understand it 'as a whole' or 'for its own sake'. The former refers to its range of concern, the second to its level of analysis.[3]

Philosophy is concerned with the whole of experience for both epistemological and ontological reasons. Every aspect of experience is integrally connected with the rest and cannot be fully understood without comprehending the whole. To detach or abstract it from the whole is to deprive it of its character and to distort it. Further, only what is 'self-complete' or 'self-subsistent' and does not owe its existence to anything external to itself is ultimately real. Only the totality of experience satisfies this criterion. As Oakeshott puts it, 'For me the only absolute individual is the universe as a whole, for this alone is self-complete without either environment or relations.'[4] As an inquiry devoted to the pursuit of definitive understanding, philosophy cannot be content with anything less than the totality of experience.

Philosophy aims to understand not only the whole of experience but also experience *as a whole* or for its own sake. For Oakeshott, as for all Idealists, every limited standpoint arrests experience. It necessarily rests on specific assumptions or presuppositions which it does not question. Since philosophy aims at a definitive account of experience, it avoids all limited standpoints and therefore all assumptions. Indeed, according to Oakeshott, a constant and relentless critique of assumptions could be said to be the most distinguishing characteristic of philosophy. Philosophy is unique among all intellectual inquiries in being radical, self-conscious and self-critical: radical because it avoids all abstract and partial standpoints and aims to grasp the whole *as* a whole; self-conscious because it constantly 'turns back' on itself to examine its own nature and methods; and critical because it elucidates and scrutinizes its assumptions at each stage of its investigation.

While the totality of experience must be viewed as a whole if one's account of it is to be fully satisfactory, it may also be arrested and viewed from limited standpoints. Such standpoints Oakeshott calls 'modes', for they rest on specific assumptions and modify the character of the totality of experience. There are many such modes, of which Oakeshott takes three to be the most important, namely, practice, history and science. Like philosophy, modes deal with the whole of experience but differ from it in analysing experience from limited points of view. A mode rests on specific assumptions, which it does not and cannot question. On the basis of these postulates and the categories of understanding which they 'imply, call forth and maintain', each mode constructs a unique world of ideas, including its own distinctive criteria of reality, fact, evidence and truth, as well as methods of investigation, modes of discourse and ways of reaching and validating its conclusions. It articulates the totality of experience in terms of these and offers its own characteristic understanding of it.

The practical mode views the totality of experience *sub specie voluntatis*. It postulates that the natural individual is a self-contained whole, that he can be neatly separated from the natural world and other selves, that the world can be judged in terms of good and bad and the desired and the desirable, and so on. From the standpoint of practice a human being is essentially a creature of desires and needs, judging the world in terms of its 'habitableness' and understanding the totality of experience in terms of such categories as 'self', 'the other', 'change', 'desire', 'ought', 'good', 'bad', 'pleasure' and 'pain'. From the standpoint of practice, reality is what can be grasped sensually, and truth is what works.

History views the whole of experience *sub specie praeteritorum*. It rests on such postulates as that change is real, that every event is related to certain other events and is not separated from them by an 'absolute hiatus', and that we can account *for* change by means of a full account *of* change. On the basis of these and other postulates, the historian constructs categories of historical understanding and his own characteristic views of the past, truth, reality, cause, explanation and so on. Unlike practice and history, the scientific mode of experience views the world in relation not to human desires and needs, nor to the temporality and the uniqueness of each event, but *sub specie quantitatis*. For science the totality of experience is amenable to quantitative methods and concepts. 'Whatever cannot be conceived quantitatively cannot belong to scientific knowledge.'

For Oakeshott science aims to develop an 'absolutely stable and communicable' body of knowledge and is necessarily driven by its basic objective to reduce the totality of experience to mathematically expressible laws and statistical generalizations. In the pursuit of this type of knowledge, it develops its own appropriate structural concepts, methods of investigation and criteria of truth, reality, proof, explanation and knowledge.

For Oakeshott each mode of experience represents a distinct way of understanding the totality of experience. It is 'homogeneous' in the sense that its 'structural concepts', congruous both with one another and with its postulates, constitute a logically coherent world of ideas. It is 'self-contained' in the sense that its categories and methods are adequate for its purpose. It is also 'sovereign' within its own world of ideas and 'wholly and absolutely independent' of the others. What one mode regards as a fact, truth, evidence or argument is 'nothing at all' for another.[5] Since the modes are 'tight, exclusive, insular' and 'wholly irrelevant' to one another, there can be 'neither dispute nor agreement' between them. A historical explanation, for example, can be judged only by historical and not by practical or scientific criteria. To pass in argument from one mode of reasoning to another is to commit the fallacy of *ignoratio elenchi*, for Oakeshott the most common and dangerous of all fallacies. Every intelligent and intelligible statement is necessarily made in the language of a specific world of ideas.

Just as the modes are mutually irrelevant, so too are philosophy and the modes. Philosophy has nothing to learn from them. It is concerned with experience as a whole, of which the modes present an abstract account. Since their conclusions and findings are secured from abstract standpoints, they are necessarily defective and can have no value or validity for philosophy. Philosophy cannot, therefore, be a synthesis of the conclusions of the various modes, as is often maintained, nor can a philosophical argument or doctrine be criticized on the basis of such conclusions. Just as philosophy has nothing to learn from the modes, they do not have anything to learn from it. Each mode is sovereign and self-contained. A historian, a scientist or a practical man does not need the philosopher to tell him how to go about his business. Philosophy cannot compete with a mode on its own ground, nor do its job for it. If we want a quantitative, historical or practical understanding of experience, we must turn to science, history or practice, and not to philosophy.

Philosophy, then, is concerned to understand the totality of experience in terms of a coherent system of logically interrelated, concrete concepts. Since the modes exist and necessarily overreach themselves, a second task devolves upon philosophy. It consists in analysing the logical structures of modes, comprehending them in their totality, demarcating their conceptual territories, elucidating their postulates and demonstrating that none of them, despite their claims to the contrary, can offer a definitive account of the totality of experience as a whole. The two tasks are interdependent. Only because it is concerned with the totality of experience as a whole is philosophy able to recognize and criticize the inadequacies of the modes. And, conversely, since experience is ordinarily arrested and viewed from limited perspectives, a 'clear and unclouded' view of it can be attained only by criticizing and superseding such arrests. While insisting on the importance of both tasks, Oakeshott places greater emphasis on the critical function of philosophy, on the ground that in a world cluttered up with abstract modes, criticism is necessary both to remind ourselves continually of their inadequacies and to pave the way for the constructive endeavour.

In *On Human Conduct,* published in 1975, we have Oakeshott's latest statement of the nature of philosophy in general and political philosophy in particular. As in *Experience and its Modes,* he emphasizes both the critical and the constructive tasks of philosophy, defines it as the pursuit of unconditional and definitive understanding, stresses its radical, self-conscious and fully critical nature, and argues that it is concerned to examine and to explain its subject matter in terms of its postulates or conditions. He argues also that philosophy is a purely explanatory form of inquiry, mocks at the view that it can ever entail practical recommendations and insists that a philosopher is not a *philosophe*, nor is a theorist a 'theoretician'.[6]

Oakeshott also, however, modifies some of his earlier views and introduces over a dozen new categories. His increasing dissatisfaction over the years with the term 'philosophy' comes to a head. He only occasionally uses the term and prefers the term 'theory'. He chooses to say that a philosopher theorizes rather than philosophizes, describes him as an unconditional theorist rather than a philosopher, and calls the outcome of his investigations a theory rather than a philosophy of the relevant subject matter. Oakeshott also argues that not only philosophy but all intellectual inquiries, including science and history, theorize – that is, explain their subject matter in terms of its postulates and thus share a basic structure or direction of investigation. He argues that theorizing consists in exploring further, and raising to another level, the initial, confused understanding of an experience. It is a 'transitive engagement' and hence one does not theorize *about* but theorizes an experience and develops not the concept *of,* say, state or society but the concept state or society.[7] He argues too that all human activities, including the theoretical, involve practice and are 'practical' in the sense that they involve 'knowing how to participate in a practice'. The opposite of theory, therefore, is conduct, not practice.[8]

Instead of 'experience', the dominant category in *Experience and its Modes,* he now refers to a 'going-on' as the subject matter of theoretical investigation. True to the practice, relatively absent in his earlier but more and more evident in recent writings of dividing everything neatly into two, he argues that the goings-on in the world belong to two 'categorially different' types, namely, those which 'exhibit intelligence' and those which do not. Human conduct belongs to the former and natural processes, including animal behaviour, to the latter. Each 'predicates' a categorially different 'order of inquiry'. Within each order of inquiry there are different 'idioms of inquiry' dealing either with different subject matter or with the same subject matter from different points of view. Such different idioms of inquiry as physics, chemistry and botany belong to one order of inquiry, and ethics, jurisprudence and aesthetics to another.

For Oakeshott to theorize something is to relate it to, and explain it in terms of, its postulates. A theoretical inquiry consists of two stages, namely, identification and the elucidation of postulates. In order to theorize a going-on, one must first identify it, that is, determine its 'ideal' or 'essential' character. An ideal character specifies the characteristics which uniquely belong to a going-on and articulates its 'identity'. Having elucidated the identity of a going-on, one may do two things. One may similarly elucidate the identities of other goings-on and relate, group, combine, compare and contrast them. If one is primarily interested in comparing, classifying or manipulating identities, as are the practical man and students of some types of comparative inquiry, the degree of intelligibility offered by this level of understanding is 'equal' to one's 'needs'. One may, therefore, build a theoretical home on this 'platform of understanding' and provide a coherent, though rather poor, understanding of the goings-on in question.

A theoretical inquiry proper begins when one is puzzled by an identity and wonders what it really is, why it has a certain character and how it is possible. To say that John is considering which hat to buy is at one level unproblematic, for we all know what the statement means and how to choose and buy hats. At another level, however, it is problematic, for we may wonder what it means to choose, how it is possible to chose and what the activities of choice and deliberation involve. Similarly, we all know what a thunderstorm is and how to recognize and describe it to a stranger. However, one may wonder why and how it occurs, and why it is accompanied by such specific features as lightning and noise. A theorist is concerned to understand an identity which has become problematic, and, obviously, comparing and contrasting it with other identities is of no help to him. What he can and must do is to 'interrogate' it, elucidate and examine its postulates and, in their light, explain why it has a certain character. For example, by analysing what it is to reflect, deliberate, choose, think and so on, a theorist can give a coherent account of what it means for someone to choose a hat. And, similarly, having identified a set of goings-on such as noise, flashes of light and torrents of rain as a thunderstorm, a scientist understands and explains the latter in terms of its postulates, namely, the laws relating to electrical discharges. The explanation that a theorist offers of a going-on Oakeshott calls a 'theorem'. For him a theorist explains an identity in terms of theorems constructed on the basis of its postulates.[9]

Although a theorist may be content to analyse the postulates of an identity and to build a world of theoretical ideas on this 'platform of understanding', he is, if he is curious, driven further. Just as his inquiry begins when he realizes that an identity he has been assuming to be self-evident is, in fact, problematic, its postulates, which he has hitherto accepted as unproblematic, are, in fact, not so. They rest on other postulates. For example, is man really capable of free will, so that my friend John can be said to deliberate and to choose? A theorist must therefore pursue his investigation yet further, until he arrives at an unconditional and definitive understanding of the kind outlined by Oakeshott in *Experience and its Modes*. A theorist committed to the pursuit of unconditional understanding is a philosopher.

Oakeshott's view of philosophy as unconditional theorizing raises the paradox he noticed but did not resolve in *Experience and its Modes*. A philosopher concerned with unconditional theorizing moves further and further away from, and is eventually driven 'far out of sight' of, the original going-on with which he began his inquiry.[10] The ideal character is one move away from it; its postulates, two; their postulates, three; and so on. When a theorist reaches the highest, metaphysical stage, he is concerned only with the general and permanent features of the totality of experience, and specific goings-on, including politics, are no longer visible to him. This means that political philosophy is an inherently precarious and fragile form of inquiry. The more philosophical it becomes, the further it moves away from politics! Oakeshott argues that a theorist of civil society must realize that if he were to launch himself into the adventure of unconditional theorizing, he would be carried 'far out of sight' of his subject matter. He must come to terms with the inherently conditional and 'intermediate' nature of his enterprise, 'forswear metaphysics' and occupy a 'platform of understanding' which is 'equal to his needs' and from which he can focus his full attention on civil society.[11]

Which 'platform of understanding' is adequate for his needs Oakeshott determines as follows. Given his view of theory, the task of a theory of civil association is twofold: to determine the ideal character of civil association, and to analyse its postulates. Now, civil association is a relationship between human beings, and hence a form of human conduct. A theorist of civil association, therefore, needs to determine as well the ideal character of human conduct and its postulates. If he were to go beyond human conduct and concern himself with man's relation to nature, God and so forth, he would be preoccupied with the universe as a whole and would not be able to focus his gaze on civil association. Human conduct offers him the widest, most appropriate and most self-contained context within which to locate his subject matter. The 'programme of inquiry' Oakeshott lays down for the theorist of civil association (and, by definition, for himself), then, is this: to analyse the ideal character and postulates of human conduct and, in their light, the ideal character and postulates of civil association.

2

Human conduct is *inter homines*. For Oakeshott it is defined by the activity of intelligent agents pursuing their imagined and desired satisfaction in specific and understood situations by eliciting specific responses from each other.[12] Schematically, every interpersonal action, of which human conduct is the ideal character, has several necessary features. It occurs in a specific situation; the agent understands the situation in a certain manner and finds it unacceptable; he believes that the 'unacceptability' can be removed and imagines, wishes for and intends to experience a specific satisfaction; the satisfaction desired depends upon another agent or agents; the agent deliberates and undertakes a specific action or utterance deemed capable of evoking the desired response from others; his deliberation and action take account of the practices regulating interpersonal intercourse, especially moral practices; and, finally, every action involves self-disclosure and self-enactment. Human conduct so identified rests on several postulates, such as the capacity for free agency, reflective consciousness, deliberation, persuasion, practice and morality. Oakeshott analyses both the features and the postulates with considerable subtlety and thoroughness. Since we are concerned with his theory of civil association, we shall ignore his discussion of human conduct and begin with a brief outline of his concept of practice, the basis of his discussion of civil association.

When men live together and interact on a relatively permanent basis, their relations cannot be episodic or 'transactional' but need to be structured in terms of what Oakeshott calls 'practices'. 'A practice may be identified as a set of considerations, manners, uses, observances, customs, canons, maxims, principles, rules, and offices specifying useful procedures or denoting obligations or duties which relate to human actions and utterances.'[13]

A practice lays down a norm of conduct and is general in nature. In Oakeshott's view, a practice can never entail a specific action, that is, require an agent to make a specific substantive choice; it specifies only the conditions or considerations which he must take into account in whatever he chooses to say or do.[14] A practice is 'a set of conditions which qualify performances'. Oakeshott calls these conditions 'considerations', 'because they qualify but do not determine performance'. A practice is like a language. Even as a language does not tell us what to say but instead provides resources in the light of which we can choose what to say and how, a practice can never tell an agent what to do. Even the least ambiguous duty does not specify a substantive action and can be fulfilled only by the choice of action of a free agent. This is so for several reasons.

First, a practice is, by its nature, general; hence it cannot enjoin a specific action. The practice that requires me to be honest or truthful cannot tell me *what* to do or to say in specific situations. It lays down only that whatever I choose to do or say must be decided in the light of the demands of these practices. Secondly, since a practice is general in nature, an agent needs to interpret it, determine its range of application and decide whether his action falls within this range. Thirdly, practice presupposes, and is logically parasitic upon, human actions. It is because men are engaged in specific actions that practice becomes necessary and has a point. Since every action aims at a specific satisfaction, no action can ever consist in merely following a practice. I cannot follow the practice of punctuality in the abstract; I can only make it a point to be punctual when I attend my office, go out for a walk or do whatever else I do. And, similarly, I cannot resolve to practise honesty, that is, to be honest in the abstract. I can only resolve to say honestly whatever I decide to say. Oakeshott advances the fascinating thesis that I can *never* undertake a moral action or be faced with a moral choice; I can only act or choose morally.[15] There is no class of actions or choices called 'moral'. There are only substantive actions undertaken in adequate subscription to moral practices, rules and duties. In short, a practice or rule can never be *executed or carried out,* only subscribed to in the choice of substantive actions. Since practices presuppose and regulate substantive actions, they are basically 'adverbial' qualifications of actions and are best represented by adverbs rather than 'faded' abstract nouns or even adjectives.[16]

Practices differ greatly in their complexity, stringency, origin, range of application and so on and can be classified in many different ways. Oakeshott classifies them as 'prudential' and 'moral'. A prudential practice is instrumental in nature. It is designed to achieve a specific substantive purpose and is modified or discarded when it hinders its realization. An office routine, a railway timetable or the rules of a school, a factory or an army belong to this category. A moral practice is very different in nature. It is 'a practice without an extrinsic purpose'.[17] It is accepted as 'authoritative' or binding and is 'not instrumental to the achievement of any substantive purpose or to the satisfaction of any substantive want'. No doubt, a moral practice may, and generally does, have beneficial consequences; honesty is often the best policy, and truth generally sustains human relationships. However, neither practice is a means to the achievement of these and other advantages, and neither stands condemned if these fail to accrue. Its authority is inherent in it and not derived from anything external.

Every human association is structured in terms of practices. As we have seen, practices are either prudentdial or moral. Prudential practices serve a common substantive purpose or purposes, whereas moral practices are non-instrumental in nature. This means that there are two 'categorially distinct *modes* of human association': prudential or 'enterprise' association, united in terms of a 'common purpose', and moral or 'practice-based' association, 'united in terms of the acknowledgement of the 'authority of common practices'. The former is 'substantial, concerned with the satisfaction of chosen wants', while the latter is 'formal and in terms of the considerations which compose a practice'. According to Oakeshott, a hospital, an army, an orchestra, a school, a sect, a fire station, a political party, a guild and a factory belong to the former category, and friendship, a neighbourhood, the speakers of a common language and the associations of historians or chemists to the latter category. Although the two modes of association have several features in common, they are qualitatively different in their forms of constitution.[18]

The members of enterprise association are united 'in terms of the pursuit of some common purpose, some substantive condition of things to be jointly procured, or some common interest to be continuously satisfied'. The common purpose may consist in the promotion of a common faith or cause, the pursuit of a common productive undertaking or a trade, the protection of a common interest or fear of a common enemy. The purpose may be simple or complex, and the ties of association may be close, like those of a corporation, or loose, like those of a partnership or an alliance. What basically distinguishes enterprise association is the fact that it has a common purpose which it is designed to realize. Obviously, it has a structure of authority. However, this authority derives its legitimacy and justification from the common purpose and is structured so as to facilitate its realization. Not the recognition of the authority but the acceptance of the purpose is the unifying principle of enterprise association. Further, since it is united in terms of a common purpose, enterprise association has an overall 'policy' to which all its activities are geared. And governing it is a 'managerial' engagement, involving decisions concerning how to execute the policy and what substantive actions to require of its members. Enterprise association does, no doubt, involve a moral relationship. However, since it is not constituted in moral terms, it is not itself moral association.

Practice-based or moral association is very different. It is held together by the acceptance not of a common purpose but of the authority of common practices. Its members share nothing save the recognition of the authority of these practices and remain free to pursue their self-chosen substantive purposes, provided, of course, that they subscribe adequately to the considerations and 'compunctions' of the practices concerned. The speakers of a common language, for example, are bound together not by a common purpose but by a common practice and are free to say what they like as long as they subscribe to the general requirements of their language. And, similarly, friends are bound together by common allegiance to certain moral practices. Unlike enterprise association, practice-based or moral association is purely formal in nature.

Given that human relationships can be constituted in 'two categorially discrete modes', Oakeshott asks to which of the two modes civil association belongs.[19] The question is not entirely proper and, as we shall see, rather loaded, for Oakeshott has at best shown that the two modes are mutually exclusive but not that they are collectively exhaustive, and therefore one could rejoin that civil association belongs to some third type of association. Oakeshott is convinced that civil association cannot be enterprise association for the following reasons, some rather strange.[20] First it is difficult to see what common purposes civil association exists to realize. If peace and security are mentioned as likely candidates, Oakeshott contends that they are not substantive purposes. Although he does not make clear the distinction between purpose and substantive purpose, he seems to think that, like happiness and excellence, security and peace are too general and too indeterminate to constitute the objectives of government actions. Even as one cannot seek happiness but only specific satisfactions, civil association cannot pursue security in the abstract but only by enforcing specific laws. Second, if civil association were an enterprise association, it would not be an association of equals, for its members would have different degrees of importance and, therefore, unequal rights and obligations corresponding to their contributions to the common purpose. Third, if civil association had a common purpose, it would not be able to tolerate individuals or groups wedded to purposes different from its own. Oakeshott observes, 'It is not easy to rebut the view that the logic of a state thus constituted assigns to the office of its government the authority to exterminate associates whose continued existence is judged to be irredeemably prejudicial to the pursuit of its purpose.' For purpose-based association its subjects are its human resources, to be mobilized for the realization of its purposes. For Oakeshott a purposive civil association is necessarily collectivist, although for various reasons it may not become so in practice. Fourth, if civil association were enterprise association, it would consist of managers not rulers, role performers not subjects, instrumental rules not laws, and so on. It is difficult to see how such an association differs from a factory, a business concern or a development corporation, and why it should be called 'civil'.

Fifth, and this is his 'main' argument, Oakeshott contends that it is inconsistent with the nature of civil association to have a common purpose.[21] A purposive association is 'necessarily' voluntary, in the sense that its members have chosen to belong to it and are free to leave it when they no longer share its purposes. As Oakeshott says, 'compulsory enterprise association is a self-contradiction.'[22] Now, civil association is by its very nature 'comprehensive, compulsory and exclusive'.[23] It is conprehensive, presumably, in the sense that its laws apply to all within its jurisdiction, compulsory in that it requires subscription to its *lex* on pain of punishment, irrespective of whether or not its citizens *(cives)* approve of it, and exclusive in the sense that a *civis* cannot be subject to two different sovereign jurisdictions. Since civil association is non-optional and exclusive, it cannot have a common substantive purpose, for it would then have to allow its members to withdraw when they could no longer share its purposes, and no civil association can allow this option. Compulsory enterprise association forces men to subscribe to purposes that they have not themselves chosen and in which they may not believe. By breaking 'the link between belief and conduct which constitutes moral agency', it violates freedom and moral autonomy and commits 'a moral enormity'.[24]

Civil association, then, cannot be understood or identified as enterprise association. Oakeshott contends that it can only be practice-based or moral association; 'the conditions of civil association are moral conditions in not being instrumental to the satisfaction of substantive wants.'[25] The practices in terms of which civil association is constituted consist not of vague and indeterminate practices but 'entirely' of rules, that is, authoritative prescriptions laying down norms of conduct. Civil association is 'rule-articulated association'. The rules constituting the civil association, which Oakeshott calls *lex,* are of various kinds.[26] Some relate to offices of authority and specify their modes of constitution, powers, duties, procedures and so on. Some are enacted by the designated legislative authority. Others lay down how *lex* and the rules arranging offices of authority can be altered. Some consist of judicial and administrative decisions. Others lay down who can occupy specific offices and exercise the powers vested in them.

Oakeshott uses the term *respublica* to refer to the entire system of rules of conduct to which *cives* subscribe in their relations with one another. Civil association is constituted by the common recognition of the authority of *respublica.* Oakeshott observes, 'What relates *cives* to one another and constitutes civil association is the acknowledgement of the authority of *respublica* and the recognition of subscription to its conditions as an obligation.'[27] In relation to *respublica, cives* put by all that differentiates them from one another and acknowledge themselves as formal equals. As *cives,* they share nothing except the 'practice of civility' and have no obligations to one another save to be civil or civilly just. They are not partners or comrades in an enterprise with a common purpose but participants in a common practice defined by formal rules. Of all the rules constituting *respublica, lex* is the most important. It is unique to civil association and constitutes its very basis. *Lex* is not a mere collection but a self-contained and internally co-ordinated system of rules enacted by the highest law-making authority. It prescribes the rights and responsibilities of *cives* and unites otherwise unrelated men. *Lex* lays down norms of conduct which, like all general norms, do not enjoin specific actions but only describe the conditions to be subscribed to by *cives* in making their choices of actions and utterances and in terms of which their choices may be civilly justified or indicated. *Lex* cannot be obeyed, only subscribed to or not subscribed to.

Since civil association needs to ensure that its *lex* is adequately subscribed to by its *cives*, it requires 'ruling' and an 'apparatus of rule'. Unlike legislation, which only lays down the conditions of general subscription and does not deal with substantive actions by specific persons, ruling deals with specific actions. Ruling consists of two types of activity, namely adjudication, and administration. Adjudication consists in elucidating the meaning of *lex* in cases of dispute, condemning inadequate subscription and requiring or forbidding an identified agent to undertake a specific action. Adjudication is a 'ruling' based on *lex* and is injunctive in nature. Secondly, the prescriptions of *lex* need to be administered. This consists in 'policing' civil association by engaging in such activities as detecting and preventing crimes, maintaining order and enforcing the law. For Oakeshott the adjudicator and the police are engaged in 'ruling', one in addressing orders to specific persons and the other in enforcing them. The two constitute an 'apparatus of rule'.[28] For Oakeshott law making and ruling are the two most basic activities of civil association. He cannot see why, except to meet the threat of war, civil association should need the all too familiar executive apparatus.

For Oakeshott *cives* have an obligation to observe *lex* because it is made by authorized men according to established procedures. To recognize an authority is to accept an obligation to subscribe to its norms of conduct. Civil laws are morally binding because they are authoritative. A *civis* need not approve of them (that is, believe that they are right or good). He need only recognize their authority and adequately subscribe to their prescriptions. His approval or disapproval is entirely irrelevant to their authority and neither increases nor decreases his obligation to observe them.[29] This means, further, that civil rulers expect observance of the laws on the ground that they are laws. They do not have to show that the laws are good or deserving of popular support, for laws are inherently binding and need no external assistance. Indeed, if civil rulers were to seek to persuade their subjects to obey laws by pointing to their virtues, by promises of better things to come or by reproaching, coaxing, cajoling and bribing them, they would cease to be rulers and become managers. The art of persuasive leadership 'corrupts' and has no place in civil association.[30]

Like the modes of experience discussed earlier, a *respublica*, then, constitutes a self-contained, self-sufficient, homogeneous and 'self-authenticating' world of interdependent and interlocked rules. Rulings and administrative requisitions have authority because of the rules which permit them to be made and which specify their jurisdiction. An office has authority because of the rules which constitute it and specify its powers. The occupant of an office has authority because he occupies it in accordance with rules. *Lex* has authority because it is made by authorized people in adequate subscription to prescribed procedures. If a specific rule were to be questioned, we could move up the 'scale of authorizations' and show how it serived its authority. There is, however, no single rule or procedure which, like Kelsen's *Grundnorm*, as it were, lies at the basis of *respublica* and constitutes its ultimate source of authority. Although rules vary in importance and in their degree of dependence on other rules, they are all interdependent.

Rules constituting *respublica*, then derive their authority from each other. It may be asked how *respublica* derives its own authority. In Oakeshott's view, its authority is derived from the 'continuous acknowledgement of *cives*', an acknowledgement expressed not in their acts of obedience but in their recognition of the obligation to subscribe to its prescriptions. If they were to cease to recognize its rules as binding upon them, its authority would 'lapse'. The authority of *respublica* is not a once-and-for-all endowment made by *cives* at some specific point in time, as some Contractualists naïvely imagined, but the result of a slow and painful historical process. The European states took centuries to establish a single legitimate and generally acknowledged civil authority within their territorial boundaries. In Oakeshott's view, the manner in which the Marylebone Cricket Club, founded in 1787 as a private club and with no power to enforce its decisions, gradually acquired complete authority over the rules of cricket provides an instructive 'analogue'. Its authority 'was acquired solely by being acknowledged to have it'.[31]

As we saw, the rules constituting *respublica* are obligatory because of their authoritative nature, and *cives* need not evaluate and approve of them. However, the conditions prescribed in *respublica* may be examined and criticized in terms of their desirability. This activity, the critical inspection of some items of *respublica*, Oakeshott calls politics. Politics is thinking about the rules of civil intercourse 'in a manner which assents to, but (because it is concerned with desirability) does not refer to, their authority'.[32] *Cives* may engage in politics, although it is primarily the concern of the occupants of legislative office. Politics is at once both an acquiescent and a critical activity; it accepts the authority of *respublica* and criticizes its specific rules.[33] Political deliberation is guided by the considerations of *bonum civile*, that is, what is civilly just or desirable and can be required to be subscribed to by all *cives* under threat of civil penalty. It must relate to the 'possible' conditions of *respublica*, and therefore several types of concern are 'not merely contingently [but] necessarily excluded by the character of *respublica*'. For example, a political proposal cannot be concerned with such objectives as creating a perfect society or bettering the lot of mankind (for civil association is not enterprise association and *cannot* accommodate such proposals), nor with distributive justice (for civil rulers have 'nothing to distribute'), nor with the 'interest of the community' (which for Oakeshott 'does not exist'), nor with imposing specific moral beliefs (for civil association is concerned only with rules of conduct).[34] Civil morality is autonomous and distinct from personal and social morality. Unlike the latter, it is backed by force, deliberately enacted and concerned only with the civil aspect of human conduct. Oakeshott does not specify the positive considerations in terms of which civil morality may be debated beyond saying that a civil rule must, by its very nature, be equally applicable to all *cives*, enforceable, on balance beneficial, consistent with prevailing practices and a reflection of what is currently held to be civilly desirable. In his view, it is a rationalist fallacy to believe that one can discuss political proposals in terms of abstract principle and ideals, for, among other things, such ideals are too general and indeterminate to be integrated into the life of a community. Politics in civil association is the correction of incoherence, not the pursuit of perfection, and therefore a political proposal must be 'intimated' by the established tradition of behaviour and must show regard for the 'etymological decencies and syntactical properties' of the prevailing vernacular language of civil intercourse.[35]

For Oakeshott politics may occur in civil association but need not, as it adds nothing significant to civil life. Civil association exists to provide civil freedom – that is, freedom to pursue only those purposes that one has chosen for oneself and to be restrained by nothing save general and formal civil norms of conduct. This freedom is neither increased by the freedom to participate in political deliberation nor diminished by its absence. Those who have participated in the making of a law do not enjoy any more freedom that those who have not. Both alike have an equal obligation, namely, to subscribe adequately to the prescriptions of *lex,* and equal freedom to pursue their chosen purposes within the framework of *lex.*[36]

For Oakeshott, then, civil association is necessarily a three-dimensional institution.[37] First, it has a specific *modus foederis,* 'mode of association', signifying the 'terms and conditions' on which it is constituted. Secondly, it has an 'office of authority', a generally accepted manner of conducting and deciding its affairs. Authority inheres in an office and has nothing to do with the character of the occupant or the quality of his actions. It is derived from the continuous acknowledgement of *cives* and expressed in their continuous recognition of obligation. Thirdly, it has a 'machinery of government', or 'an apparatus of power' or of 'ruling'. Unlike authority, power is concerned with 'substantive conduct' and refers to the 'ability to procure with certainty a wished-for response in the conduct of another'. Power and authority are categorially different and independent of each other. Of the three aspects of civil association, the first represents its character or 'identity', the second its 'shape', 'form' or 'appearance', and the third its manner of survival. For Oakeshott the first is the most important of the three, and hence he defines the ideal character of civil society in terms of it. Although all three are integrally connected, they are categorially different. Each has its own logic and requires a distinct language of description. In addition to its three necessary structural properties, civil association *may* also accommodate the practice of politics which, again, is categorially different from all three and has its own distinct vocabulary.

Oakeshott contends that the differences between these four have not been fully appreciated by political theorists or, of course, by ordinary men, with the result that the words belonging to one of four vocabularies have been allowed to wander freely into the others and to create confusion and mystification. For example, politics relates to the desirability of the rules of conduct of the *respublica,* and neither to its authority nor to the apparatus of power. Therefore the words belonging to the vocabulary of politics cannot be combined with those designating authority or power. In the course of a dazzling exercise in conceptual cartography, Oakeshott argues that such expressions as *de facto* and 'charismatic authority', 'sovereign government', 'bureaucracy', 'democratic rule', 'political authority', 'political obligation', 'political institutions', 'political power', 'power politics' and even his own earlier inventions, 'nomocracy' and 'telocracy', are all 'muddles' and 'impossible to construe'. He clears the 'chaos' by dismissing many of these 'bastard' expressions and assigning the rest their proper 'homes'.[38]

As we have seen, with respect to its mode of association civil association can be identified and understood in terms of two ideal characters, namely, rule-based association and enterprise association. In Oakeshott's view, European political consciousness since the emergence of the modern states in the sixteenth century has been polarized between the two modes of identification. Some European political theorists, such as Machiavelli, Hobbes, Locke, Spinoza, Montesquieu, Tocqueville, Burke, Paine, Kant, Fichte and Hegel, understood the state as *societas* or rule-based association, whereas others, such as Calvin, Bacon, St Simon, Fourier, Sismondi, Marx, Lenin and the Webbs, identified it as *universitas* or enterprise association, although, of course, they disagreed about the nature of enterprise. Rulers and their subjects have also been torn between the two images of the state. By and large the European states have moved increasingly in the direction of enterprise association, largely under the impact of such factors as the enormous expansion of the apparatus of ruling, the lingering influence of the medieval notion of 'lordship', colonialism, wars and, above all, the emergence of the vast masses of men who, showing 'slavish concern for benefits' and lacking the disposition and ability to cherish and exercise their autonomy, have provided the 'human postulates' of the 'servile state'. That the state is regarded as enterprise association or a development corporation in the communist and most of the Third World countries is obvious. It has also moved a long way in this direction in the Western European countries, as is evident from such practices as government direction of production, the management of the economy, preoccupation with full employment and a guaranteed income, compulsory generalized education and the receipt of assured benefits in a 'welfare' state. The pull in the contrary direction is not entirely absent but is comparatively weak.

For Oakeshott every modern state is a mixture of the two modes of association and contains tendencies towards both civil and enterprise association. One is a tendency towards freedom and springs from respect for one's own and others' individuality; the other is a tendency towards servility and commands the allegiance of 'half-men' lacking respect for their own and others' autonomy. In Oakeshott's view, the conflict between the two tendencies is the fundamental 'postulate' of modern states and offers a better key to the understanding of their physiognomy than such familiar ideological labels as right and left, free enterprise and collectivist planning, or reactionary and progressive.[39]

3

I have offered above a brief outline of Oakeshott's political philosophy. He is one of the few twentieth-century philosophers to have developed a distinct vocabulary of his own and to have contributed several new concepts, some of which are likely to prove of lasting value. His view that political philosophy investigates the structural concepts and postulates of civil society and arbitrates between conflicting explanations of it makes a fresh contribution to the current debate on the nature of political philosophy. Oakeshott is probably the only philosopher in the history of political thought to have noticed that political philosophy is an inherently limited and precarious form of inquiry, which must find its own appropriate level of reflection. If it falls below this level, it is not political *philosophy*; if it goes much beyond it, it loses sight of politics and ceases to be *political* philosophy. Politics is a limited and conditional activity, whereas philosophy aims to offer unconditional understanding of the totality of experience. If a political philosopher is not sensitive to this tension, he will concentrate on the large and general questions about man and the world, which, by their very nature, will prevent him from fixing his gaze on, and even noticing, the specific character of his subject matter.

Although he himself does not make this point, Oakeshott's last essay in *Human Conduct,* seems to extend the scope of political philosophy in a new direction. In this essay he analyses the character and postulates of the modern state. He examines the different ways in which political writers and the ordinary man have attempted to understand the modern state since the sixteenth century onwards and concludes that they have been informed by two different images of it. Some understand it as civil association, the others as enterprise association. In Oakeshott's view, the interaction between the two images explains the history of the modern state. One can press Oakeshott's analysis of the modern state in a direction intimated but not pursued by him. Just as a political philosopher elucidates the character of the *modern* state, there is no reason why he cannot elucidate the character of a *specific* state such as Britain, France and India. He may examine its structure, institutions, language of political discourse, the way in which its citizens understand it, the demands they make upon it, the policies pursued by its government and so on and may eludiate its basic forms of self-understanding as well as the general limits within which its political consciousness moves. Just as Oakeshott uncovers the inner structure and tensions of the modern state, one may uncover the structure and tensions of modern Britain or of France and use the theoretical insights so gained to explain its institutions and practices. This is both a possible and an important area of investigation, and no form of inquiry other than political philosophy is equipped to undertake it. When so understood, political philosophy regains its Socratic character. It is able to illuminate the general assumptions underlying the ideas and practices of a specific state and bring to its citizens the gift of self-knowledge. Political philosophy does not remain only a connoisseur of voices but acquires a distinct voice of its own and makes its own unique contribution to the understanding of contemporary political life.

As for Oakeshott's analysis of human conduct in general and civil association in particular, a good deal of it is illuminating and insightful. One of his greatest achievements is to have developed a carefully worked out philosophy of individuality. He does not merely defend individuality, as its greatest advocate John Stuart Mill did, but also shows that it is an *inseparable* component of human conduct and that the latter simply cannot be adequately accounted for without invoking the concept of individuality. On the basis of his illuminating distinction between individuality and individualism, he is able to show that a stable framework of traditions and practices is not inimical to, but is a necessary condition of, individuality. Even as individuality requires settled practices, the latter require individuality as their necessary correlative. An action based on a practice is necessarily a performance bearing the distinctive stamp of the agent's individuality. An action is an act, and an agent is an actor displaying his virtuosity in picking his way through a labyrinth of social practices and developing an appropriate response to his unique situation. Further, as Oakeshott rightly emphasizes, an action not only expresses an agent's individuality but is also a language in which he converses with others, conveying his sympathies and antipathies and communicating his views and beliefs. The language of action has its own syntax, vocabulary, idioms, style, metaphors, symbols, rules of speech, grammar, dialects and so on and is spoken well or ill, simply or idiomatically, crudely or elegantly, in prose or in verse depending on the agent's mastery of it. Oakeshott's view that an action is a mode of self-disclosure and a language of conversation is a considerable improvement on the traditional theories of action and opens up several new areas of investigation.

In viewing political life from the perspective of his theory of individuality, Oakeshott is able to explore a neglected theoretical terrain, namely, civil condition. He charts the area with considerable skill and develops a vocabulary capable of describing its sensitively demarcated conceptual space. This enables him both to criticize traditional and contemporary political thought and to construct a new theory of his own. He is able to show that several political philosophers have come to grief because of their confusion of authority with purpose, civil society with politics, the making of rules with ruling, the structure of authority with the composition of government, law with command, and so on. He offers a new 'political' theory which, despite its limitations, is coherent and compels attention. From his fresh and original perspective, he argues that civil relationship is not one of command and obedience, nor the pursuit of a collective purpose, but participation in the practice of civility and in several respects similar to that obtaining between the speakers of a common language. To live in civil association is to learn to converse in the language of civility and to acquire a modicum of civilization. Such a novel view of civil society enables Oakeshott to provide new and illuminating insights into the nature of law, authority, citizenship, government, political activity, civil freedom, moral autonomy, the nature of political discourse and the nature and autonomy of civil morality. It enables him also to define and classify political terms. Although his classification is somewhat over-schematic, it is without a precedent in the history of political philosophy and paves the way for clear thinking.

Despite its many profound and original insights, Oakeshott's views of philosophy and civil society are not free from difficulties. His view of philosophy in general and of political philosophy in particular seems open to two criticisms.

First, Oakeshott takes theory to be a generic category and argues that all intellectual inquiries engage in theorizing in one way or another. Now, as he himself recognizes, science, history and philosophy are very different forms of inquiry. The first two use postulates, although in their own different ways, whereas philosophy elucidates and criticizes them. If we are to claim that all three are theoretical inquiries, we need to specify their shared features. Oakeshott does not indicate what form of understanding and/or type of investigation characterizes them all. He sometimes suggests that they are all concerned to understand rather than to make practical responses. This is surely not enough, since not every attempt to understand is theoretical. Trying to understand why a friend behaves in a particular manner is certainly not a theoretical inquiry. One therefore needs to specify what form or level of understanding counts as the theoretical.

Further, the ideal character, the basic unit of theoretical

investigation, seems to play little if any part in history. On Oakeshott's own account, a historian explains human actions in terms of other such actions. And no distinction can be made between them such that one is a feature and the other a postulate. History, therefore, would not seem to be a theoretical inquiry at all. The scientific is certainly a theoretical inquiry, although one may wonder if its distinctive theoretical character can be fully expressed in the language of postulates or conditions. The laws of thermo-dynamics are not the postulates or even the conditions of a thunderstorm, at least not in the sense in which the capacity for choice is the condition of selecting a shirt.

Second, Oakeshott says that philosophy is concerned to under-stand, not to prescribe. It is entirely explanatory in nature and has no recommendatory orientation or implication. Although he formulates it differently on different occasions, Oakeshott's basic thesis seems to be twofold. First, the philosophical understanding of an activity cannot 'supersede and... take the place of' the practical understanding necessary for the conduct of it. The philosopher is not an 'expert' in it and is in no way qualified to issue *detailed* injunctions and recommendations concerning how to organize and conduct the activity in question. Second, the philosophical under-standing of an activity cannot have even *general* normative implications for the conduct of it.

Of the two, the first thesis is true but rather trivial. If we exclude some part of Plato's Dialogues and some of the Utopian writers, it is difficult to think of any political philosopher who has ever thought that he was an 'expert' in the conduct of public affairs and qualified to tell politicians what to do in specific situations. To the extent that some may have entertained such pretensions, they were obviously wrong, for the reasons Oakeshott gives.

As for Oakeshott's second and far more interesting thesis, it is difficult to see how it can be sustained. The philosophical under-standing of an activity is an understanding of its nature, assump-tions, basic concepts and structure. It indicates how to think about the activity, what properly belongs to it, what demands and expectations can be accommodated by it, what is and is not congruent with its character, how to argue and reason about it, what considerations are relevant to it and so on. In indicating all this, philosophical understanding does not remain wholly explanatory and acquires a normative dimension. Oakeshott's own analysis of civil association is an interesting example of this. He argues that civil association is constituted in a certain manner and hence capable of accommodating only certain types of demand. It cannot, for example, provide substantive satisfactions, pursue social justice or aim to create a perfect society. His philosophical understanding of it enables him to rule out a large body of political proposals and doctrines. If one takes into account Oakeshott's views on freedom, moral autonomy and human dignity, even stronger conclusions follow, as is evident from his attacks on the 'spiritual indigence' of 'helf-men', the 'moral enormity' of the state constituted as enterprise association and the moral impropriety of certain types of government activity.

To accept Oakeshott's philosophical account of human agency, human dignity, moral autonomy and civil association is to see the modern state, analyse political events and evaluate political situations and possibilities in a certain manner, to recognize certain types of demand or government activity as threats to human dignity, to feel 'shame', 'guilt' or 'pride' about certain trends in modern society and so on. To be persuaded by Oakeshott's philosophical theory of human conduct and civil association, then, is not only to see and judge but also to be disposed to act and feel in a particular manner. It would be inconsistent to accept his theory and then go on to demand large-scale nationalization, join the Communist Party, take pride in the rise of the collectivist state or feel guilty about the dismantling of the 'welfare' state. The actions of a man who did so would imply a marked incoherence in the way he understood and responded to the modern state. No doubt, men are not always coherent, but they do search for greater coherence in their lives and know that beyond a certain point incoherence threatens their intellectual and moral integrity.

Sometimes Oakeshott seems to appreciate all this and is content to argue that philosophical understanding does not *logically* entail recommendation. One may make two points in response. One may argue that it does not matter *how* recommendations are related to explanations as long as it is admitted that there is a connection between the two. The nature of their connection is a subordinate question and can be seriously discussed once the *fact* of the connection is conceded. One may also make a different response. One may ask what Oakeshott means by 'logically' when he says that an explanation cannot 'logically' entail recommendation. Although he is not entirely clear, he seems to have formal deduction in mind, as when he says that a recommendation cannot be deduced from an explanation. Perhaps he is right, but there is no reason why the logical relation between them must be deductive. Logical relations are of many different types. Deduction is only one of them and does not obtain anywhere except in some areas of formal logic.

Let us now briefly consider Oakeshott's theories of morality and civil association. Oakeshott's account of morality is somewhat ambiguous and seems to leave several questions unanswered. We use the term 'moral' in opposition to either 'non-moral' or 'immoral'. Oakeshott's primary concern is to distinguish the moral from the non-moral. As we have seen, he identifies two types of practice. Some are instrumentally and the others intrinsically authoritative. Sometimes he seems to say that all intrinsically authoritative practices are moral. He must have this sense in mind when he says, rather strangely, that the speakers of a common language 'constitute...a moral relationship'. On other occasions he seems to suggest that of the intrinsically authoritative practices, only some are moral, but he does not specify the distinguishing principle. Good table manners, the practice of cleaning the house once a week, wearing a black dress at a funeral and forms of social greeting are all accepted by most men as intrinsically authoritative. Oakeshott does not seem to regard them as moral practices, but he does not say why, nor how they differ from such moral practices as keeping promises, telling the truth and helping a man in need. Further, in his view, moral practices can be defined in purely formal terms, and this is questionable. If a man saw no difference between kicking a stone and kicking a man, or between hammering a nail into a wall and into a man's skull, we would have little hesitation in saying that he lacked the elementary capacity to distinguish between the moral and the non-moral. We do not feel the need to inquire if he may not perhaps be acting according to some strange and unfamiliar authoritative practice. In other words, some minimal moral content, some conception of what is due to a human being and perhaps some reference to human well-being is built into the very definition of a moral practice.

Oakeshott says that morality is 'indifferent to the achievement of any substantive purpose', and that moral practices are intrinsically binding, irrespective of their consequences. It is difficult to see how such a view can be sustained. A practice, be it moral or otherwise, is necessarily two-dimensional. It is a *practice* and, as such, has the authority inherent in a settled mode of behaviour. However, it arises and exists within the wider context of human purposes from which it derives its significance and part of its authority. Hence we ask of a practice what its 'point' or 'rationale' is – that is, not what its 'end' is but how it relates to the purposes and satisfaction of the agents affected by it. A practice without a point is an empty ritual. This is how we generally criticize apartheid, racialism, anti-Semitism or untouchability, pointing out in each case that the victims of each practice suffer both materially and psychologically and are prevented from realizing their self-chosen purposes and from procuring substantive satisfaction. And this is also how moral practices evolve and change. As social relations and human purposes change, the old moral practices appear restrictive, rigid, unduly demanding, frustrating, unable to promote the substantive satisfaction that men now seek and so on. Increasingly, they are breached, lose their authority and appeal and eventually cease to command the allegiance of the bulk of the community.

As for Oakeshott's theory of civil society, some of its basic theses fail to carry conviction. As we have seen, he distinguishes two modes of association, namely, civil and enterprise. Civil association is practice-based, whereas enterprise association is purpose-based. In his view, the state can be organized as civil or enterprise association. For him only the state organized as civil association respects its citizens' moral autonomy, whereas one organized as enterprise association is guilty of 'moral enormity'.

Oakeshott distinguishes between practice and purpose-based association. It is difficult to see where the association between husband and wife or between two lovers belongs. *Prima facie,* they are united in terms of neither purpose nor practice. They come together and remain together because they love each other and part company when their love dries up. Unless practice were so defined as to include human emotions and sentiments and thus rendered vacuous, it is difficult to think of love as a practice laying down the considerations to which one subscribes. One does not think that one ought to treat another person in a certain manner *because* one loves him or her. Indeed, an action based on a sense of duty or a rule would seem to signify the *absence* of love. The relation between two lovers or between husband and wife is, no doubt, *regulated* by practice but not wholly, and in any case it is not *constituted* in terms of or only held together by allegiance to a practice. The family seems to be another association which is neither practice- nor purpose-based. Parents and children are not united in terms of purpose. And although practice regulates their relationship, it does so to a limited degree and cannot be said to constitute it. Friendship would seem to be another such relationship. Friends are united in terms of common interests, mutual affection and so on. Their relations are regulated by, but not constituted in terms of, commonly accepted practices. It is because they are already friends that they accept certain practices. Their friendship is conceptually prior to whatever practices regulate the relations between friends in a given community.

One may also wonder if it is not the case that practice and purpose dovetail, so that most human associations are based on both. Men initially associated in terms of practice may, over time, develop common interests, affection, mutual concern, common purposes and so on, such that their association is sustained not only by allegiance to a common practice but also by the sharing of common purposes. The opposite also often happens. Men may come together to pursue a common purpose and set up a system of practices. Over time the practices acquire their own independent character and momentum and are considered binding not because they serve a specific purpose but because they are part of their association's tradition, history and collective identity. Some of them may not be changed even when they frustrate the realization of a purpose. This happens in many human associations, especially those with a long history, for example, ancient colleges and universities, the Churches, the Civil Service and even the army. In such associations practices and purposes build up a complex relationship and shape each other. Purposes are pursued only within the framework of established practices, and certain ways of pursuing them are ruled out if they conflict with established practices. At the same practices are altered when they demonstrably hinder the realization of agreed purposes. It is difficult to say whether an Oxford college or the Roman Catholic Church is purpose-or practice-based.

Even if the distinction between practice- and purpose-based association could be maintained *in general*, it is difficult to see how it can be sustained with respect to the state. Whatever else it may be, a state is, by definition, an association of men held together by their common acknowledgement of a system of authority. It simply cannot be constituted otherwise. Enterprise association lapses when its members cease to accept its basic purposes. This is never possible in a state. Even the Soviet Union, for Oakeshott enterprise association *par excellence,* is united or constituted in terms of a specific system of authority. No doubt, it pursues large purposes and requires its citizens to promote them. However, it is not united in terms of these purposes; what unites all its citizens is the fact that they are all bound by the established system of authority. True, some of them may not freely acknowledge it, but then this is also true of civil association, whose citizens are all bound by its authority, although some may refuse to acknowledge it. The state constituted as enterprise association in Oakeshott's sense is an impossible institution. Oakeshott draws a general distinction between civil and enterprise association and applies it to the state without asking if it is a kind of collectivity to which the distinction can apply.

Oakeshott argues that civil association respects its citizens' moral autonomy. For him it is constituted solely in terms of practice and, since practices do not require substantive actions, it preserves the freedom of its citizens. As Oakeshott says, there is *'nothing* in civil association to threaten the link between belief and conduct which constitutes "free" agency'. It is difficult to see how this is so. First, although civil association is not constituted in terms of purposes, it cannot avoid pursuing them and is therefore bound to compromise the moral autonomy of those disapproving of its purposes. Even a civil association that may do little more than eliminate a long-festering grievance or relieve distress commits 'moral enormity' in respect to those who believe that poverty is a divine punishment for sin or a proof of failure in the battle for survival. Oakeshott's arguments against the state constituted as enterprise association therefore apply to civil association as well.

Second, for Oakeshott practice-based association preserves freedom, because he thinks that a practice, by its very nature, can never require a substantive action. While this is true of some practices sometimes, it cannot be accepted as a necessary truth about the nature of practice. For example, Oakeshott says that a criminal law prohibits not killing but killing murderously, not setting fire but doing so arsonically. This is odd, for murder is not a way of killing but a type of killing. It is deliberate and unauthorized killing in forbidden circumstances and hence a substantive act. Similarly, arson does not adverbially qualify the act of lighting fire; it is a certain type of setting fire. Again the law forbids not copulating rapishly but rape, sexual intercourse without the consent of the person concerned or with someone below a certain age. Further, such laws as those requiring the payment of taxes, jury service, conscription and voting in an election require substantive acts and do not merely specify the considerations to be subscribed to. Even civil association, some of whose laws necessarily require substantive action, cannot therefore safeguard moral autonomy and freedom.

Even as civil association cannot fully preserve moral autonomy, enterprise association cannot wholly abolish it either. First, a state geared to the realization of a single, overarching purpose is inherently impossible. Such purposes as increasing the gross national product, promoting economic development, creating a classless society and even winning a war are too general and too indeterminate to form the goal of government actions and must be articulated as a cluster of interrelated and loosely connected purposes. The state organized as enterprise association is not therefore qualitatively different from civil association. Second, like practices, purposes vary in their specificity. Some purposes do not require substantive actions. They specify the considerations to be subscribed to and leave room for choice. Helping India to develop economically or helping Britain to win the war, or increase productivity, or fight inflation does not tell me which one of several possible substantive courses of action to adopt. It is because Oakeshott seems to appreciate this that he sometimes talks of substantive purposes rather than purposes *per se*. However, it is not entirely clear how he proposes to distinguish the two. Every purpose is realized by other, less general purposes, and each of these in turn by other, less general purposes, and so on until one arrives at a substantive action. It is difficult to see which of these is a general and which a substantive purpose.

It would therefore seem that the difference between civil and enterprise association is not one of kind but at best one of degree. Each is constituted in terms of a commonly acknowledged authority, and there is no distinction between the two in that respect. Further, each pursues purposes, some of which some citizens are bound to disapprove of. This is the inescapable price we pay for living in an organized society. And it is unrealistic, even Utopian, to imagine that there can ever by a form of organized life in which the price does not have to be paid and the tragic limitations of social existence can be wholly eliminated. This is not at all to say that what Oakeshott calls civil and enterprise association do not represent profoundly different ways of life. Only that the difference does not lie in their modes of constitution, nor in the alleged fact that one fully preserves and the other entirely destroys moral autonomy and freedom.

6

Karl Popper

Karl Popper is one of the few contemporary philosophers to have made important contributions in a variety of fields. As far as political theory is concerned, his contribution is limited largely to *Open Society and its Enemies*. The book made a considerable impact not only because it captured the post-war ethos, but also because it contained a sustained and polemical statement of his political theory and grounded it in a carefully thought out theory of knowledge. Accordingly, it will be useful to begin with a brief outline of his philosophical system.

1

For Popper both science and philosophy are concerned with what he calls the 'problem of cosmology'. By this he means 'the problem of understanding the world, including ourselves, and our knowledge, as part of the world'.[1] For Popper the main interest of philosophy, as of science, 'lies solely in its bold attempt to add to our knowledge of the world, and to the theory of our knowledge of the world'. In his view, then, philosophers are concerned with two interconnected types of problem, namely, the cosmological and the epistemological. This is true not only of the great philosophers of the past but also of such rebels as Wittgenstein. Popper argues that Wittgenstein's *Tractatus* was 'a cosmological treatise (although a crude one)' and his theory of knowledge was 'closely linked with his cosmology'.

For Popper espistemological problems are uniquely philosophical. As for cosmological problems, they may be dealt with in one of two ways: by means of empirically testable theories, or by rational reflection. Popper calls the first a scientific and the second a metaphysical way of dealing with cosmological problems. The latter belongs to philosophy. For Popper, then, metaphysical and epistemological problems are philosophical problems *par excellence*. We shall take each in turn.

Popper proposes refutability or falsifiability as the criterion of demarcation between science and metaphysics. A system of thought is scientific 'only if it makes assertions which may clash with observations'.[2] We can test a scientific theory by producing evidence for or against it, that is, by attempting to verify or to falsify it. Popper proposes that the latter is a better procedure. Some confirming evidence can always be obtained 'for nearly every theory', and therefore verification can never help us decide whether or not to accept it. Further, universal statements, which is what all theoretical statements are, can never be conclusively verified, but they can be conclusively falsified. This is so because they can never be derived from, but can be contradicted by, singular statements. This means that from the truth of a singular statement we can deduce the falsity but not the truth of a relevant universal statement. Given that universal statements have this 'logical form', there is an 'asymmetry' between verification and falsification, and the latter is the only reliable way to test them. As Popper puts it, 'Testability is the same as refutability, and can therefore likewise be taken as a criterion of demarcation.' He recognizes that the criterion of demarcation cannot be 'absolutely sharp', for testability is a matter of degree, and different types of theory are testable in different degrees. Popper calls wholly non-testable theories 'metaphysical'.[3] This does not mean that metaphysical theories are meaningless, for Popper's falsifiability criterion is a criterion not of meaning but of demarcation; it means only that they are not empirical or scientific. Nor does it mean that they are uncriticizable, for they can be criticized and even shown to be false, only that their criticism cannot take the form of falsification or refutation.

For Popper, then, metaphysical statements are non-testable. This is true of various other types of statement as well, however, and cannot therefore distinguish a metaphysical statement. Although Popper is not entirely clear, he seems to think that in addition to irrefutability, metaphysical statements and problems are 'general', 'abstract' and concerned with the 'rational understanding' of a class of phenomena.[4] For example, Parmenides was puzzled by the phenomenon of change. If an entity T changes, then clearly it is not the same T after the change as before. On the other hand, one cannot say that T changes without implying that it persists during the change, and that it is therefore the same T after the change as before. Parmenides found it impossible to understand and to give a coherent 'account of change'.[5] For Popper both his problem and his solution of it were metasphysical in nature. In his view, Plato's theory of Forms was also a metaphysical theory. Although it had logical, empirical and other components, its basic concern to give a 'rational account' of the nature of the perceptible world was metaphysical. Many of Kant's problems and theories were metaphysical also.[6] He was perplexed by Newtonian physics and wondered how Newton could attain such a universal body of knowledge, how pure natural science was possible and how a mathematical, demonstrable, general and precisely formulated theory could ever provide a causal explanation of the chaotic phenomenal world. In the course of grappling with such metaphysical problems, he developed his metaphysical theories of space, time, man's relation to nature and so on. For Popper determinism, idealism, materialism and irrationalism are all metaphysical theories.[7] They are all concerned to understand and make intellectual sense of some specific aspect of the world and to propose general, irrefutable but rationally discussible accounts of it.

Popper argues that although non-empirical, metaphysical theories are not at all trivial or uninteresting. They often deal with genuine and disturbing problems. Parmenides' perplexity about the nature of change, Plato's perplexity about the nature of the phenomenal world and Kant's bewilderment about Newton's achievements are all serious philosophical problems, and their solutions are of the greatest philosophical interest. Further, many a metaphysical theory contains illuminating ideas and inspires fruitful scientific investigations. Sometimes a metaphysical theory may even offer a 'new approach towards the world' and provide a 'theoretical framework' within which the scientist can pursue his inquiries.[8] In Popper's view, Democritus' metaphysical theory of change was 'fundamental to the whole development of physics'. As he puts it:[9]

> it is a fact that purely metaphysical ideas – and therefore philosophical ideas – have been of the greatest importance for cosmology. From Thales to Einstein, from ancient atomism to Descartes's speculation about matter, from the speculations of Gilbert and Newton and Leibniz and Boscovic about forces to those of Faraday and Einstein about fields of forces, metaphysical ideas have shown the way.

For Popper philosophy is concerned with not only metaphysical but also epistemological problems. As he understands it, epistemology is concerned not with the so-called foundations or sources of knowledge for, as we shall see, none exists, nor with such psychological questions as how an individual perceives the world, forms concepts or comes by new ideas. For Popper epistemology is basically 'a theory of the growth of knowledge', a theory about the nature and conditions of the 'progress' of knowledge. For Popper the growth of knowledge can best be studied by examining the growth of scientific knowledge for at least three important reasons.[10] First, scientific knowledge is the paradigm of all knowledge, in the sense that it represents the final form which all knowledge ultimately aims to attain. Second, scientific knowledge is pursued in an organized, systematic and public manner. Thus its growth is the 'most important and interesting' case of the growth of knowledge and offers most illuminating insights into the manner of the growth of knowledge in general. And, third, Popper advances the somewhat strange view that the growth of knowledge is essential to the very existence of science in a way that it is not to any other form of knowledge. In his view, science has a 'need' to grow and progress. If it stopped growing and were not constantly criticized, revised and even overhauled, it would become a dogma and would lose its scientific character. As he puts it, 'I assert that continued growth is essential to the rational and empirical character of scientific knowledge, that if science ceases to grow, it must lose that character.'[11]

For Popper epistemology is concerned with the growth of knowledge in general and that of scientific knowledge in particular. Therefore its basic objective is to analyse the growth of scientific knowledge and to develop a body of rules capable of facilitating and promoting it.[12] As he says, epistemology attempts to answer the following fundamental question: 'How should we proceed if we wish to contribute to the growth of scientific knowledge?'[13] In Popper's view, the clear and unambiguous demarcation between science and non-science is the first and most important step in this direction. Accordingly, he calls the criterion of demarcation the 'supreme rule'. It 'serves as a kind of norm for deciding upon the remaining rules' and is a 'rule of a higher type'. It lays down that the rest of the rules that we formulate should not protect any statement in a scientific theory against falsification or whatever other criterion of demarcation is accepted. Since the rules concerning the growth of knowledge are systematically formulated, subjected to the criterion of demarcation and constitute a coherent system, Popper says that we may refer to them as a *theory of method* or simply methodology.

For Popper, then, epistemology is ultimately methodology, the technology of the growth of science.[14] It is explicitly normative in its orientation and concerned to stipulate what scientists *ought* to do if they are to reach their 'goal' or 'aim' of making progress in knowledge. In his *Logic of Scientific Discovery* and other writings, Popper proposes a number of rules designed to facilitate and expedite the growth of knowledge. His writings abound in such statements as 'I propose the rule...', 'We shall adopt the methodological rule...', and 'We shall make the convention....' Since Popper is largely preoccupied with the technology of scientific knowledge, he generally takes it for granted that scientific knowledge grows, that we can give a non-circular definition of the growth of knowledge, and that the choice of the criterion of demarcation, upon which the entire methodology rests, is relatively unproblematic.

As we have seen, Popper takes the view that philosophy consists of two interrelated types of inquiry, the metaphysical and the epistemological. He seems to think that of the two, only the latter is relevant to the study of politics, but he does not give any reasons. *Prima facie,* political life would seem to raise several perplexing questions which require rational understanding and are no less obvious that the nature of change, the perceptible world and the scientific knowledge that perplexed and prompted the metaphysical theories of Parmenides, Plato and Kant respectively. However, Popper does not think that this is so and discusses politics almost entirely in epistemological or methodological terms. Before considering his political theory, it would be helpful, therefore, to offer a brief outline of his epistemology.

2

Popper's theory of knowledge can best be understood against the background of his critique of most of the traditional theories of knowledge. He criticizes them on several grounds.

First, many of them are authoritarian in nature.[15] They seek to ground knowledge in some allegedly unshakeable foundation, be it the senses, reason, intuition, experience, intellect or God. For Popper there are no unshakeable and infallible foundations of knowledge, for each of them may turn to be mistaken. Our intuitions and reason sometimes mislead us. And as for observation and experiment, they do not consist of pure data or indubitable experience but are theoretically interpreted. Popper argues, further, that the search for authoritative foundations is logically incoherent, since they cannot themselves tell us which are authoritative and why. Since no authority can be self-authenticating, its acceptance must ultimately depend upon blind commitment or faith. All authoritarianism rests ultimately on irrationalism.

Second, and this is only a further implication of the first, most traditional theories of knowledge are preoccupied with the 'sources' or 'origins' of knowledge and confuse the validity of knowledge with its source.[16] They assume that an item of knowledge derives its validity from its source and is valid if its source is reliable or pure. In Popper's view, the idealists, the empiricists, the religious writers, the Marxists and others are all guilty of the genetic fallacy. He argues that there are 'no ultimate sources of knowledge', and that every source is 'admissible and may be used, but none has any authority'. Knowledge cannot therefore be 'legitimized by its pedigree'. Further, like the appeal to authority, the appeal to a source of knowledge involves an irrational act of faith. A source of knowledge cannot itself tell us whether or not it is reliable and, if so, to what degree; hence its acceptance can only be based on blind faith.

Third, Popper argues that traditional theories of knowledge are absolutist, in the sense that they seek, and claim to offer, incorrigible and infallible knowledge. In his view, Plato's immutable truths, the Christian Revelation, the empiricist sense data and the Marxist laws of history are all examples of this. For Popper the history of science and philosophy shows, beyond a shadow of doubt, that 'every bit' of our knowledge is fallible and 'may be overthrown'. Although Popper rejects absolutism of the traditional kind, he claims to subscribe to his own peculiar brand of it, which he paradoxically calls 'fallibilistic absolutism'.[17] By this he seems to mean two things. First, although our knowledge is fallible and open to revision, our mistakes are absolute, in the sencsense that if a theory is shown to be false, it is absolutely false. Second, the ideas of truth and of falling short of it are 'absolute standards', in the sense that they are integral to the very pursuit of knowledge and can never be abandoned.

Fourth, most traditional theories of knowledge assume that truth is manifest.[18] Plato held that the Ideas appeared in their pristine purity to the philosophically cultivated mind. Bacon believed in *veracitas naturae* and held that we only needed to read with an unprejudiced mind the book of nature lying open before us. Descartes believed in *veracitas dei* and maintained that clear and distinct ideas revealed the truth. Since the truth was manifest for these and other philosophers, they had difficulty in explaining ignorance, which they conveniently attributed to the influence of passions, prejudices, illiteracy, the Church, bourgeois indoctrination and so on. For Popper truth is not manifest.[19] All knowledge is theoretically mediated, and all theories may turn out to be mistaken. The world reveals its secrets only to those who ask questions, and the character of its answers is determined by that of the questions.

Finally, traditional theories are justificationist in orientation. For them a theory is true and a decision is rational if they can be justified, that is, conclusively established and shown to follow from indubitable premises. In Popper's view, the demand for justification is a logical corollary to the authoritarian character of most traditional theories of knowledge. As they claim to ground knowledge in allegedly solid foundations, they encourage the belief that no knowledge is reliable unless it is thoroughly well founded or well established. Since Popper rejects the idea of foundation, he rejects the idea of justification. As he says, 'We can never justify our theories rationally...and cannot even prove that they are probable.'[20] All that we can do is to subject them to the most severe criticisms and tests and tentatively accept those that best stand up to them. There is 'no justification which goes beyond this'.[21] Accordingly, Popper replaces the concept of justification by that of criticism and links rationality with criticism as opposed to justification.[22] For him a theory or a decision is rational or worth accepting not because it can be justified but because it stands up to criticism.

Since he finds traditional theories of knowledge unsatisfactory, Popper offers an alternative non-authoritarian, non-genetic, non-justificationist and non-absolutist theory of his own.[23] He calls it 'critical and progressive fallibilism' and himself a 'criticist'. Since Popper's theory has been widely discussed and its complex and technical details are not relevant to us, we shall do no more than highlight its four essential features, namely, its rationalism, criticism and fallibilism and its emphasis on problems.

In Popper's view, one of the main reasons for the authoritarianism of traditional theories of knowledge was their radical scepticism. They doubted that we can know anything at all and hence felt it necessary to establish knowledge on solid foundations. In Popper's view, a throughgoing doubt calls for an equally throughgoing authoritarianism. He cannot see why we should begin with radical scepticism. Although we do not know everything, we do know something. Besides we know some things better than other things. And we know better those things which we knew less well before. The proper question to ask, therefore, is how we progress not from absolute ignorance to absolute truth but rather from less reliable to more reliable knowledge. As Popper says, 'Knowledge cannot start with nothing.... The advance of knowledge consists, mainly, in the modification of earlier knowledge.'

For Popper all knowledge grows through criticism. Criticism takes different forms depending upon the type of theory or statement involved. Popper divides theories into three categories, namely, the logical and mathematical, the empirical and scientific, and the philosophical or metaphysical.[24] As far as the first type of theory is concerned, criticism is largely formal and internal in nature and consists in examining the validity of deductions. The second type of theory is also amenable to this kind of criticism. However, since it makes statements about the world, the most important way to criticize it is to subject it to empirical tests. When a theory has withstood rigorous attempts to refute it, it deserves to be accepted. Such a theory is not necessarily true, nor even probable; it is only well corroborated. Popper recognizes that falsification is an extremely complex process. It is a matter of degree, and most theories cannot be conclusively disproved.[25] Further, a theory consists of different types of statement with different degrees of importance. A theorist, therefore, needs to decide which of them must be falsified in order for a theory to be falsified, how much weight to assign to counter-examples and so on. We cannot go into all this here and need observe only that for Popper science is a system of well corroborated theories, not a body of certain knowledge. And it grows not by the collection of observations but by the development of theories that have ever-increasing explanatory content and have been subjected to the most stringent attempts to refute them.

Popper is not entirely clear as to how philosophical theories can be criticized. He seems to think that they can be criticized in three different ways. First, although they are not empirical in nature, they are never wholly devoid of some empirical content, and this can be tested. Second, they can be criticized in terms of their internal consistency, the validity of their arguments and so on. The third and, for Popper, the most satisfactory way to criticize them is to examine them in relation to their central problems. As we have seen in connection with Parmenides, Plato and Kant, every philosophical theory attempts to solve a particular problem or cluster of problems. We can therefore ask if the problem is genuine, if its underlying assumptions are tenable, if it is unambiguously formulated and so on. And we can also ask if the theory concerned really solves the problem or only shifts it, if its solution is better than that proposed by another theory, if it contradicts other theories, if its solution is fruitful and opens up a new direction of inquiry and so on.[26]

For Popper, then, no theory is immune to rational criticism. To criticize it is to expose its mistakes, and every recognition of a mistake represents a diminution of ignorance and an increase in knowledge.[27] Further, by criticizing established theories we challenge people to offer better theories, which in turn can be criticized and rejected or modified. In this way our knowledge of the world and of ourselves grows. Our knowledge is never final and certain. We may come nearer the truth, but we never attain it. The progress of knowledge has no final resting point; it is what Popper calls an 'unending quest'.

For 'popper criticism is 'the life blood of all rational thought' and the basis of objectivity and impartiality. Only by subjecting our views to each other's criticisms are we able to notice and eliminate our prejudices and biases. The natural sciences offer more objective and reliable knowledge than the social sciences, not because natural scientists are more impartial and self-critical than social scientists, nor because their prejudices and preferences do not enter into their work, but because they have higher standards of rational criticism. They avoid talking at cross-purposes by speaking the same conceptual language and by appealing to the common authority of observation and experiment. And they have institutionalized public criticism in the form of scientific journals and congresses, where every claim to knowledge is rigorously scrutinized. As Popper says, scientific objectivity in the natural and social sciences is wholly a product of 'the inter-subjectivity of scientific method' and 'lies in the objectivity of the critical method'.[28]

Popper calls himself a rationalist. Although he frequently uses the terms 'reason', 'rational' and 'rationality', he defines them differently on different occasions. He seems to use the term 'rational' in at least three different senses.

In its first sense he uses it to mean 'reasonable'.[29] As he says, rationalism is an 'attitude of reasonableness'. A rationalist attempts to reach decision by argument and compromise. He 'would rather be unsuccessful in convincing another man by argument than successful in crushing him by force, by intimidation and threats, or even by persuasive propaganda'. Basically, rationalism, as Popper understands it, involves discussion, readiness to learn from others, an 'attitude of give and take', intellectual humility, the acknowledgement of fallibility, respect for each individual as a 'potential source of argument and of reasonable information' and the recognition of his right to be heard. Popper uses the term 'rational' in this sense in his *Open Society, Conjectures and Refutations* and other writings. In his later works he calls this a 'personal or psychological or subjective sense of "rational"' and says that it is 'less important and in any case pretty vague'.

In its second sense, Popper equates the term 'rationality' with criticism. He says that the discovery of a new problem is 'the result of criticism' and *therefore* 'rational in a high degree'. Popper calls it 'rationality in the objective sense'. Mathematics is rational because its propositions 'can be rationally, that is, critically discussed'. Since the theories of the natural sciences, moral standards and so on can also be critically discussed, they too are said to belong to the 'rational' domain of world 3 which consists of objective and public knowledge. By contrast, the works of art and artistic standards which also belong to world 3 are not, or rather are not 'fully within the domain of rationality', because they do not admit of *'comparable and arguable* standards'.[30]

Popper also uses the term rational in a third sense. Here reason is conceived in instrumental or technological terms and represents the capacity to relate means to ends. He frequently refers to the 'problem-solving character of rationality' and says, 'We can judge the rationality of an action only in relation to some aims or ends.'[31] To be rational is to be clear about one's aims or 'goals' and to choose the best means to realize them. It is because Popper understands rationality in this way that he attempts to analyse human actions in terms of the logic of their situations. He elucidates the aims and means that a rational man placed in a specific situation will adopt and uses these as standards for assessing the rationality of the actions of the agent involved.[32] As we shall see, this view of reason dominates Popper's social and political thought.

The three senses in which Popper uses the term 'reason' are obviously distinct, and although they sometimes overlap, they also conflict. Willingness to submit a dispute to arbitration, an attitude of give and take and readiness to compromise make sense in social and political life but not at all in scientific and philosophical discussions. Einstein could not conceivably approach Newton in a spirit of give and take, and nor could theoretical disputes between proponents of wave and particle theories of light be resolved by means of arbitration. Further, Popper's second sense of rationality is distinctly odd. It is strange and confusing to say that mathematics is rational, or that it is more rational than aesthetics, or that a scientific theory is more rational than an artistic object or a poem. In its first sense the term 'rational' should perhaps be replaced by the term 'reasonable'. This leaves us with the third sense. Not surprisingly, it is this fairly common usage of the term that dominates Popper's writings. Popper frequently says that a debate is rational 'only when it is problem-orientated', a theory is rational only 'in so far as it tries to solve certain problems' and can be rationally discussed 'only by discussing' its problems.[33] He says that a musical piece should be seen as the musician not expressing his emotions but 'struggling to solve musical problems'.[34] As we shall see, Popper defines social and political rationality in similar terms.

Given Popper's view of reason, it is easy to see why the concept of problem is central to his epistemology. For him the pursuit of knowledge springs from the need to solve specific problems. He goes further and gives the activity of problem solving a metaphysical status. He observes: 'While I think that... there are no sharp limits between living and dead matter, I also feel... that with life there came into existence things entirely new: problems and problem solving.'[35] To be faced with problems and to be forced to solve them is the 'most characteristic and specific property of life'. A soap bubble has no problems; an amoeba has. Its most basic problem is to find food. The higher the organism, the more complex are its problems, and the less they are connected with its survival. 'All organisms are constantly, day and night, engaged in problem solving.' They may not consciously formulate their problems and may not even be aware of them. However, their problems can be 'hypothetically reconstructed'. Only such a reconstruction can explain and give coherence to their apparently random movements. The complex world of science, philosophy and so on is 'merely a belated outcome on the human level of the existence of problems and of problem solving'.[36]

For Popper there is only one way to solve a problem, namely, the method of trial and error. By definition a problem arises when we do not know what to do in a specific situation. The only way we can deal with a problem, therefore, is to propose solutions to it, to eliminate the erroneous ones and to select the most effective one. The lower organisms try out solutions at random. The higher organisms, especially man, consciously and systematically apply the method of trial and error. Thanks to their unique capacity for descriptive and argumentative language, human beings have the capacity for self-consciousness and criticism and the objective knowledge characteristic of world 3. Thus they can formulate their problems verbally and devise carefully planned ways in which to criticize and eliminate mistaken solutions. As Popper puts it, from the amoeba to Einstein there is 'just one stop', namely, the 'conscious and critical search for one's errors'.[37]

Popper argues that the evolution of the living organisms can best be explained in terms of their problem situations. They tend to evolve in the direction of greater adaptation to their environment. Biological mutation occurs in response to the need for problem solving. Every mutation is like an experiment or a trial, which may succeed and lead to greater biological fitness or fail and lead to extinction. An organism's sense organs and modes of perceiving and responding to its environment are developed under evolutionary pressures and contain solutions to its life problems. It is born equipped with a central control system, which it owes to the evolutionary process of trial and error through which its ancestors have succeeded in coping with similar conditions. Thus it is born with a good deal of physiologically incorporated 'foreknowledge' of appropriate ways of dealing with its environment and the expectations that grow out of it. A new-born baby does not wait for the environment or society to inculcate certain beliefs in it; it 'expects' to be fed and 'knows' what to do when presented with a nipple. For Popper the sense organs are not mere receptacles, collecting impressions that require subsequent mental processing; rather, they are an 'epistemic apparatus' providing the organism with the type of pre-digested information it needs for its task of problem solving.[38] The activity of interpretation, therefore, begins at the physiological level, in the sense organs themselves. Sense perception is necessarily selective, and its selectivity is 'problem-dependent and problem-solving', especially in the higher organisms. As Popper puts it, 'I think that nothing is "first known through the senses". The senses themselves interpret and theorize...they are literally only the feelers of the central nervous system, which is a problem-solver.'[39] For Popper sense organs embody theories, and theories are like 'endosomatic organs' and function similarly. Both help us to adjust to and to change the world.

Popper sees the self-conscious mind as an evolutionary product of the human brain but transcending it and actively directing and assessing its processes. For him the self or the mind controls the brain, as is evident when we see an optical illusion and are aware that we are seeing one, or when we switch at will the way we 'read' an illusory figure. The self 'plays on the brain, as a pianist plays on a piano or as a driver plays on the controls of a car'. Popper introduces the hypothesis of an active and immaterial self interacting with the material world, admits to the self being a 'ghost in the machine' and appropriately entitles his book *The Self and its Brain*. He carries his Cartesianism and its interactionist dualism to its logical conclusion when he speaks of the 'liaison brain' as both the area and the result of interaction between the brain and the self. The liaison brain is the Popperian equivalent of Descartes's pineal gland. For Popper the self owes its origin to, and draws its ontological sustenance from, the

Platonic world 3. The uneasy combination of Platonism and Cartesianism makes Popper's epistemology a fascinating, if not wholly persuasive, philosophical achievement.[40]

3

As we have seen, Popper defines rationality in terms of problem solving. To be rational is to formulate one's aims clearly and to explore the best means of realizing them.[41] This is as true of a theoretical inquiry as of a practical activity. As we have seen too, this is how Popper defines the task of the theory of scientific method. It is concerned to elucidate and analyse the basic aims of science and to devise a body of rules capable of promoting them. In Popper's view, political philosophy should ask similar questions about politics. First, it should inquire into what he calls the 'legitimate aims' of the state; for him this the 'fundamental question' of political life.[42] And, second, it should explore the institutional structure best suited to realizing these aims.

Popper argues that we cannot discuss political life 'rationally' unless we approach it 'from the point of view of a fairly clear and definite aim'. Political institutions are 'always...designed with certain aims in mind'. Once we have identified their aims, we can formulate 'political demands' and 'proposals' and devise institutions accordingly. Even as Popper reduces epistemology to methodology and the philosophy of science to scientific method, he reduces political philosophy to political methodology. Further, like his philosophy of science, his philosophy of politics is normative in orientation. It aims to tell us what the state should do and how it should be constituted. Since for Popper to approach a question rationally is to approach it 'from a technological point of view', it is hardly surprising that his political theory should have a technological orientation.[43]

Popper criticizes traditional political philosophy for not defining its task in this way. He argues that, like traditional theories of knowledge, traditional political philosophy was authoritarian and justificationist in orientation. And even as the former looked for infallible sources of knowledge, traditional political philosophy asked questions which were authoritarian and absolutist in orientation. Many political philosophers, including the most liberal and anti-authoritarian, asked such questions as *who* is best qualified to rule, or *who* ought to wield the ultimate authority, or *where* the sovereign power is ultimately located.[44] Popper argues that such authoritarian questions could only elicit such authoritarian and illiberal answers as that the wise, the best, the philosophers or the proletariat should rule, that sovereign power is located in and derived from God, the nation, the people, the laws of the universe or of history and so on. In Popper's view, there are no infallible men or institutions, any more than there are infallible sources of knowledge. A ruler, however wise, may turn out to be bad, and every source of authority, however reliable, may turn out to be fallible. What is more, authoritarian questions rest on the false assumption that rationality is the property of an isolated individual, whereas, as we saw above, it is a product of an inter-subjective and critical method of discussion. It is located not in an individual but in the process of mutual criticism occurring *between* individuals. Even as Popper rejects authoritarian epistemology, he rejects authoritarian political philosophy and aims to construct a non-authoritarian political philosophy on the basis of his non-authoritarian epistemology.

According to Popper, political philosophers have formulated the aims of the state in several different ways. For some it should aim at promoting or maximizing human happiness. For others it should aim at creating a fully human, or perfect, or virtuous, or classless society. For yet others its aims are much more modest; they are limited to maintaining a peaceful and orderly social existence. In Popper's view, all but the last are mistaken.

Popper argues that 'of all political ideas that of making the people happy is perhaps the most dangerous one.'[45] Different people find their happiness in different things, and there never is, nor can there be, general agreement on what it consists in or even whether it is the highest political ideal. Any attempt to use the state to promote human happiness, therefore, necessarily involves interference with individual liberties and judgements. It also involves coercing men to do what they may not wish to do (and, indeed, what they may strongly disapprove of) and produces a considerable amount of unhappiness. It may be argued that the unhappiness caused to some may be outweighed by the far greater amount of happiness offered to the rest. Popper rejoins that the argument rests on the fallacious assumptions that pain and pleasure can be abstracted from human agents and that pain is only the negative of pleasure. Pleasure and pain cannot be assessed and quantified in the abstract. They do not exist by themselves but only as the experiences of actual human beings. And human beings cannot be traded off against each other. Further, pleasure and pain do not form a 'continuum' and are very different in nature. Pleasure is not the mere absence of pain, nor is pain the absence of pleasure. Both are independent and positive states of mind. Since we cannot 'treat degrees of pain as negative degrees of pleasure', it is a mistake to argue that pain can be outweighed or compensated by pleasure.

In Popper's view, pleasure and pain are morally asymmetrical. Pain or human suffering 'makes a direct moral appeal...for help', whereas there is 'no similar call' to increase the happiness of a man already doing reasonably well. Further, the reduction of suffering has a moral urgency which the increase of happiness does not have. Again, diminishing a man's suffering does not involve imposing our values upon him, whereas increasing his happiness does. Unlike happiness, suffering is relatively self-evident, easily identifiable, and, as it were, dictates the lines of our response. We can deal with it, therefore, in a manner that respects the values and judgements of the person involved.

Pleasure and pain are also epistemologically asymmetrical. Misery and suffering are universally familiar experiences, and there is a certain uniformity about their causes. We therefore have a reliable body of knowledge about how to deal with them. By contrast, the causes and conditions of human happiness are infinite and various, and hence we can never be sure whether, and to what degree, our actions will make others happy.[46] Moreover, since suffering is a relatively specific form of human experience, we can ascertain its existence and check whether or not our response to it is effective and adequate, and whether and when we have succeeded in eliminating it. By contrast, happiness is hypothetical and indeterminate, difficult to define and identify. In order to increase other's happiness we need intimate knowledge of them, and they should be able to get rid of us if they think that we are mistaken or intrusive. These conditions obtain only in close personal relationships. Increasing others' happiness can therefore be a legitimate goal in private life but not at all in the political sphere.

For these and other reasons Popper proposes that not the greatest happiness of the greatest number but 'the least amount of avoidable suffering for all' should be our aim. Just as in science we aim at the 'elimination of false theories...rather than the attainment of established truths', we should in moral and political life 'demand the elimination of suffering rather than the promotion of happiness'.[47] As Popper understands it, the minimization of suffering is not a negative formulation of the well-known utilitarian formula but an independent principle. Popper's formula rejects the fundamental assumptions of its utilitarian cousin, namely, that pleasure and pain are homogeneous, form a continuum and can be traded off. It is wrong, therefore, to describe it as 'negative utilitarianism'.

For Popper, then, moral and political demands should be formulated negatively if they are to be amenable to rational discussion.[48] Negatively formulated demands highlight the fact of human suffering, emphasize the urgency of response, present a clear target and can command general support. For example, it is easier to discuss how to minimize, even eliminate, the disadvantages of poor children than to decide how to maximize their opportunities or create an abstract and indeterminate equality of opportunity. We can easily ascertain and demonstrate the disadvantages from which such shildren suffer and why they need to be, and how they can be, removed. Our discussion has a focus, is subject to empirical check, proceeds in a controlled and systematic manner and occurs within an agreed framework. These conditions are absent when we pursue such general and inherently vague objectives as social and economic equality or even equality of opportunity.

Even as Popper rejects the pursuit of human happiness as the legitimate aim of the state, he rejects the revolutionary proposal to replace the established social order with a truly human, just, classless or perfect society.[49] He advances eight reasons for his rejection.

First, such abstract goals as the fullest realization of man, perfect equality and justice and a truly human society are 'theoretical, unreal things' about which it is difficult to form an opinion. We do not know what they mean and involve or how to go about achieving them.

Second, such ultimate goals are too general and too abstract to be clearly formulated, and hence they are incapable of elucidation through rational discussion. What is more, they are too distant to enable us to make rational choices in complex, specific situations. Indeed, they can be used to justify almost any course of action.

Third, Popper argues that the language of ultimate ends is logically incoherent. The ends we pursue must be relevant to the situations in which we need to act. Since all situations are specific, so are the ends we aim at. Specific and concrete ends have unforeseen consequences and constantly require us to reformulate our subsequent aims. In other words, the very activity of realizing ultimate ends calls for their constant reformulation, and hence they cannot be formulated and fixed for ever.

Fourth, even people who agree about allegedly ultimate ends are bound to disagree about them when new facts and problems come to light during the course of their realization. By its very nature, the process of realizing them takes a very long time, and it is extremely difficult to sustain a fanatical commitment to them.

Those initially pledged to them begin to have second thoughts. And this cannot but lead to mutual suspicion, hostility, intolerance, prohibition of dissent and the persecution of dissidents.

Fifth, the Utopian and revolutionary approach to politics rests on the mistaken assumption that social and political institutions form an integrated whole, such that none of them can be changed without changing the entire social structure. Popper argues that the so-called social whole is a fiction. It does not exist independently of, and is nothing more than, the totality of specific institutions and practices. Further, although interrelated, social and political institutions are also autonomous and distinct and not only can be but must be examined and changed separately. In Popper's view, it is only by changing one social institution at a time that we can ensure that our actions correspond to our intentions and can identify and control their unintended consequences.

Sixth, every elimination of an evil 'must necessarily produce' as its unintended consequence a host of new, though possibly lesser, evils. This means that 'all politics consists in chosing the lesser evil' and requires a 'proper evaluation of competing evils'.[50] Since we can never produce good without producing at least some evil in the process, it is naïve to imagine that one can ever achieve an absolutely good or perfect society.

Seventh, it is impossible to control *all* social relationships. In the course of controlling one set of relationships, we necessarily create a whole host of other relationships which now need to be controlled. And in the process of controlling them, we create yet other sets of relationships. In other words, we cannot create a society in which all conflicts and problems of arbitrary power can be altogether eliminated. As Popper says, this is 'quite impossible' and 'the impossibility is a logical impossibility'.

Finally, Popper argues that the revolutionary attempt to create a perfect society involves investing the state with an enormous amount of power. This not only poses a grave danger to individual liberty but also creates the very inequalities of power and social conditions which the revolutionary is so concerned to eliminate.

Since the 'Utopian method' of social engineering 'violates the principles of scientific method', Popper proposes to replace it with what, following Roscoe Pound, he calls 'piecemeal social engineering'.[51] As opposed to the 'canvas-cleaning' approach of the Utopian revolutionary, which aims to change the entire social structure in one clean sweep on the basis of an abstract blueprint, piecemeal social engineering consists in identifying and tackling specific problems one at a time. Contrary to what some commentators have maintained, Poper's piecemeal social engineering is distinguished by its *method of approach* and not by its *aims*.[52] It is not necessarily confined to 'smallish' problems and may pursue 'bold' objectives as long as they are pursued in a cautious, experimental, gradual and self-critical manner.[53]

In Popper's view, piecemeal social engineering is 'methodologically sound' and represents 'the only rational' way to conduct politics.[54] He argues that an engineer is able to desigcn complicated machines because he has acquired the relevant knowledge by means of repeated experiments. We have no such knowledge of social and political machines. As he puts it, 'The fact that such a social science hardly exists so far... is one of the strongest arguments against the possibility of large-scale or Utopian social engineering.' All our knowledge, including our knowledge of society, is acquired by means of repeated experiments involving trial and error. Piecemeal social engineering meets this epistemological requirement. It allows us to make 'repeated experiments', to isolate irrelevant factors, to disentangle complex causes, to establish correlations between causes and effects, to compare our expectations with the consequences of our actions and so on.[55] Piecemeal social engineering has the further methodological advantage that we can reach a consensus on what counts as success or failure, try out the method of trial and error and provide the controlled conditions needed for social experiments. The method is also less costly, since we can change our policies without much risk when their consequences turn out to be contrary to our intentions. In short, piecemeal social engineering is the only rational method of building up, over time, a reliable body of social and political knowledge.[56]

Popper's epistemological defence of piecemeal social engineering implies that once we have acquired a reliable body of social and political knowledge, an 'empirical social technology' as he calls it, we do not need to be so cautious and may undertake bold projects of large-scale social engineering. Popper lends support to this view when he says, 'We must reform... little by little *until* we have more experience in social engineering.'[57] In his view, the scale of social change that can be rationally undertaken is governed 'by the degree of our experience gained in conscious and systematic piecemeal engineering'. As our experience and knowledge improves, we can undertake 'bold' projects. Our knowledge is, of course, never wholly free of error. However, just as the possible fallibility of his knowledge does not deter an engineer from designing complicated machines, there is no reason why it should deter a social engineer either. Personally, of course, Popper wishes to change society 'little by little'.[58] However, his personal preference is not supported by his methodology, which *in principle* sanctions revolutionary social reconstruction.

Popper argues, then, largely on epistemological grounds, that the aims of the government should be limited and negative. It is methodologically sounder to reduce human suffering than to promote human happiness, and to proceed in a cautious, controlled, gradual and experimental manner. In his view, the aims of the state can be summed up in one word, namely, protection.[59] Men are self-determining beings who can and wish to pursue their own purposes and run their lives themselves. In order that they can do so, they require certain general conditions, some of which can only be met by the state. These are the protection of life, liberty and property from aggression by other men as well as the agencies of government, the elimination of distress and suffering and the maintenance of a certain level of general welfare. Popper calls this a 'protectionist' theory of the state.

Having identified the aims of the government, Popper asks what social and political institutions are best equipped to realize them. The institutions are basically 'means that serve certain ends'. As 'social technologists', we should therefore design social and political institutions capable of realizing the limited ends outlined earlier. Popper's institutional proposals boil down to what he, following Bergson, calls an 'open society'.[60]

Popper uses the terms 'open' and 'closed' in this context rather loosely and in several different senses.[61] By a closed or tribal society, he generally means a society based on uncritically accepted customs and taboos. It is essentially like a 'cage', and its members lack the capacit for rational criticism and for taking personal responsibility for their decisions.[62] By contrast, an open society is 'rational and critical'. It is characterized by 'faith in reason and liberty'. Its members define themselves as rational and responsible individuals who wish to run their lives themselves and to accept responsibility for their decisions. In an open society the citizens resolve their differences through debate and discussion. Every citizen is respected as a potential source of ideas and arguments, and his right to speak and to be heard is fully safeguarded. Diversity of opinions is not only respected but also encouraged. The government's policies are not accepted uncritically but subjected to the test of reason and experience and amended in the light of criticism. Politicians show 'scientific readiness' to learn from experience and to 'look for their mistakes instead of trying to explain them away'.[63]

For Popper an open society is democratic in its structure of government. He divides all forms of government into two, namely, democracy and dictatorship or tyranny.[64] In the former the rulers can be dismissed by the ruled 'without bloodshed'; in the latter they cannot be. Popper argues that although democracy involves acceptance of the procedural principle of taking decisions by majority vote, this is not its most distinctive feature. For him democracy is the political expression and institutionalization of the scientific method. It is essentially a 'method', a method of so conducting the affairs of a community that the ruled can criticize and remove the rulers. Its essential and most distinctive feature is its commitment to 'free institutions', that is, the institutions of free speech and free elections.

Popper argues that this way of defining democracy avoids the paradox that bedevils the traditional definition of it in terms of majority rule. If the majority were to elect a tyrant, the principle of majority rule would tell us *both* that we should obey him (because he is elected by the majority) *and* that we should disobey him (because he stands for the rejection of majority rule).[65] When defined in terms of majority rule, democracy turns out to be a paradoxical and self-contradictory form of government. Popper claims that his view of democracy avoids the paradox. For him the heart of democracy lies in its free institutions, and a democrat's primary commitment is to their preservation. The democrat, therefore, is not always bound by the majority's decisions and remains free to oppose them if they result in the establishment of a tyrannical government.

Popper argues that since democracy institutionalizes freedom, reason and criticism, every rational man has a 'moral obligation' to support it. To abandon it for economic gain is irrational since, once it is lost, even economic advantages 'persist only on sufferance'. For Popper any attempt to overthrow a democratic government is a 'crime', and the ensuing government 'a dangerous gang of criminals'. The citizens have 'not only a right but also a duty' to resist the latter, by violence if necessary.[66] Popper goes even further. He argues that a democratic government does not have a duty to tolerate those committed to replacing it with an undemocratic form of government. In his view, the principle of tolerance involves a paradox, in the sense that tolerating all, including the intolerant, can lead to a situation in which the latter may gain power and put an end to the practice of tolerance. Popper resolves the paradox by arguing that we can 'claim, in the name of tolerance, the right not to tolerate the intolerant'.[67]

In Popper's view, an open society requires a free market.[68]

Without a free market no economic system can serve its 'only rational purpose', namely, 'to satisfy the demands of the consumer'. Unles producers compete for the favour of consumers, the latter's choice is drastically reduced. The competitive market, however, has a tendency to create such semi-political organizations as business monopolies, trusts and unions, which severely restrict competition among producers. Popper argues that a democratic government, which is committed to safeguarding freedom, should legislate against them. A free market also tends to create poverty and suffering and encourages the misuse of economic power. The government should therefore intervene in economic life. Even as it should protect citizens from physical coercion, it should protect them from economic coercion. It should limit the working day, guarantee a livelihood to everyone willing and able to work, insure all its citizens against disability, unemployment and old age and in general ensure that no one is forced to enter into an inequitable arrangement out of fear of starvation or economic ruin.[69] Economic intervention by the government increases its power and is 'extremely dangerous', for 'if freedom is lost, everything is lost.' Following Hayek, Popper therefore proposes that economic intervention should be institutional and indirect and not personal and direct. Rather than empower the executive organs of the government to act as they please in order to realize agreed ends, the government should design a legal framework of protective institutions and lay down by law what its citizens may or may not do and within what limits. This measure would be not only more conducive to freedom but also more 'rational', in the sense that it would allow for adjustments in the light of experience, would minimize unexpected consequences and would apply the method of trial and error to government policies.[70]

Popper's discussion of open society is informed by one overriding concern, that social and political life should be so organized that it promotes the 'growth of reason' and facilitates effective problem solving. For him the institutional preconditions for the achievement of these ends are the same in science and in society, namely, inter-subjective criticism, controlled experiments, clarity of aim, the method of trial and error, freedom to make mistakes and so on. Political debate is not fundamentally different from scientific, and the logic of political problem solving is no different from that of scientific problem solving. According to Popper, an open society, an idealized version of the Western liberal democracy, subjects society to reason as far as is humanly possible and best provides the institutional preconditions of progress.[71] As he puts it, 'I assert that our own free world is by far the best society which has come into existence during the course of human history.'[72]

It will have been noted that Popper's political theory is remarkably congruent with his epistemology. He himself says that *Open Society* and *The Poverty of Historicism* 'grew out of the theory of knowledge' outlined in his *Logic,* and that there are 'a number of common ideas' in his social and political theory and his theory of scientific method.[73] In both he is concerned with progress, and progress consists in the 'growth of reason'. In both his mode of inquiry is normative in character and designed to formulate rules for promoting progress. Further, the rules are basically the same in each, namely, the formulation of a problem, inter-subjective criticism of its proposed solutions, the method of trial and error, the elimination of error, the test of reason and experience and so on. Both his social and his scientific theory are articulated in terms of such structural concepts as decision, proposal and problem. According to Popper, in science we *decide* what propositions to accept as basic, how to distinguish between science and non-science, how to test theories, what is to count as adequate corroboration of a theory and so on. Similarly, in political life we *decide* what objectives the government should pursue, what demands we should make upon it, what institutions to establish, what moral rules to adopt and so on. Even as Popper refuses to ask essentialist questions in philosophy, he declines to ask them in politics. And even as we get closer to the truth and make scientific progress by eliminating error, we get closer to the good society and make social progress by eliminating human suffering. Again, Popper sees the essence of science in its method; as he says, 'It is advisable to characterize science by its method rather than by its results.' He similarly sees the essence of democracy in its method. For him science *is* scientific method, and democracy *is* democratic method.

It is sometimes suggested that despite these and other similarities, there is 'an asymmetry and strain' between Popper's scientific and political theory, especially between his gradualist view of politics and his revolutionary view of science.[74] Popper himself lends support to this view when he observes, 'My *social theory* (which favours gradual and piecemeal reform...) contrasts sharply with my *theory of method,* which happens to be a theory of scientific and intellectual revolutions.'[75]

The contrast between Popper's evolutionary politics and revolutionary science seems to be exaggerated. As we have seen, his political theory is not as gradualist as it appears to be. One of his main reasons for advocating piecemeal social engineering is that the social sciences have not yet built up an adequate body of knowledge about methods of designing social machines and the long-term consequences of human actions. When they do, and Popper does not rule out the possibility, radical social change becomes logically permissible. Even as Popper's political theory is not very gradualist, his theory of science is not very revolutionary. Unlike some philosophers, Popper is in no doubt that the natural sciences offer objective and reliable knowledge of the world, that scientific knowledge grows over time, that scientific method, as it has evolved in the West, will not one day undergo radical change and so on. Indeed, he takes all this for granted without much argument. Further, he insists that although everything that the scientist knows is in principle open to doubt, he recognizes that not everything can be doubted at once. At any given point in time we must take the bulk of scientific knowledge for granted. As he himself says, we can never say in science that we are not making much progress and should therefore 'sweep away all science and start afresh'. The 'rational procedure' in science is always 'to correct', not to reject, the prevailing body of knowledge.[76] So-called scientific revolution is never total and sweeping; it is, by its very nature, limited and partial. This is precisely what Popper says about society. Although all social institutions can be changed, they cannot all be changed at once.[77] The scale and pace of change in both science and society are determined by the same principle, namely, the extent and reliability of available knowledge. Certainly, Popper argues that our social and political knowledge is unlikely to be as certain and as reliable as our scientific knowledge, and that since social and political actions affect human beings, we cannot be as adventurous in social and political life as in scientific investigation. However, for him the difference between the two is at most one of degree.

4

Popper's philosophical achievements are considerable. Although seen by some commentators principally as a philosopher of science, he is, in fact, a philosopher in the great tradition. His ambition is nothing less than to construct a general and substantive theory offering a comprehensive and systematic account of man and the world. For Popper, as for the great philosophers, a philosophical system includes the four major departments of metaphysics, ontology, epistemology and logic. Popper has made important contributions in each of these areas. His bold speculations on the nature and evolution of the material world and consciousness, his three-world ontology, his fascinating ideas about the nature and constitution of the human self, the relationship between the self, the body, the mind and the world, the nature and growth of knowledge, man, society, state, history and so forth are all ample evidence of the range of his philosophical ambition and achievements.

Unlike some naïve rationalists, Popper recognizes that a general theory of the world cannot be constructed without full knowledge of the findings of the natural sciences. At the same time he is aware of the limits of the natural sciences and appreciates that they throw up problems which they cannot solve and which call for metaphysics. Accordingly, Popper regards metaphysics as an extremely important inquiry and insists upon its close relation to the natural sciences. Along with Russell, Whitehead and a few others, Popper shares the honour of sustaining the metaphysical tradition not only through his powerful defence of it against the misguided criticisms of the logical positivists, the linguistic philosophers and others but also through his practice of it.

Although Popper exaggerates both the authoritarian character of traditional epistemology and his differences with it, many of his criticisms of it are well taken. He rightly rejects the radical epistemological scepticism so beloved of traditional philosophy and shows conclusively why it is incoherent and leads to a curious blend of authoritarianism and irrationalism. He is no less right to question the post-Cartesian confusion between epistemology and psychology and to orientate epistemology towards the nature and growth of knowledge rather than the nature and mechanism of perception. His criticisms of the traditional preoccupation with the 'foundations' and 'justification' of knowledge are sound and have deservedly been recognized as path-breaking. The merits and limitations of Popper's own 'criticist' and falsificationist epistemology have been widely commented upon and do not concern us here.

Popper's other important contribution lies in his fascinating theories of reason and criticism. His concern to link rationality with criticism rather than with justification is novel and puts an end to many an unnecessary controversy. As he points out, an action, proposal, theory or decision is rational not because it can be derived from some indisputably self-evident principle discovered by *reason,* as Plato, Aristotle and others thought; nor because it can be shown to follow from the agent's process of *reasoning,* as the nominalist and subjectivist philosophers maintained; nor because *reasons* can be given for it, as Wittgenstein, Winch and others have argued. It is rational if it can be discussed and criticized intersubjectively, if the reasons given for it are discussible and criticizable – in short, if *arguments* can be presented for and against it. In his view, rationality is located not in reason, reasoning or reasons but in arguments. For Popper reason is inherently argumentative and critical, and a theory of reason is necessarily a theory of criticism.

Popper's theory of criticism contains many useful insights.[78] Although he does not integrate them into a general theory, he distinguishes four different levels and forms of criticism, namely, the empirical, the logical, the immanent and the transcendental, and argues that one or more of them can be invoked according to the nature of the subject matter to be criticized. Further, as he rightly argues, nothing is beyond criticism and discussion, not even so-called paradigms and conceptual frameworks. They can be criticized in terms of their coherence, explanatory power, basic assumptions, capacity to open up fruitful lines of inquiry, explicit or implicit empirical assertions about the world and so on. Popper advances what I might call a 'piecemeal' theory of criticism. Although we may not be able to criticize a philosophical system as a whole, we can criticize specific parts of it and cast doubt on its validity. Popper rightly observes that we are not prisoners of any framework of thought, and that all forms of relativism, including Kuhn's paradigmatic version, are questionable.[79]

As for Popper's social and political theory, which is our main concern, his achievements are less impressive. His refutations of what he calls 'historicism' and 'naïve rationalism' are conclusive. His criticisms of what he calls 'Utopian social engineering' are persuasive. Although ultimately unsatisfactory, his methodological individualism is an interesting way of explaining social and political actions. At a different level Popper's defence of liberalism is ingenious, even if not wholly convincing. He defends it on meta-physical and epistemological grounds. Since problem solving is for him an inescapable feature of human existence (and, indeed, of all existence), one cannot survive, let alone progress, without the freedom to experiment with and criticize different ways of solving a problem. Wherever there is life, there is a problem, and wherever there is a problem, experiment and criticism are essential. Popper gives liberalism not only a metaphysical but also a biological basis.

Popper defends liberalism on epistemological grounds as well. As we have seen, he argues that criticism is the life blood of knowledge and rationality. Knowledge grows by eliminating errors, and errors can only be eliminated by subjecting ideas to inter-subjective discussion and criticism. Further, for Popper rationality is located in arguments. An action or a proposal is rational if it can be argued, and our confidence in its rationality is strengthened if it stands up to criticism. Indeed, Popper argues that men develop rationality only by participating directly or indirectly in the process of inter-subjective criticism. As he says, they 'owe' their rationality to world 3. For him rationality can develop and 'grow' only if inter-subjective criticism is institutionalized, and this is possible only in a free society.

Despite these and other insights, Popper's political theory is fundamentally inadequate. He is primarily interested in prescribing the aims of government and the best methods of realizing them. He makes no attempt to *understand* the nature and structure of political life. He never asks how organized life is possible, how men holding conflicting moral and political beliefs can sustain a common system of authority, how they acquire a sense of collective identity, how one man can acquire authority over another, how citizens can be free within a state which sometimes requires them to do things that are at odds with their moral beliefs, how men can be morally asked to die for causes or to pay taxes for purposes they wholly disapprove of, and so on. It is such questions that have been the principal concern of political philosophy over the centuries. Popper's political theory may tell us how to organize political life but not how to understand and explain it. As we have noted, Popper's failure to ask these questions is not inherent in his view of philosophy. His discussions of Parmenides, Plato, Kant, and others amply demonstrate that he fully appreciates the importance of the questions which spring from intellectual perplexity and seek what he calls 'rational understanding'. For reasons never made clear, Popper somehow does not see that political life too raises such questions. As a result, his political theory remains almost entirely didactic.

Even as Popper reduces epistemology to the technology of the growth of science, he reduces political philosophy to social tech-nology. He assumes that a human society is basically like a machine, its government like an engineer and governing a country like attending to the social machine by means of piecemeal engineering. On the basis of this wholly misleading view of society, he argues that political philosophy is concerned to determine the aims of govern-ment and institutional ways of realizing them. As we shall see, his view of society is false, as is his view of the nature of government. Further Popper treats the question of the aims of government as unproblematic and fails to notice its complexity. He does not appreciate that we cannot discuss the question without undertaking an inquiry into the kinds of obligation men have to one another, which of these can and should be enforced by law, the nature of the state, the nature and limits of law, the relation between law and morality, the complex relations between different human goals, a conception of how men wish and ought to live, and so on. It is these types of question that political philosophers have asked and that Popper's technological approach to politics prevents him from asking. In so far as it fails to ask them, Popper's theory is inadequately grounded and remains unsatisfactory.

While Popper's non-authoritarian political philosophy has the advantage of dismissing some improper questions, it has several inherent limitations. Thanks to his non-authoritarian perspective, questions relating to the nature of authority, law, obligation, duty and right simply do not engage his attention. As a result, Popper's political theory contains large gaps. He examines the nature of public discussion and criticism but not the structure and basis of authority; he discusses what objectives government or law should aim at but not what government and law are. Since questions relating to the nature of authority are crucial, Popper cannot avoid answering them. However, since he does not formulate them explicitly and carefully, his answers remain rather simple-minded. He says, for example, that because a law is made by public authority, we cannot assume that it is right. We must criticize it and judge for ourselves whether it is right or rational. Popper treats the law as if it were a proposal or a hypothesis to be subjected to, and accepted only if it withstands, stringent inter-subjective criticism. This is wholly to misunderstand its nature. Again, Popper says that unless it is totally irrational, a law should be obeyed, as otherwise orderly social life is endangered. That a law is not a piece of advice but an authoritative directive which a citizen has a *prima facie* obligation to obey, that its form is as important as its content never enters into Popper's argument. His technological and instrumental approach is inherently ill-equipped to grasp the *formal* nature of rules, law and authority.[80]

As for Popper's view of political life, its limitations are closely connected with those of his brand of rationalism. He thinks that there are no differences which rational men cannot resolve. A discussion is a matter of presenting arguments for and against the issue involved and accepting those with superior logical force. Popper abstracts reason from the complex human personality and treats it as if it were an independent and self-subsistent faculty. In so doing he fails to notice the subtle and complex ways in which an individual's values, interests, language and forms of thought shape his reason. A rational discussion is inescapably subject to the limits imposed by the diversity of values. Rationality cannot be defined in 'objective' and abstract terms. Whether a particular view or conduct is rational or otherwise depends on the wider context of the form of life within which it occurs. Men holding different views of life disagree profoundly about the nature and criteria of rationality and also, therefore, in their analyses of situations, the factors they consider relevant and the degree of importance they assign to them. It is difficult to see how one could convince an anti-vivisectionist, a strict vegetarian, an anti-abortionist or a radical egalitarian that his cause is wholly misconceived.

Even if Popper were right that such disputes can 'in principle' be resolved by patient and open-minded discussion, it is difficult to see how his argument is relevant to politics. The patient resolution of profound moral and political differences requires intellectual openness, a relatively neutral language of communication, the ability and willingness to engage in searching and sustained discussions, a lack of urgency and so on. These conditions are met in an academic seminar but never in political life. Political problems are urgent and require immediate attention. They are highly complex, and it is often difficult to distinguish genuine disagreement from mere rationalization and special pleading. The parties to a dispute lack the capacity, training and leisure to engage in sustained and critical discussion. Deep conflicts of interest generate mutual suspicion and discourage them from looking at issues impartially and from each other's perspective. Dominant classes and groups so shape the language of public discourse as to prevent the formulation of certain types of issue and argument. In short, the background conditions necessary for a rational and critical debate are generally conspicuous by their absence from political life.

Since Popper does not fully appreciate all this, he mistakenly extends to political life his general theory of rational criticism. As a result his political theory remains naïve and *simpliste*. He sees a society as if it were a community of scientists, the newspapers as if they were scientific periodicals, the sessions of a legislative assembly as if they were scientific congresses and the government as if it were engaged in conducting political experiments designed to falsify political proposals. He contends that citizens must resolve their differences by discussion and must refrain from vigorously pursuing their own interests. Indeed, he says that a rational citizen will rather lose an argument than coerce, coax or even persuade his opponent![81] Popper treats the *method* of criticism as sacrosanct and allows only those goals that can be realized by means of it. This is to turn method into a fetish and to make it the arbiter of human goals.

Since Popper does not appreciate the political limits of rationalism, his rationalism turns into its opposite and becomes Utopian. It bears no relation to the present or, indeed, any conceivable form of human society.

Thanks to his conception of reason, Popper views politics as if it were a form of rational problem solving. For him 'rational' or 'sane' politics consists in isolating and identifying problems, defining them in unambiguous terms and proposing and criticizing solutions to them. This is a strange view of politics. In political life there are no problems in Popper's sense. Unlike theoretical problems, political problems owe their origin to the ways in which men perceive and define their situations, and they disappear if men can be persuaded or induced to define them differently. If restless slaves can be persuaded that they deserve their lot in life, the problem of dealing with their potential disobedience disappears. And the problem of inflation which breaks one government may not even pose a problem for its successor if it could somehow induce the workers to make 'patriotic' sacrifices or to believe that demands for higher wages lead to unemployment.

Further, political 'problems' cannot be isolated in a way that theoretical problems can be. They occur within the context of the social whole, and their 'solutions' have profound consequences for several other areas. We cannot ask how 'best' we can solve the 'problem' of abolishing the independent schools or the House of Lords, for neither problem exists *as a problem* in isolation. In itself private education is not a problem. It is a problem in the eyes of certain members of society because it offers access to certain types of privilege, nourishes a certain type of social structure and cultural ethos and so on. Its 'solution', therefore, necessarily requires us to deal with a whole complex of social and political institutions. Further, we cannot 'objectively' decide which solution is rational, for that depends upon how it is presented to the people, what they perceive to be its likely consequences, what they are prepared to accept, what price we consider worth paying and so on. It is also misleading to think of established institutions and practices as products of the method of trial and error, consciously or unconsciously applied. They have grown up as a result of human choices, inertia, social pressures, manipulations by dominant interests and so on and, over time, have become part of the established way of life. Alternatives to them have rarely been tried out and rejected as unsuitable. The concept of falsification and even the apparently more popular concept of historical induction do not make sense in social and political life.

The limitation of Popper's view of reason are evident also in what he takes to be the aims of government. Some of what he says about the negative character of moral principles is persuasive. However, in its generalized form his moral theory pulls in two conflicting directions. Interpreted in one way, it is highly restrictive. For example, no one suffers in the absence of sports grounds, swimming pools, theatres, operas, public libraries, public parks, an aesthetically pleasing environment and so on, and therefore Popper would have to rule out the public provision of these. No obvious suffering is involved in the public display of pornographic material, and therefore, again, Popper would have to rule out government action in these areas. We provide certain public amenities and disallow certain forms of conduct because we cherish a particular way of life and value certain forms of human excellence. Popper's negative and individualistic approach prevents him from appreciating the importance of public goods and a shared conception of human excellence.

While at one level the elimination of suffering rules out all but minimal government action, at another level it has the opposite implication. Suffering and even distress encompass a broad sphere and arise from many different sources. The poor may suffer because they have to make do without a number of basic amenities. They may also suffer because the very presence of conspicuous waste by the rich offends their dignity and sense of justice, or because their sense of their own worth or self-esteem is violated by great inequalities of power and wealth. Interpreted broadly, the principle of the minimization of suffering calls for profound changes in the structure of social relationships. Popper gives no valid reason why we should interpret it in very narrow, almost wholly material terms.

7

John Rawls

John Rawls' work has justly received wide acclaim. No other contemporary work has aroused as much interest and comment as his majestic *Theory of Justice*. He is a moral and political philosopher in the grand tradition and practises moral and political philosophy in the manner of distinguished philosophers from Aristotle to Sidgwick. Unlike some of them, he does not undertake a systematic inquiry into the nature of philosophy in general and moral and political philosophy in particular. Nevertheless, a fairly clear and carefully defended view of philosophy informs his attempt to construct a theory of justice.

Unlike some contemporary philosophers, Rawls believes that a philosopher interested in examining the nature of justice is concerned not so much to analyse the concept as to construct a substantive theory of justice. By a substantive theory of justice he means one that examines the nature and structure of the human capacity for justice, its relations to other capacities, its place in moral life, the conditions under which the questions of justice arise, the principles by which they generally are and ought to be answered, the specific institutions and practices in which the principles are best realized and so on. As Rawls understands it, such a substantive theory is neither wholly formal nor wholly empirical. It cannot be wholly empirical, since it is concerned to analyse the conept of justice, to relate it to other moral and political concepts and to examine critically its criteria. It cannot be wholly formal either, since it is concerned to analyse the structures of man's moral capacities, to articulate the criteria of justice as revealed in moral actions and judgements and to outline the types of social practices and institutions in which they are fully realized. Furthermore, a theory of justice is interested not in justice *sans phrase* but in human justice, that is, justice as it applies not to 'pure intelligences' but to men as we know them. Thus Rawls thinks that it must be grounded in adequate empirical knowledge of the way men think and feel, the ends they pursue, the means necessary to realize them and so on.[1]

As moral beings, men constantly make judgements about the justice and injustice of their actions, social practices and institutions.[2] For Rawls these judgements constitute the philosopher's subject matter. The moral philosopher aims to analyse them, to examine the human capacities revealed by them and to elucidate and assess their 'regulative principles' or standards. Like our moral judgements in general, our judgements of justice and injustice vary considerably in the degree of confidence with which we make them. We feel certain about some of them, are in considerable doubt about some others and cannot make up our minds at all about the rest. Rawls is convinced that the philosopher should take into account only what he calls 'considered judgements'. By these he means 'judgements rendered under conditions favourable to the exercise of the sense of judgement, and therefore under circumstances where the more common excuses and explanations for making a mistake do not obtain'. Judgements made with hesitation or when we are upset or frightened, or those in which we have little confidence or which put us in a position to gain one way or another do not represent well considered judgements and can be ignored. By contrast, judgements made by us when we possess the ability, the opportunity and the desire to reach correct decisions are well considered.

Even considered judgements, however, are subject to 'irregularities and distortions', are likely to rest on conflicting principles and cannot be regarded as incorrigible.[3] It is possible, therefore, that we might revise them if someone were systematically to analyse them and to show either that they do not cohere with our other judgements or that they rest on principles that we reject in other case; indeed, this is a common experience. Rawls argues that the 'best account' of a man's conception of justice is not one which fits his judgements *prior* to his consideration of a systematic account of it but rather one which matches his judgements in what Rawls calls 'reflective equilibrium'.[4] As he puts it:[5]

> Moral philosophy is Socratic; we may want to change our present considered judgements once their regulative principles are brought to light. And we may want to do this even though these principles are a perfect fit. A knowledge of these principles may suggest further reflections that lead us to revise our judgements. This feature is not peculiar though to moral philosophy, or to the study of other philosophical principles such as those of induction and scientific method.

Rawls maintains that almost every theory of justice matches at least some of our judgements in reflective equilibrium. Each may, therefore, appear convincing when taken in isolation but inadequate when compared with others. A moral philosopher cannot rest content to show that his theory matches our considered judgements; he must critically examine its rivals and demonstrate that his is 'the best approximation overall'.[6] He has obviously no means of knowing what new theories may be developed in the future. All that he can claim is that his theory offers a better account of our moral judgements than any other that he can think of. However well considered it might be, every moral theory at best 'moves us closer to the philosophical ideal: it does not, of course, achieve it.'[7]

For Rawls, then, a philosophical theory of justice is concerned to analyse and explain our judgements of justice and injustice. By elucidating their regulative principles it not only explains to us why we make specific judgements but also extrapolates them in an acceptable way and guides us in areas where we are confused or in doubt. In other words, a philosophical theory of justice is not only explanatory but also critical and normative. Obviously, it cannot tell us what to do in specific situations, for that requires a detailed knowledge of the context. Rather, it offers a guiding principle, clears our vision, 'defines a perspective', 'identifies' the considerations relevant to a situation and helps us to assign them their 'correct weights', at least in the more important instances.[8] A theory of justice also explains the complex ways in which a public sense of justice comes into being and is maintained, and indicates the acts and institutions necessary for its continued existence. In these and other ways it provides 'some guidance' as to how to act and live justly.[9]

In the light of our brief discussion of Rawls' views about the nature and task of a philosophical theory of justice, it is easy to see why his own theory, as articulated in his *magnum opus,* has a specific character and structure. Rawls' theory is both formal and empirical and involves both conceptual analysis and empirical generalizations about men and society. He examines the nature of the human capacity for justice, and relates it to other human capacities and ultimately to man's moral nature. He elucidates and systematizes the principles of justice that underlie our considered judgements. He discusses other theories of justice and claims to show this his own matches best our considered judgements in reflective equilibrium. Given his view of the nature of moral theory, Rawls' book is, by its very nature, a Socratic dialogue between him and his readers. He tells them what their principles of justice are and invites them to consider whether these principles really do match their considered judgements and guide them in moments of doubt in an acceptable manner. Finally, by its very nature, Rawls' theory of justice presupposes what he calls a 'consensus', broad agreement about the nature and content of the considered judgements to which he and his readers can appeal.[10] Thus Rawls' theory cannot avoid becoming both critical and uncritical. It criticizes and revises some of our judgements. At the same time it is uncritical of most of our considered judgements.

1

For Rawls human society is distinguished by both harmony and a conflict of interests: harmony because social co-operation makes possible a better life for all than any man would have if each were to live solely by himself, and a conflict of interests because each is keenly interested in his share in the fruits of social co-operation and prefers a larger to a smaller share. Every society, therefore, needs a set of general principles to guide its choices between the various ways of determining the proper distributive shares of its members. These principles are the principles of social justice. They constitute its fundamental charter and provide the 'common point of view' from which its citizens debate the merits of prevailing social institutions and practices.[11]

As will have been noted, Rawls uses the term 'justice' to refer to the distribution not only of legal rights and duties, as most philosophers have done, but also of social and economic opportunities, advantages, wealth, abilities and indeed almost everything that can be shown to be the 'result' or 'fruit' of social co-operation. For him the question of justice arises 'whenever there is an allotment of something regarded as advantageous' and is ultimately about the 'division' and 'distribution' of the 'benefits' of social life.[12] As Rawls put it, 'The primary subject of justice is the basic structure of society,' and a theory of justice is basically a theory of 'social justice'.[13]

Rawls, then, defines the term 'justice' very widely to cover far more than what is generally taken to be its proper concern. He defends his controversial view that the basic social structure is the 'primary' subject of justice on two grounds. First, the effects of the social structure are 'profound and present from the start'. The social structure consists of different social positions to which unequal opportunities and advantages are attached and which affect the initial chances of life, the aspirations, the desires, the self-image and so on of those born in them. Since the social structure contains 'deep inequalities' and profoundly shapes the lives of its members, it raises questions of justice and makes it 'crucial' to inquire into the general principles upon which it is, and ought to be, based.

Second, the basic social structure constitutes the background conditions against which the actions of individuals and groups take place and cannot be ignored, therefore, by a theory of justice.[14] If we were to ignore the social structure altogether, we would have to say that justice is entirely a matter of agreements between the parties involved. Such a view is untenable, for such agreements might be coerced or unfair. We would need to say, therefore, that justice is a matter of agreements freely and fairly arrived at. This raises the question of *when* they can be said to be so arrived at and requires the specification of background conditions. Such background conditions refer to the social and economic positions of the parties involved and, ultimately, to the social structure. In Rawls' view, this is evident from the fact we do not consider voluntary market transactions fair unless the antecedent distribution of income and wealth and the structure of the market are also fair.

When carefully examined, neither argument turns out to be persuasive. First, there is no reason why a social structure should raise questions of justice simply because its effects are profoundly unequal unless it is assumed that equality is the natural and proper relation between men, and that inequality is undesirable or somehow improper and needs justification. Rawls, of course, makes this assumption but does not show why it must be made. Rawls' second argument is even less satisfactory, for one can easily give an adequate account of a fair and free agreement without raising larger questions about the justice or injustice of the social structure. An agreement between two sane adults need not necessarily be fair, only free. And even if it were to be argued that it should be fair, its fairness would not require that the distribution of wealth and income in the society at large, or between the parties involved, should be fair. Rawls is right to take the view that the social structure *is* a subject of justice, but his reasons are unsatisfactory and do not meet the objections raised by Hayek, Friedman and Nozick.

The social structure can be based on several different principles of justice. This raises the question of how we are to choose among them. In the light of our earlier discussions, it is obvious that, in Rawls' view, those principles should be preferred which, among other things, give the most coherent account of our considered judgements on matters of justice. Therefore Rawls could have proceeded in one of two ways. Either he could have outlined and analysed these judgements and showed what general principles underlay and informed them, or he could have stated what, in his view, such principles were and showed that they best accounted for our considered judgements. For reasons not entirely clear, Rawls has not adopted either procedure. Instead he deploys a rather complex two-stage strategy. His first step is designed to 'arrive at' or 'formulate' principles of justice; his second step is to subject these principles to 'severe' tests and 'confirm' or 'justify' them.[15]

For Rawls principles of justice are neither given by God nor deducible from the laws of history, the structure of the universe or man's immutable reason; they are products of human choice. This choice is most likely to yield fair principles if made under ideally fair conditions, that is, if it is subject to no constraints other than those inherent in the choice of moral principles.[16] Principles of justice are 'ethical' in nature and are intended to apply to human beings as we know them. Thus a choice between alternative principles is subject to three interconnected types of constraint.

First, we are concerned to choose *principles* of justice, and principles, by their very nature, must be general and public in nature, universal in application, capable of adjudicating between and ordering conflicting claims and accepted as the final court of appeal in practical reasoning.

Second, they are *moral* principles and must be chosen in a moral manner. For Rawls, to reason morally is to rise above one's personal biases and prejudices and to think in an impartial and disinterested manner. Ideally, to think morally is to ignore one's social circumstances, interests, views, indeed everything that distinguishes one from others and is therefore likely to generate a bias.[17] For Rawls, as we shall see later, to think morally is to think behind 'a veil of ignorance'. A moral choice between principles of justice requires, therefore, that those choosing them should transcend their specific personal and social circumstances and think about them in an impartial and disinterested manner.

Third, principles of justice are designed to regulate relations between men. Now, men are not 'pure intelligences', as Kant imagined, but beings with specific natural desires, interests and capacities. Their choice of principles of justice must therefore be based on knowledge of the relevant basic facts about human beings. Their knowledge must not be too detailed and specific, for there is then a danger of their being biased towards a specific generation, social structure, historical epoch or social group. In Rawls' view, we should take into account only those facts about men which are general in nature and true of all men. For him these include such facts as that human existence is characterized by moderate scarcity and that men seek to pursue their own interests, are rational in the sense of seeking to 'maximize' their interests and adopting 'the most affective means of given ends', entertain different conceptions of good life and are all agreed upon such primary goods as rights, liberties, opportunities, powers, income, wealth and self-respect, which every 'rational man wants, whatever else he wants'.[18]

For Rawls, then, principles of justice must be chosen under the three sets of constraints outlined above. His concept of 'original position' is intended to provide a vivid and picturesque presentation of these constraints. As Rawls puts it, it 'unites in one conception' the 'totality' of the 'ethical constraints' to which the choice of moral principles is subject.[19] To examine a social structure, institution or practice 'from the perspective' of the original position *is* to reason about it in a truly just manner. Indeed, says Rawls, we do, as a matter of fact, frequently 'simulate the original position in everyday life when we try to conduct ourselves in moral argument'.[20]

Since the original position is intended to bring together the ethical constraints to which the choice of principles of justice is subject, Rawls' description of it is not difficult to imagine. According to it, men are all formally free and equal; capable of a 'conception of their good' and capable of a 'sense of justice'; free of envy, vanity, greed and the urge to gamble; and unaware of their natural abilities, social status, colour, religion, culture, family background, class positions, the generation to which they belong, their specific conceptions of the good life, their ambitions, aspirations, plans for life and so on. In short, they are denuded of everything that sets one man apart from another.[21] Such more or less identically constituted and situated men deliberate about principles of justice and choose those that they are prepared to accept as binding upon them for ever and under all conditions. They are all concerned to advance their respective interests and 'win for them-selves the highest index of primary social goods', no matter where in society they may later find themselves or what abilities and temperaments they may come to be endowed with. Rawls is convinced that, as rational maximizers deciding about totally unpredictable situations, they will adopt what he calls the 'maximin rule'. Acting in accordance with the principle of *maximum minimorum*, they will attempt to cover themselves against the worst eventualities and will choose principles which will give them the best possible bargain even if their places in society were to be assigned by their enemies.

Having used the procedural device of the original position to arrive at his principles of justice, Rawls goes on to justify or confirm them. His mode of justification is not easy to follow. He invokes different and rather disparate considerations, among which he does not establish any clear or systematic relationship.[22]

First, he argues that principles of justice must match the fixed points of our considered judgements better than their alternatives, and must lead to us 'to revise and extrapolate' them in what seem, on reflection, to be more satisfactory ways. Rawls shows that the types of institution enjoined by his principles and the kinds of obligation imposed by them match our considered judgements in a reflective equilibrium. Since his principles – to be discussed below – 'hang together reasonably well' with these judgements and represent the 'best approximation overall', they stand confirmed.

Second, Rawls argues that principles should cohere with 'our nature as noumenal beings'. Men are noumenal beings in the sense that they are capable of rational self-determination and enjoy 'freedom from contingency and happenstance'. They can rise above 'natural contingencies and social accidents', as represented by their natural endowments and social positions, and may freely decide upon their principles of conduct. When men choose principles out of regard for personal or group interests, they behave as though they were heteronomous and belonged to 'a lower order'. By contrast, when they adopt principles chosen in total ignorance of their phenomenal characteristics, they act in a manner worthy of their free and autonomous moral nature. In Rawls' view, his principles of justice meet this condition. They are accepted as binding under all conditions. And the 'veil of ignorance' behind which they are chosen in the original position is intended to block out knowledge of natural and social contingencies and stands as a symbolic expression of man's noumenal nature.

Third, Rawls argues that principles of justice must meet the 'criterion of stability', in the sense that the scheme of social co-operation suggested by them should prove stable and lasting. In his view, a conception of justice meets this criterion if, among other things, its moral conception is clear, its ideals are attractive, it appeals to common and reasonably strong inclinations and it can elicit the willing co-operation of everyone. Rawls argues that his principles possess these features to a much greater degree than do their rivals.

Fourth, Rawls argues that social life, requires not only justice but also efficiency, harmony, civic friendship, a sense of community and so on. We cannot judge a conception of justice by 'its distributive role alone', therefore, but must also consider its effects upon the other desirable qualities of social life. As Rawls puts it, 'Other things being equal, one conception of justice is preferable to another when its consequences are more desirable.'[23] In his view, his principles of justice meet this quasi-utilitarian requirement better than do most others.

Fifth, principles of justice must be 'workable' or 'practicable' in at least two senses. First, they should not encourage those human propensities and aspirations which a social order may have to disappoint, or even repress, in order to survive. And, second, men should be able to live up to them in 'all relevant and foreseeable circumstances'. In Rawls' view, his principles meet both these requirements.

From time to time Rawls also introduces various other considerations, of which one deserves brief mention. Human existence is characterized by such apparently irrational and arbitrary facts as differences in natural endowments, luck and social origin. Rawls argues that, as rational and moral beings, men feel troubled by such differences, especially by the considerable influence they exert upon the distribution of social and economic opportunities. While men cannot altogether eliminate these differences, they can at least make them bearable by reducing their influence and subordinating them to rational purposes. Since a theory of justice has human inequalities as its subject matter, we turn to it to 'reconcile us to the dispositions of the natural order and the conditions of human life'. Rawls thinks that his theory performs this metaphysical function better than most. Thanks to its requirements that the natural and social inequalities should be beneficial to the worst-off members of society, the 'natural distribution of assets and the contingencies of social circumstances can more easily be accepted', and we are 'more ready to dwell upon our good fortune now that these differences are made to work to our advantage rather than to be downcast'.[24] Needless to say, Rawls seeks reconciliation only for, or at least from, the standpoint of the underprivileged.

2

Rawls is convinced that men in the original position will choose the following general conception of justice:[25]

> All social primary goods – liberty and opportunity, income and wealth, and the bases of self-respect – are to be distributed equally unless an unequal distribution of any or all of these goods is to the advantage of the least favoured.

The general conception involves the following two principles of justice. The first principle is concerned with the distinction of liberty, the second with that of the other primary goods. Rawls formulates the first principle as follows:[26]

> Each person is to have an equal right to the most extensive total system of equal basic liberties compatible with a similar system of liberty for all.

The second principle is formulated thus:

> Social and economic inequalities are to be arranged so that they are both:
> (a) to the greatest benefit of the least advantaged, consistent with the just savings principle, and
> (b) attached to offices and positions open to all under conditions of fair equality of opportunity.

Since the two principles, as well as the two parts of the second principle, may conflict, Rawls lays down what he calls 'priority rules'. With one exception (to be noted below), they stipulate that the first principle is prior to the second and, within the latter, the second part is prior to the first.

The two principles and the two priority rules have been extensively discussed by Rawls' commentators, hence a few words about them should suffice.

As for the first principle, three points of clarification are in order. First, Rawls thinks of various liberties as capable of existing independently of, and coming into conflict with, one another. He therefore proposes that liberties should be balanced against one another in such a way that the resulting combination is one of as much liberty, equally distributed, as possible. He does not say much concerning how these liberties can be compared and balanced, what he means by a system of liberty, how we are to ascertain that we have secured the most extensive system of liberties or what we are to do if considerations of maximization and equality conflict.

Second, under 'basic liberties' Rawls includes four: first, political liberty, including the right to vote and to stand for public office and freedom of speech and assembly; second, liberty of conscience, including freedom of thought and belief; third, freedom of the person and the right to hold personal property; and fourth, freedom from arbitrary arrest and seizure, as defined by the concept of the rule of law.[27] It is worth noting that Rawls deliberately excludes from the basic liberties the right to ownership of the means of production and freedom of contract, as understood by *laissez-faire* liberals.

Third, Rawls draws a distinction between liberty and the worth of liberty.[28] In his view, the inability to take advantage of one's liberty as a result of poverty, ignorance or the lack of necessary means affects not liberty itself but its worth or value to the individual concerned. Compensating a man for the lesser worth of liberty is not the same as making good unequal liberty. For Rawls the principle of equal liberty requires that all citizens should enjoy equal basic liberties, and that the social structure should be so designed as to ensure that their liberties have more or less equal worth.

Rawls' second principle is fairly straightforward. He is not against social and economic inequalities *per se*, only those that cannot be justified. Social and economic inequality is justified under two conditions. First, it should conduce to the benefit of the least advantaged. By the least advantaged Rawls does not mean 'literally the worst-off individual' but rather any citizen falling below a national average of income and wealth. Rawls introduces the just savings principle in order to ensure that the prospects of the least advantaged in the present generation are not improved at the expense of the savings and investmant needed for future growth. Second, social inequality is justified if the office or position to which it is attached is open to all. For Rawls it is not enough that men are formally free to compete for offices and positions; they should also enjoy 'fair' equality of opportunity to acquire the relevant qualifications.

Rawls' priority rules are relatively unproblematic. For him the first principle is prior to, or morally higher than, the second. However, he adds the ambiguous proviso that this system of priority comes into effect only after a certain level of economic development or 'civilization' has been reached. Up to that point it is not unjust to distribute unequally, or require citizens to surrender, some of the fundamental liberties for the sake of social and economic gains.[29] Rawls thinks that once the level of social well-being reaches the point at which basic needs are all met, men begin to cherish liberty as the highest good. They pursue spiritual and cultural interests, are less preoccupied with their relative social positions and material possessions and are most concerned to choose their plans of life themselves. While these and other questionable generalizations at best show that it might be desirable, even perhaps in some sense rational, to prefer liberty, Rawls nowhere explains why such a preference is a matter of justice.

Of the two parts of the second principle, Rawls argues that the second has priority over the first. This means that the principle of equal opportunity cannot be sacrificed for the sake of potential gains for the worst-off representative men, or (and this amounts to the same thing) that the claims of those with similar talents and inclinations to attain commensurate positions cannot be overridden in the interests of general efficiency or the betterment of the worst-off.[30] Rawls rejects the views of such men as Burke, Hegel and Keynes who, in his view, drastically restricted equality of economic and political opportunity on the ground that such restrictions were needed to create a class of politically wise and talented men or to build up capital. In Rawls' view, which is nowhere clearly developed, the case for fair equality of opportunity rests on the ground that otherwise those qualified, or capable of being qualified, for specific positions would be denied both the material rewards attached to the positions and the 'realization of self' that comes from occupying offices commensurate with one's abilities.[31] He argues that the infringement of the principle of fair equality of opportunity may be justified only if it can be shown that otherwise the opportunities of the least fortunate sections of the community would be still more limited. For Rawls justice enjoys priority over both efficiency and a greater sum of material advantages.

Rawls imagines that after they have adopted principles of justice, parties in the original position move through three more stages. At each stage the 'veil of ignorance' is progressively lifted in order to facilitate the intelligent application of the principles of to the kinds of question of justice involved. After principles of justice are chosen, the parties in the original position choose a just constitution, by which Rawls means a constitution that 'satisfies the principles of justice and is best calculated to lead to just and effective legislation'.[32] Of the two principles of justice, only the first is relevant at this stage. After the constitutional stage comes the legislative stage, when the justice of laws and policies is the subject of consideration. At this stage the second principle of justice is crucial. It requires that social and economic policies should aim to maximize the long-term expectations of the least advantaged under conditions of fair equality of opportunity and subject to the maintenance of equal basic liberties. At the fourth and final stage the application of laws to particular cases by the judges and the administrators is the subject of consideration. At this stage the 'veil of ignorance' is removed. As Rawls understands it, the four-stage sequence is a 'device' for increasingly narrowing the application of principles of justice and specifying the 'points of view' from which to settle relevant problems of justice.[33] Since we are interested primarily in Rawls' political thought, we shall concentrate on his idea of a just political system.

3

For Rawls, in a just political system law-making authority should be vested in a representative body elected for a limited period of office on the basis of universal franchise.[34] The principle of equal liberty requires that each member of the legislature should represent an equal number of voters. It also requires that legislative decisions should be taken by the majority.[35] Rawls argues that the constitution may limit the scope and authority of the majority, either by requiring a greater plurality for certain types of legislative measure or through a constitutionally entrenched Bill of Rights. Equal political liberty is then rendered less extensive, but also more secure. In a just political system all citizens should enjoy an equal right of participation, and their political liberties should have equal worth. In order to assure this, Rawls proposes a number of measures.

All citizens should enjoy equal access to full information about political issues. They should also have a fair chance to add alternative proposals of their own to the political agenda. Political liberty loses much of its value when those with greater private means are able to control the course of public debate and to exert disproportionate influence over the development of legislation. In order to preserve the 'fair value' of the equal political liberties of all citizens, Rawls proposes such measures as encouraging a wider distribution of property and wealth, providing public funds on a regular basis to encourage public discussion of important issues and reducing the dependence of political parties on private financial contribution by allotting to each a proportionate share of public money. Rawls argues that it is only when these and similar measures are adopted that each member of the community will be said to enoy the 'common status of equal citizen'.

According to Rawls, discussion in the legislative assembly should be informed by a desire to determine the piece of legislation that is most just in relation to a specific matter. The representatives should not pursue their own or their constituents' private interests but should adopt the standpoint of the ideal legislator. They should rise above their prejudices and social circumstances and should debate and vote 'solely' according to what, in their view, the principles of justice dictate. The outcome of their votes is a reliable indication of what is most likely to be in harmony with the principles of justice. The majority is not necessarily right, and a citizen may disagree with a decision. However, a law resulting from the deliberations of rational legislators conscientiously trying to follow the principles of justice is more likely to be morally right. For Rawls there is a profound difference between the 'ideal market process' and the 'ideal political process'. The market achieves an efficient and desirable outcome even if – indeed, only if – everyone pursues his own interest. By contrast, political life can deliver the best results only when the citizens and their representatives transcend narrow personal and group interests.

As we have seen, the second principle of justice requires that the government should ensure fair and effective equality of opportunity. This implies a number of things. The government should ensure equal chances of education and culture for those similarly endowed and motivated, either by subsidizing private schools or by establishing a public school system. It should also promote equality of economic and social opportunities by policing the conduct of firms and private associations and by preventing the establishment of monopolistic barriers to entry to the more desirable occupations. It should also guarantee a minimum income either through family allowances and special payments for sickness and unemployment or through such devices as a graded income supplement.

In establishing these and other 'background institutions', Rawls argues that the government may be thought of as divided into four branches or, rather, engaged in four sets of functions, namely, allocation, stabilization, transfer and distribution.[36] The first consists in keeping the price system workably competitive, preventing the formation of unreasonable market power and correcting, by means of suitable taxes and subsidies, the failure of prices to reflect social benefits and costs. Stabilization consists in bringing about reasonably full employment and free choice of occupation. The third function consists in guaranteeing a minimum income and ensuring that the total income of the least advantaged is such as to maximize their long-run expectations. Since the competitive market system gives no consideration to human needs and does not meet the demands of justice, Rawls argues that the government needs to make 'transfer payments' in order to guarantee this minimum income. Once the minimum is provided by the government, Rawls thinks that it is perfectly fair to leave the rest of the distribution of income to be settled by the market mechanism.

Distribution, the fourth function, consists in preserving approximate equality of distributive shares by means of taxation and necessary adjustments in the rights of property. When inequalities of wealth exceed a certain limit, the principles of equal liberty and equality of opportunity are threatened. As we have seen, the rich are then able to exercise undue influence over the character of political debate and the content of legislation, and the liberties of those with limited means lose their worth and value. Further, chances of education and culture are no longer equally available to those equally endowed and motivated, and social positions and offices are no longer equally open to all. Rawls argues, therefore, that the distribution of wealth needs to be corrected by such means as inheritance, gift and proportional expenditure taxes.

The whole area of government subsidies to universities, the arts, theatres and the realm of culture in general seems to give Rawls some difficulty. In his discussion of the functions of government he studiously avoids what he calls 'perfectionism' – that is, prescribing a specific way of life as excellent or morally more worthy that any other. In his view, such moral preferences are basically like aesthetic preferences; they rest on 'personal feelings' and are inherently subjective in nature. This means that Rawls cannot accept the argument that universities, opera houses and theatres are *intrinsically* valuable and should enjoy government subsidies. They can be subsidized only if they can be shown to secure the equal liberties of all and advance the long-term interests of the least advantaged. Rawls is convinced that this can be easily shown but does not offer any argument in support of his view.

Although he is not entirely clear, he seems to argue that while universities, institutes, opera and the theatre can justly be subsidized, the 'arts and sciences', or what he calls the area of 'culture', cannot be, but he gives no reasons.[37] He recognizes that citizens may prefer cultural goods and services to be provided publicly rather than through the mechanism of the market and suggests that ways should be found for the government to provide them. In his view, the government does not have a duty to provide them, for they fall outside considerations of justice. As he puts it, there is 'no more justification for using the state apparatus to compel some citizens to pay for unwanted benefits that others desire than there is to force them to reimburse others for their private expenses'. For Rawls the government may arrange for the provision of cultural goods, perhaps by setting up an independent co-ordinating body, provided that the expense involved is met collectively by the citizens enjoying them. He thinks that even if all the citizens were to ask for them, the government could not be required to provide them unless the citizens collectively and specifically decided to tax themselves for this purpose. According to Rawls, this is the only way we can ensure that in matters of personal preferences 'no one is taxed without his consent.'

Rawls' discussion of political obligation raises interesting and novel issues. For him an obligation has several characteristics which distinguish it from other moral requirements. First, an obligation arises from a voluntary act of the obligated agent.[38] The act may be the giving of an express or tacit undertaking, as in the case of a promise or a contract, or it may simply consist in accepting benefits. Second, the content of an obligation is defined by the institution or practice governing the act to which it owes its origin. And, third, an obligation is normally owed to specific individuals, namely, those co-operating to maintain the institution or practice in question. For example, a man holding a public office incurs an obligation because he has freely run or applied for it. His obligation consists in fulfilling the duties of the office, as laid down by the rules that establish and govern its conduct. and he owes this obligation to the individuals connected with the institutional structure of which his office is an integral part.

Given his analysis of the nature of obligation, Rawls argues that an average citizen can have no political obligation. As he puts it, 'There is, I believe, no political obligation, strictly speaking, for citizens generally.'[39] Those holding public offices have obligations, but citizenship is not an office and a citizen is not an official. An obligation is created by a voluntary act, and Rawls argues that in the case of a citizen, 'It is not clear what is the requisite binding action and who has performed it.' It may be argued that he has accepted the benefits accruing from his membership of the state, and that the benefits are, on Rawls' own account, source of obligations. Rawls rejoins that the benefits generate obligations only when their acceptance is voluntary, and that this is not the case with the state, 'into which we are born and begin our lives' and which we never voluntarily join.[40] Even if it could be shown that a citizen has political obligations arising out of his receipt of benefits and the principle of fairness, Rawls argues that they are too tenuous to form the basis of a political society. We have no means of knowing whether a citizen who has accepted benefits intends to continue accepting them and therefore no assurance that he will continue to retain his obligation to the political system. Without such mutual and general assurances, the political system lacks stability.

Rawls argues that although a citizen has no political obligations even under a just constitution, he has *natural duties*.[41] Natural duties are very different from obligations. They apply to us without regard to our voluntary acts. They have no necessary connections with, and their content is not specified by, social institutions and practices. They hold between persons, irrespective of their institutional relationships. And they are owed to all men, not only to specific individuals.[42] According to Rawls, a human being has several natural duties – for example, the duties not to inflict unnecessary suffering on others and to help men in need provided that one can do so without excessive risk or loss to oneself. From the standpoint of justice, 'a fundamental natural duty is the duty of justice.' It consists in supporting and complying with the just institutions that exist and apply to us and furthering the realization of those not yet established. If the basic structure of society is just, everyone has a natural duty to uphold it and to do his part independently of his voluntary acts.

For Rawls, then, there is an important division between citizens in terms of the character of their ties to each other. Ordinary citizens generally have no political obligations to each other or to the government; they have only natural duties of justice. As for those holding public offices, they have, in addition, political obligations arising from the principle of fairness. They have sought after and attained the offices they occupy, and such voluntary acts generate specific obligations. As Rawls puts it: 'There is, then, another sense of *noblesse oblige*: namely, that those who are more privileged are likely to acquire obligations tying them even more strongly to a just scheme.'[43]

For Rawls an obligation can arise only from the voluntary act of an agent. This does not, however, mean that every voluntary action generates an obligation, for one can have no obligations if the institution one has joined, or whose benefits one has accepted, is itself not just. As Rawls puts it, 'Acquiescence in, or even consent to, clearly unjust institutions does not give rise to obligations.' This is why conquest and violence can generate no obligations among their victims. One can, similarly, have no obligations to autocratic and arbitrary governments because the background conditions under which consensual acts generate obligations are absent. Extorted promises are void. For Rawls unjust social arrangements are 'a kind of extortion, even violence, and consent to them does not bind'. One may obey such governments for prudential and other reasons, but one has no obligation to do so.

According to Rawls, citizens have a natural duty to comply with just laws enacted under a just constitution. Both the principle of natural duty and the principle of fairness require this. If the basic social structure is just, even unjust laws are binding, provided that they do not cross the acceptable limits of injustice. No constitutional procedure, however perfect, can guarantee that all laws made will always be just. The majority may lack relevant knowledge and judgement, or it may be guided by self-interest, or it may lack a perfect sense of justice.[44] We have a 'natural duty of civility' not to use the inevitable faults of a social arrangement as too ready an excuse for refusing to comply with its laws. However, when, in an otherwise just society a law or a policy is blatantly unjust or represents a manifest abuse of trust and power, the general duty to tolerate human imperfections lapses and a citizen has both a 'duty' and a 'right' to disobey.[45] He has a duty to do so because he has a natural duty to uphold just institutions and a 'duty to oppose injustice'. And he has a right because 'to employ the coercive apparatus of the state in order to maintain manifestly unjust institutions is itself a form of illegitimate force that men in due course have a right to resist.'[46]

For Rawls a citizen's disobedience must in the first instance take the form of civil disobedience. Civil disobedience is a public, non-violent, conscientious and political act, the deliberate violation of a specific law in order to bring about a desired change in a specific policy or law of the government. It is a public act in the sense that it is undertaken in public and appeals to the public sense of justice; it is civil in the sense that while disobeying the law, the individual concerned fully acknowledges the authority of the government and accepts the legal consequences of his action; and it is a political act in the sense that it is addressed to the majority and is justified in terms not of religious or personal morality but of the commonly shared conception of justice underlying the political order. For Rawls civil disobedience is a 'mode of address' to the majority's sense of justice and a declaration that, in the considered opinion of those engaged in it, the principles of social co-operation are not being respected.

According to Rawls, civil disobedience is subject to three limiting conditions.

First, it should be directed against clear and substantial acts of injustice.[47] The infringement of the principles of justice should be 'clear', since otherwise the objection lacks focus and cannot appeal to the majority's sense of justice, and substantial, since minor violations are generally unavoidable and difficult to agree upon. In Rawls' view, violations of the second principle of justice are often very difficult to demonstrate. They raise highly complex issues, require a wealth of supporting statistics, call for complex theoretical analyses and relate to areas in which the influences of self-interest and prejudice are often too difficult and insidious to check. Accordingly, Rawls argues that civil disobedience is best restricted to violations of the principle of equal liberty and best directed against the blatant infringements of such rights as the minority's right to vote, to hold office and to own property.

Rawls asks if a minority which does not itself believe in tolerance is justified in resorting to civil disobedience when its equal basic liberties are curtailed by law. In his view, while the majority should be guided by its own principles of justice and should tolerate the intolerant, it may restrict their liberties if the safety of free institutions so requires. The intolerant are like 'free-riders'. They 'seek the advantages of just institutions while not doing their share to uphold them' and 'exploit' the majority's sense of justice for their own private ends. A shared and public sense of justice is a vital collective asset built up and sustained by the constant co-operation of all. The intolerant make no contribution to this process, and hence they are not entitled to resort to civil disobedience or to appeal to the majority's sense of justice.

The second restriction to which civil disobedience is subject is that it should generally be resorted to only after legal means of redress and appeals to the majority have proved to be of no avail. It is not necessary that these should have been exhausted, for they never really can be; one can always keep writing letters to the government or campaigning for one's cause in the hope that these measures might one day yield the desired results. If their past actions have shown the government or the majority to be callous and apathetic, further appeals to them may reasonably be thought pointless. In Rawls' view, some cases may be so extreme that one may even have no duty to use legal remedies. For example, if the legislature were to forbid the religion of a minority, the latter may not oppose the law by normal political methods. It may resort to civil disobedience straightaway, and even that might be 'much too mild'.[48]

The third condition restricting civil disobedience is more tactical than moral in nature. It is conceivable, although unlikely in a just society, that several groups may have an 'equally sound case' for resorting to civil disobedience. If they were all to resort to it, there would be a serious breakdown in the general respect for law and a decline in the effectiveness of civil disobedience. In Rawls' view, there is always an unmistakable, though not easily definable, 'upper bound' on the ability to handle simultaneous expressions of dissent. It is important, therefore, for minorities to realize that, like any other right, the exercise of the right to dissent is limited by the similar right of others. In Rawls' view, the 'ideal' solution is for them to devise an equitable way of ordering the various claims to civil disobedience and by regulating the overall level of dissent by means of a co-operative political alliance.[49]

Rawls argues that sometimes civil disobedience may not be enough, and a citizen may be justified in resorting to militant action and forcible resistance. A citizen is clearly free to resort to them against an unjust social structure or constitution. As we have noted, an individual has no natural duty to uphold, and indeed a natural duty to combat, unjust institutions. Rawls argues that even in a just or nearly just society, civil disobedience may sometimes not be enough. If the majority were to behave in a 'wantonly unjust and overtly hostile' manner in its relations with other groups, or if civil disobedience were to fail to achieve its objective of redressing the violations of the two principles of justice, especially the first, forceful resistance may become necessary.[50]

Rawls argues that the idea of justice as fairness needs not be confined to relations between citizens within a political community but might be extended to cover relations between states as well. We could define the original position to include not only private individuals but also representatives of different nations working behind the 'veil of ignorance' and agreeing upon universally and eternally binding principles of international justice. Rawls thinks that such principles would include the equality of nations, the right of national self-determination, the right of self-defence against external attack, the duty to observe treaties, the inadmissibility of certain forms of violence in war, a strict and limited definition of national interest and the exclusion of economic gains, territorial expansion and national glory as justifiable reasons for war. These and other public principles of international justice would not only regulate relations between states but would also provide the standards by which citizens might judge the actions of their governments. A citizen might appeal to them to justify his conscientious refusal to take part in an unjust war. A soldier might refuse to engage in certain acts if he 'reasonably and conscientiously' believed that they violated the principles governing the conduct of war. And he might refuse to take part in a war altogether if he could show that it violated the principles of international justice, and that, all things considered, 'his natural duty not to be made the agent of grave injustice and evil to another' outweighed his duty to obey his government.

Similar arguments apply in the case of conscription. Conscription is an instance of drastic interference with the basic liberties of the citizens. The principle of the priority of liberty requires that conscription can be introduced not to wage unjust wars but only in order to maintain a system of basic liberties. If a war is unjust in its aims or conduct, a citizen has a 'right' to refuse military service on the ground that he must disregard his 'legal duty' when it conflicts with his 'natural duty' not to damage the basic liberties of his own or any other society. Rawls is persuaded that the aims of the modern states (especially the large and powerful ones) in waging wars are likely to be so unjust that one may rightly decide to abjure military service altogether in the foreseeable future. Such 'contingent pacifism' admits the possibility of a just war, but not in present circumstances.[51] Rawls argues that contingent and discriminating pacifism is far more effective than the indiscriminate pacifism of the pacifists. The latter is unworldly, no more challenges the militarism of a state than the celibacy of priests challenges the sanctity of marriage and can be easily accommodated by the state's granting it privileged status and continuing with its aggressive policies. By contrast, discriminatory pacifism is realistic, challenges a government's pretensions and is likely to ensure that unjust wars will not be too easily embarked upon.

4

Rawls' theory of justice has been deservedly acclaimed as one of the most impressive achievements of twentieth-century moral and political philosophy. In its scope and level of analysis it towers above most others in the field. He shows that moral and political philosophy need not, indeed cannot, remain merely formal inquiries concerned to analyse and relate concepts but can and must become substantive inquiries capable of grappling with the substantive questions raised by moral and political life. As he rightly argues, such questions cannot be answered without systematic discussion of the nature of human capacities, aspirations, sentiments and values, the structure of the human self and of the ways in which men define and express their moral nature, preserve their integrity and build up a public world of shared values. Rawls discusses all this with considerable philosophical skill and says much that is illuminating and profound. He realizes, further, that his discussion cuts across traditional disciplinary boundaries and requires the philosopher to draw upon such very different disciplines as philosophy, logic, ethics, moral theory, psychology, sociology, political theory and economics. Rawls judiciously incorporates their insights and weaves them into a coherent and impressive theoretical fabric.

Rawls' work shows that it is possible to think about moral and political life in a systematic and coherent manner, and that moral and political philosophy can make a useful contribution to its conduct. His work is conclusive proof, if one were needed, that although a moral and political philosopher cannot tell us how to respond to specific situations, he can fruitfully analyse their context, the available alternatives, the ways in which and the principles in terms of which the alternatives can be debated, the manner in which moral and political arguments should be conducted and so on. Rawls' work is in the great tradition of moral and political philosophy. It both reaffirms the coherence of the tradition and enriches it, and it is an inspiring monument to what moral and political philosophy at its best must aspire to achieve.

As for the content of Rawls' moral and political theory, much of what he says is illuminating and interesting, even though not always persuasive. With all its limitations, his concept of the original position offers a vivid and fascinating account of the nature of moral reasoning. His analyses of the moral nature of man, the integrity of the self and the character and constitution of man's moral capacities and sentiments are perceptive and persuasive. And his discussions of the nature of liberty and equality, the limits of tolerance, the nature of political authority, the grounds of civil disobedience and political resistance, the rule of law and so on are all full of fresh insights.

One of Rawls' important contributions consists in giving liberalism a new foundation and a new vitality. As its critics have pointed out, liberalism contains large areas of incoherence. It talks about individual development but lacks a coherent theory of how individuals develop. It talks about liberty but defines it in a narrowly negative manner and fails to appreciate its social basis and consequences. It talks about morality but fails to realize that its narrow individualism and negative liberty lead to an equally narrow and negative theory of morality. Rawls takes full account of these and other limitations of liberalism and offers a theory which overcomes at least some of them. He grounds liberty in the moral nature of man and demonstrates its close connection with man's sense of his own worth and self-respect. He shows that the self which seeks liberty is also moral in nature and that liberty and morality are inseparable. Rawls is therefore able tó give liberalism a moral depth which it has always lacked. He shows, further, that men are not only materially but also morally and ontologically interdependent, that they grow together and complete one another and that the full development of each is inseparable from the full development of all within a just society. In taking this view, Rawls is able to relate liberty, equality and justice and to elucidate the radical dimension of liberalism. In short, Rawls refines and breathes a new spirit into the major categories of liberal thought and enables them to speak in a twentieth-centruy idiom. By any standard, this is a remarkable achievement.

While these and other merits of Rawls' theory of justice have been rightly acclaimed, it suffers from several fundamental limitations.

For Rawls a social order necessarily distributes rights, obligations, opportunities, wealth, life chances and so on and requires commonly agreed principles of justice. He recognizes that men entertain very different conceptions of the good life or of human excellence. And he believes that these conceptions cannot be demonstrated in terms of universal and objective principles but must remain a matter of individual choice. Accordingly, Rawls insists that a social order should be so constructed that it is not biased towards, and does not impose a specific conception of, human excellence on its members. Given his two fundamental beliefs, that a society needs agreed principles of justice and that men entertain different conceptions of the good life, Rawls' problem is obvious, namely, to develop principles of justice which can be agreed upon by all men and yet are not biased towards a specific conception of human excellence. In order to help him answer the question satisfactorily, he introduces the ideas of pure procedural justice and the 'veil of ignorance' and insists that men in the original position should not be aware of their specific conceptions of the good life. Rawls' theory of justice must, therefore, be judged in terms of the problem he himself sets out to solve. If it could be shown to be biased towards a specific conception of the good life, he would himself have to admit that it was unsatisfactory.

It seems that Rawls' theory is not at all neutral with respect to different conceptions of human excellence. His formulation of the problem, his manner of answering it and his answers embody a specific conception of the good life. Rawls assumes that men entertain different and conflicting conceptions of the good life and that these cannot be defended objectively but must ultimately remain a matter of individual choice. Although his assumption may appear plausible, even self-evident to many of his readers, it is nothing of the kind. A devout Roman Catholic, a Jehovah's Witness and a fanatical Muslim have no doubt that there is a 'true' conception of the good life, and that it is revealed in the sacred texts, Rawls assumes, further, that principles of justice are products of human choice and must be arrived at after prolonged rational deliberations and negotiations. This apparently self-evident assumption would be strongly denied by a believer in revealed truth or by a man who held that such principles are written into, and must be read off, the structure of the universe or are deducible from the laws of evolution. In short, Rawls' very formulation of the problem only makes sense within a secular, rationalist, pluralist, and sceptical *Weltanschauung* characteristic of contemporary Western culture.

If we look at the way in which Rawls arrives at his principles of justice, we see that similar assumptions are at work. He assumes that the morally proper way to think about principles of justice is to abstract away all the differences between men and to construct a 'veil of ignorance'. This view of moral reasoning is, again, not self-evident. Different cultures define the nature of moral reasoning in very different ways. The idea that a man's social position is contingent and not part of his very essence, such that he can abstract it away and define himself independently of it, is wholly alien to ancient Athens and Rome and many Eastern societies. For Plato and Aristotle a slave's labour was qualitatively different from that of a free man, and hence they could not understand how the products of qualitatively different men could ever be compared and exchanged. For a Hindu, men belonging to different castes have different degrees of worth and are unequal *qua* men. Rawls' view of moral reasoning, which rests on the concept of abstract and formally equal men only contingently related to, and definable independently of, their natual andowments and social positions, is distinctly Christian in origin and did not become an integral part of Western moral and social theory until the seventeenth century.

Some of Rawls' crucial assumptions about men in the original position, from which his principles of justice are derived, are also distinctly liberal. As Rawls imagines them, men in the original position are rational and basically concerned to maximize their interests. His definitions of each of the three crucial concepts, namely, interest, reason and maximization, presuppose a specific conception of the good life. He defines interest in terms of what he calls 'primary goods', and these are all derived from a specific conception of the good life. Rawls says that *whatever* their conceptions of the good life, all men desire rights, liberties, opportunities, power, income, wealth and a sense of their own worth. This is a strange assertion, for most (even perhaps none) of these have any meaning for a nun, a hermit, a yogi or a Buddhist monk. Their ways of life centre on duties rather than rights, involve an irresistible inner call to surrender to the will of God and rule out freedom of choice, require neither power nor wealth and are sustained by an acute sense of sinfulness and personal unworthiness. Men devoted to these and other ways of life not only do not need Rawls' primary goods but find them a hindrance. It is also striking that Rawls' primary goods are almost all privately enjoyable and do not include a single public good that can only be enjoyed by men together.

Rawls assumes that each man in the original position wishes to pursue his own interests. None of the people listed above seems to meet this condition (nor did Albert Schweitzer or Gandhi, nor does Mother Teresa). They have no interests of their own to pursue. Their interest consists in promoting, and is therefore parasitic upon, the interests of others, and they define these interests in moral and spiritual terms. Again, Rawls says that each individual wishes to *maximize* his interests. This is not true of the kinds of religious men mentioned above. Nor is it true of many a man in the so-called Third World who is content to satisfy his basic needs. And it is becoming less and less true of many men even in the Western world who desire a life of relative comfort but not one characterized by the acquisition of the maximum number of primary goods, and who would readily give up certain primary goods if their acquisition involved the sacrifice of leisure, or the brutal exploitation of nature, or the violation of the ecological equilibrium. Rawls' views about men in the original position presuppose, and only fit, the liberal individualism of Western world.

Rawls validates his principles of justice with reference to our considered judgements. One would have thought that the bias of his principles would have been detected and exposed at this stage of the argument. However, it is not. Indeed, it is striking that *none* of the principles derived in the original position turns out to be in the slightest conflict with our considered judgements. The perfect coincidence between the two springs from the fact that the considred judgements which Rawls examines are informed by the same basic assumptions that underlie his concept of the original position. Rawls is interested only in the considered judgements of those sharing the modern secular, rationalist and pluralist outlook characteristic of liberal individualism. For example, he says that 'we' have the greatest confidence in our belief that religious intolerance and racial discrimination are wholly unjust.[52] The 'we' obviously excludes religious fanatics, Nazis, advocates of apartheid in South Africa, and racists in many other parts of the world. Again, Rawls says that it is one of 'the fixed points of our moral judgements' that no one deserves his natural talents or starting place in life. He obviously excludes the Hindus, whose doctrines of *Karma* and reincarnation maintain that every man deserves his natural endowments and place of birth because of his deeds in his previous life. And he also excludes many a conservative and neo-liberal writer who believes that the concept of desert simply does not apply to these natural facts, which are therefore neither deserved nor undeserved.

Given the ways in which Rawls both defines the problem of justice and arrives at and validates his principles of justice, it is hardly surprising that the content of the principles should turn out to be biased systematically towards a specific conception of the good life. They regulate the distribution of not only rights and obligations but also economic and social opportunities. As we have seen, Rawls has considerable difficulty defending this view, which is relatively modern (it does not go back much further than the late eighteenth century) and rests on a view of social life vigorously contested by many a conservative and neo-liberal writer. By and large, he simply assumes that the social structure is the primary subject of justice. The assumption rests on admirable moral sentimetns, but it is still an assumption and reflects a specific moral view.

Further, Rawls sees nothing wrong with considerable social, economic and political inequalities as long as they can be shown to benefit the worst-off. This quasi-egalitarian assumption rests on a specific conception of life, and Rawls never shows why it should be preferred to the thoroughgoing inegalitarianism of the social Darwinists, Hayek, Nozick and others, or to the radical egalitarianism of the Marxists. Rawls assumes that equality, not inequality, needs justification, and that rational men feel troubled by inequality unless it can be shown to be in the interests of all, especially the worst-off. He assumes, conversely, that once it is shown to have these consequences, they welcome or are at least reconciled to it. Neither is self-evident. The first assumption is contested by conservative and neo-liberal writers, who cannot see why equality and not inequality should be deemed the natural and proper condition of life, or why the justification should be in terms of social consequences rather than desert. The second assumption is questioned by socialists, who find inequalities of wealth and power inherently offensive and degrading and think that the rational man in the original position would rather forego material advantages than tolerate the indignity of inequality. Rawls does not defend this assumptions against either group of critics and is content to tread the middle path of radical liberalism.

Rawls' theory of justice, then, does not adopt a neutral stance between the different conceptions of the good life but is deeply biased towards liberal individualism. Notwithstanding his claim to the contrary, he has not provided a theory which all rational men can be persuaded to accept. Further, since Rawls' just society embodies a specific conception of the good life and imposes it upon its members, he is wrong to claim that it fully and equally respects diverse moral and political beliefs. To be sure, it does tolerate and even welcomes diversity but only as long as the latter does not exceed the range permitted by its basic assumptions. Since Rawls insists that men must first agree on principles of social justice and then form their personal ideals, his just society delimits the choice of personal ideals and rules out several forms of individual excellence as well.

Rawls' theory of justice is open to other objections as well. He rightly criticizes utilitarianism and aims to offer an alternative theory of justice. When carefully examined, however, his theory, turns out to have a marked utilitarian orientation. Rawls' whole mode of reasoning about justice is in terms of individual interest, personal benefits, maximization, instrumental rationality, compensation, justification in terms of consequences, a view of moral principles as devices for the protection of long-term interests and so on, all of which are distinctive to the utalitarian form of thought and hardly to be found in the theories of justice of Plato, Aristotle, Augustine, Aquinas, Hobbes, Locke and others. In the original position men debate and choose principles of justice on the basis of the maximization of their long-term individual interests. They accept social and economic inequalities as just 'only if they result in compensating benefits for everyone'.[53] Indeed, Rawls' very usage of the term 'justice' has a distinctly utilitarian flavour. Ordinarily we associate the ideas of desert and proportionality with justice and expect a theorist of justice to discuss questions like who deserves what and whether rewards should be proportionate to merit or effort. It is remarkable that Rawls generally bypasses these questions. He constantly defines justice in terms of what conduces to the well-being of the worst-off. This is a strange use of 'justice', for generally, and even on reflection, we would want to say that such inequality is more desirable, more beneficial, more *justified*, but not more *just*. Rawls makes justice a forward-looking virtue which, strictly speaking, it is not, and he subsumes under his concept of justice much that properly belongs to the concept of utility. This is not to say that he is a utilitarian. His emphasis on fairness, the intrinsic value of certain goods and man's noumenal nature, his rejection of the aggregate or average quantity of the desired good as a moral goal and so on distinguish him decisively from the utilitarians. However, the Kantian strand sits uneasily with the utilitarian and creates considerable tension. Further, since he does not fully probe, let alone criticize, the fundamental categories and assumptions of utilitarianism, he is able to detect and reject its Benthamite and other crude forms, but not their subtle and more elusive cousins.[54]

Rawls' theory of justice, then, is an uneasy amalgam of the utilitarian and Kantian forms of thought. As we have seen, his derivation of the principles of justice has a utilitarian basis. Men in the original position are concerned to maximize their interests and arrive at Rawlsian principles not because these best express their moral nature but because such principles seem to them most effectively to promote their own long-term interests. By contrast, Rawls' subsequent defence of his principles of justice has a distinctly Kantian orientation. When he says that men are noumenal beings, that they must rise above contingent natural and social facts, that the principles of justice express their moral nature and that in acting on them they express their dignity and moral autonomy, he speaks in the authentic Kantian idiom. His defence, however, is not wholly Kantian, for he says that self-interested men will not co-operate on any other terms, that the principles promote a stable social life, have desirable consequences and so on.

For Rawls, then, his principles of justice promote men's long-term interests and are chosen for that reason in the original position. They also, however, express men's noumenal nature. It is remarkable that, for Rawls, the calculations of men's phenomenal selves neatly coincide with the aspirations of their noumenal selves, that 'prudential' and moral choices turn out to be in perfect harmony and that the most effective hypothetical imperatives are also the noblest categorical imperatives! This curious conclusion raises the obvious question of how Rawls can claim that his theory is 'highly Kantian in nature', since Kant's form of moral reasoning is so obviously different from the utilitarian.[55] For Kant a moral principle implies 'absolute necessity' and is grounded in pure practical reason. A man is autonomous when his principles of action are derived not from his natural and social circumstances or desires but solely from reason. As he puts it:[56]

> the ground of obligation here must not be sought in the nature of man or in the circumstances in which he is placed, but sought *a priori* solely in the concepts of pure reason, and that every other precept which rests on the principles of mere experience, even a precept which is in certain respects universal, so far as it leans *in the least* on empirical grounds (perhaps *only* in regards to the *motive* involved), may be called a practical rule, but *never* a moral law.

Rawls' 'veil of ignorance' cannot accommodate Kant's view that an autonomous moral action must spring not from desires and inclinations but from respect for moral law. Not surprisingly, he is led to misinterpret Kant. He says that for Kant a moral action rules out only a particular interest but not a concern for interest itself, and that moral autonomy is safeguarded as long as the principle of one's action is not designed with a particular interest in mind. This is how he distinguishes Kant's categorical and hypothetical imperatives. For him the former is based on a 'general' and the latter on a 'specific' or 'particular' interest. For Kant the concept of interest or end, whether general or particular, has no place in moral life, for a moral action is intended not to serve an interest, however indeterminate and generalized that might be, but to express man's moral or noumenal nature. As Kant says:

> If the action is good only as a means to something else, the imperative is hypothetical, but if it is thought of as good in itself, and hence as necessary in a will which of itself conforms to reason as the principle of his will, the imperative is categorical.

It is true that Kant aimed to offer a non-anthropological understanding of rational agency and was therefore concerned to avoid all reference to the contingent facts about human nature. Rawls is right to see the difficulties involved in Kant's position.[57] However, rather than admit that Kant's moral theory is of little use to him, he misrepresents his concept of autonomy and treats his pure practical reason as if it were not different from the maximizing utilitarian reason.

We can press our criticism of Rawls a little further. If we examine his theory of justice carefully, we see that it is not really a theory of justice at all. Both historically and conceptually, the concept of justice has been closely connected with the ideas of desert and personal responsibility. We need both the concept and a theory of justice because men have different abilities, make different amounts of effort, possess different qualities and qualifications and so on, and we wonder how they should be rewarded. We believe that their efforts, industry and abilities are their personal attainments and form the basis of their claims to specific deserts. Rawls is uneasy with the idea of personal responsibility because, in his view, so little in a man's life is a product of his own efforts. A man inherits some of his basic abilities and potentialities at birth and is born into a specific social position which shapes how much he develops them and what other capacities he acquires. For Rawls even a man's qualities of character, motivation, conscientiousness, industry, and so forth are 'in large part' shaped and 'influenced' by his inherited abilities and social circumstances.[58] This means, in Rawls' view, that only a small part of what a man is, has and does can be considered his personal achievement. As the area of personal responsibility shrinks, so does the basis of desert. Since Rawls' theory of man has very limited conceptual space for the ideas of desert and personal responsibility, he obviously cannot provide a theory of justice. He stresses the role of nature, accident and luck so much that he lacks the framework within which the concept of justice can arise or a theory of justice can become necessary. Paradoxical as it may seem, the general implication of Rawls' theory of justice is that justice is a very limited, perhaps even an incoherent, concept. A well considered moral theory may need to assign it its proper and limited place but must ultimately go beyond it, as Rawls himself does when he views human abilities not as private property but as a collective asset only to be used for common well-being.

Even in Rawls' view of man there is, however, an important problem to be solved, but it is not a problem of justice. The problem relates to the best or most 'rational' way of arranging the distribution of the fruits of social co-operation, such that all the members of a society can live fulfilling lives and be persuaded to co-operate. This is a problem for a theory of rationality, not a theory of justice. Rawls himself sometimes sees it this way. As he says, the important problem for a social and political theory is to devise 'reasonable terms' of social co-operation.[59] In his view, it is 'irrational' to choose the terms on any basis other than 'reciprocal advantage'.[60] And he justifies the principles of justice on the ground that it would be most rational to adopt them in the original position. As he himself admits, a theory of justice is ultimately a part of a 'theory of rational choice'.[61] Since Rawls analyses the concept of justice in terms of rationality, he can at best offer a theory of rationality, but not one of justice. As we have seen, he justifies inequalities of income, wealth and power on the ground not that some people deserve more than others but that they are rational and have beneficial consequences for the worst-off . And he attacks the natural endowments and social circumstances of birth because they are all 'irrational', 'arbitrary' and 'contingent'. Since they are irrational, the inequalities of income, status, wealth and opportunities based on them are also irrational. For Rawls equality alone is ultimately rational. His primary concern therefore is to explore how it can be maximised, and the inescapable inequalities chartered in its service. In other words he reduces justice to equality and ultimately to rationality.

One may wonder why Rawls does not notice that he has dissolved the concept of justice into that of equality or rationality. There are several explanations, the one most relevant to our discussion lies in his almost unquestioned equation of distribution with justice. He assumes that every principle of distribution is a principle of justice. This is a false assumption for every principle of justice is a principle of distribution, but the converse is not true. We can devise different ways of distributing social goods on the grounds that they are efficient, maximise net or aggregate satisfactions, create a lively and co-operative community, and so on. None of these necessarily raises the question of justice.

Since we have already alluded to some of the basic limitations of Rawls' theory of justice, we need not dwell at length on its specifically political part. Although much of it is interesting and persuasive, parts of it fail to carry conviction. We may briefly mention three. First, since Rawls' principles of justice represent the liberal individualist conception of the good life, they cannot form the basis of a truly just state as Rawls himself defines it. At least some citizens are likely to entertain mildly or even wholly divergent conceptions of the good life and will not, therefore, be able to accept the principles as its 'fundamental charter'. It is not clear how Rawls will be able to convince them that they should offer their allegiance and loyalty to their state and obey its laws. And if, *per impossibile,* all states were to be constructed in accordance with Rawls' principles, they would not even have the option of emigration!

Second, since Rawls' entire mode of political reasoning is based on certain ideal assumptions about man and society, his theory comes to grief when confronted with the real world characterized by class conflict, the pressures of organized interests and less than ideal citizens and legislators. He cannot tell us how we are to argue with those who reject his view of moral reasoning and his concept of the 'veil of ignorance', what we are to do in a society whose language of public discourse is distorted and biased, whether we are to disobey every law passed by self-interested legislators under a biased political system, how a citizen or his representative is to co-operate with those who cannot or do not take the standpoint of the ideal citizen or legislator and so on. Rawls' beautifully constructed system turns out to be largely irrelevant to the real political world and does not offer us much practical guidance.[62]

Third, Rawls' account of political obligation raises several difficulties. For Rawls ordinary citizens have no political obligations. They have a natural duty to uphold the constitution and the laws of their community, if they are justly constituted, and a natural duty to oppose them if they are not. The natural duty devolves upon all men, and therefore Rawls seems to imply that there is no real difference between citizens and foreigners! Further, Rawls introduces quite a catalogue of natural duties without fully explaining their grounds and relations. He says, for example, that men have a natural duty to 'oppose justice'.[63] It is not clear from where the duty is derived, how far it extends, how it is to be interpreted or what is to be done when it conflicts with the other natural duties. Again, as we have noted, Rawls tends to limit civil disobedience to the violation of the principle of equal liberty. While he is right to argue that violations of other principles of justice are difficult to identify, this is a practical difficulty which bedevils even the first principle and cannot warrant the exclusion of civil disobedience to attain social and economic objectives. As for Rawls' discussion of the justification of political resistance, it is marred by a confusion between the just society and a just constitution. He says that political resistance is justified when a constitution is just, and that therefore it is not justified in such liberal democracies as Britain and the United States of America. This is strange, for, while the American political system is just, the American social structure, judged by Rawls' own criteria, is not.

8

Some Reflections

In previous chapters we outlined and commented upon the political ideas of some of the influential thinkers of our time. In the course of our discussion we raised several general questions but did not pursue them further. It would be useful to highlight and briefly to consider three of them.

1

Although they have frequently commented upon it, many twentieth-century political philosophers have shown little appreciation of the problem of ideology, let alone come to terms with some of its disturbing implications. The problem was first formulated by Marx.[1] Since it has been much misinterpreted and often wrongly formulated, a brief statement of it is in order.

Over the centuries philosophers have defined and distinguished philosophy from other forms of inquiry in several different ways. One theme, however, has remained constant, namely, that unlike the others, philosophy is a self-conscious and radically self-critical form of inquiry. Non-philosophical forms of inquiry rest on, and are constituted by, several basic assumptions which they do not and cannot question. When a form of inquiry rests on assumptions, its perception and interpretation of the world are necessarily mediated by them and are hence inherently limited and distorted. Thanks to its basic assumptions, it abstracts certain aspects of the world and ignores others, conceptualizes its subject matter in a selective manner, asks certain questions and not others, employs certain methods of investigation and not others and theorizes about the world in a specific manner.

Philosophers have argued that since non-philosophical forms of inquiry are not fully conscious of their assumptions and therefore of their limitations, they have a constant tendency to claim universal validity and to transgress into areas not their own. For example, a scientist *qua* scientist does not step out of his form of inquiry and investigate its nature and assumptions. Consequently, he tends to assume that its concepts and methods of investigation apply not only to the natural but also to the social world and that he can offer about the latter the same kind of knowledge as about the former. Such universalist claims have been made or are being made also by such other forms of inquiry as theology, aesthetics and history.

Philosophers have maintained that, unlike others, philosophy is a radically critical and fully self-conscious form of inquiry. It aims to elucidate and to criticize the assumptions underlying other forms of inquiry; it also constantly turns on itself to elucidate and to criticize its own basic assumptions. Unlike other forms of inquiry, which study their subject matter confidently, philosophy is constantly plagued by doubt. It wonders if its methods, concepts, questions and modes of investigation may not rest on unexamined assumptions and directs its attention as much as itself as at its subject matter. The investigation of assumptions has been universally recognized by philosophers to be one of their major preoccupations. And the criticism of a body of thought in terms not of its factual errors or inadequate supporting evidence but of its structural assumptions and limits has traditionally been recognized as the distinctively philosophical form of criticism.

Marx appreciated and accepted the traditional view. In his opinion, philosophers were right to argue that forms of inquiry that rested on unexamined assumptions offered a distorted account of their subject matter and that the task of philosophers was to elucidate and to criticize assumptions. However, he raised an important question. He argued that philosophers stressed ontological, epistemological and other assumptions but wholly ignored the important class of social assumptions. In his view, the philosopher is not a disembodied soul operating in a historical vacuum. He is an embodied and social being who is a member of a specific group, within a specific society, in a specific historical epoch. He grows up within his society, imbibes its values, traditions and ways of understanding man and society. Since certain beliefs and forms of thought are an integral part of his social being, they appear natural and self-evident to him, and he tends to take them for granted. They constitute his 'point of view', his way of approaching and understanding the world. Even as the historical or scientific point of view is grounded in, and constituted by, certain assumptions, so is the social point of view. And even as the scientist *qua* scientist does not know the limits of his basic assumptions, and both considers his form of thought to be self-evident and extends them beyond their legitimate areas of application, every social point of view has a tendency to take for granted its characteristic forms of thought and to claim universal validity for them. When Marx says that men unconciously universalize or 'absolutize' their ideas, he has in mind not some complicated Freudian mechanism but their tendency to assume that what is natural and self-evident to them is so *in fact*, that the limits of their world are the limits of the world itself.

Marx gives the name 'ideology' to a body of thought resulting from the universalization of a partial and narrow social point of view. An ideology understands man and society within the framework of a set of assumptions characteristic of a specific class, society or epoch. It reflects a systematic orientation of thought, a perspective, a standpoint, a point of view derived from the forms of thought and conditions of existence of a particular social group. It is structurally biased, in that it seeks to reduce the totality of human experience to the limited proportions of the categories of thought derived from a specific and narrow social point of view.

In Marx's view, much traditional epistemology did not fully appreciate the social mediation of knowledge. While it recognized the importance of conceptual, methodological and other assumptions, it more or less completely overlooked the influence of the social, largely because it viewed the knowing subject as a transcendental being in no way shaped by his society and human consciousness as a kind of free-floating power rather than a socially structured capacity. It never encouraged social theorists to ask *who* they were, where in history and society they were *situated*, how they were affected by the practical struggles going on in their society, how their society was constituted, how they were structurally related to others and how this shaped their experiences and modes of thought, what assumptions they were likely to bring to their study of man and society and so on. Since they never asked these questions, they never became fully aware of the narrow social basis of their thought and obviously took no steps to counter its influence. Not surprisingly, they unwittingly universalized the values, modes of thought, criteria of rationality and so on of their social group and/or society and ended up by claiming universal validity for what was inherently restricted in time and place. For Marx the problem of ideology consisted in exploring the complex ways in which philosophers illegitimately universalize a specific form of experience and in inquiring how this could be avoided.

Few contemporary political philosophers have appreciated the importance of Marx's problem of ideology. Most have simply dismissed it as a non-problem or have thought that it could be easily taken care of by their becoming more critical of their assumptions. Not surprisingly, their central doctrines display a systematic tendency towards illegitimate generalization. Notwithstanding his claims to the contrary, Rawls' theory of justice rests, as we have seen, on liberal assumptions about the nature of man. Popper's open or rational society is only an idealized version of the liberal society, and his views of man, reason and the technological orientation of epistemology reflect a liberal *Weltanschauung*. Berlin's negative liberty reflects and generalizes the way in which liberty is conceived and institutionalized in England. As he himself asknowledges, and as his critics have pointed out, the French, the Germans and others do not define liberty in this way.[2] As for Berlin's distinction between negative and positive liberty, it is largely a conceptualization of English and Continental views of liberty.[3] It is hardly surprising that almost all those upon whom he fathers positive liberty are Continental philosophers, whereas almost all the champions of negative liberty turn out to be English.[4] What is true of Berlin is true also of Oakeshott. His views of freedom and human dignity find limited support in the French and German, and less in non-European, experience and cultural traditions. The French have long regarded central planning as a necessary condition of their freedom. Suspicion of the state is rooted in English political tradition in a way that it is not on the continent of Europe. Oakeshott's account of the history of modern Europe in terms of the conflict between civil and enterprise associations is a generalization of English historical experience. As he says himself, after the seventeenth century 'belief in civil association' remained strong in England alone.[5]

The same basic limitations are evident in the conceptions of man advocated in the writings of many, though by no means all, twentieth-century political philosophers. Their writings are marked by the following recurrent and rarely argued themes: man is higher than the animal; he has dignity; his dignity consists in possessing certain distinctive capacities, especially reason; self-direction, or the capacity to choose his purposes, is the hallmark of man's humanity; freedom of choice is the highest value; man has certain natural or moral rights derived from his nature; and the individual is the ultimate unit of moral and political life. While all, or at any rate most, of these beliefs appear self-evident to most of us, this is not, in fact, the case.

It is not clear how one can show that man is *higher* than the other animals. Such a judgement is passed by man, and he cannot be both a judge and a party to the dispute. Only God is able to make this judgement. Further, logically such a judgement requires a criterion independent of the capacities possessed by both men and other animals, and the criterion is, by definition, not available. Often philosophers abstract a particular human capacity such as reason or self-direction, call it a 'higher' capacity, show that only man has it and contend, therefore, that he is higher than other animals! The history of philosophy is replete with such circular arguments.[6] To argue for man's dignity on such a basis is to make a very weak case for it. What is more, we are now beginning to 'respect' the animals and to invest them with rights. As they rise in moral esteem, and as the moral distance between them and men diminishes, one wonders if the traditional basis of human dignity can retain its appeal much longer.

Not only the concept of human dignity but also the concepts of choice, purpose, reason, self-direction and natural rights raise several difficult and unnoticed problems. Since we cannot analyse them all, we shall concentrate on the crucial concept of the individual.

Although much contemporary moral and political philosophy is grounded in individualism, it has rarely examined the concept of the individual. The individual is not given but is a social construction. A man is inseparably connected with other men and nature. To individuate him is to decide where to draw the boundary between him on the one hand and other men and nature on the other. Different philosophers and societies individuate men differently. The ancient Athenians saw man as an integral part of nature and society and thought that a man, *taken together with* his land and political rights, constituted an individual. For the Indians the set of social relations into which he is born as a member of a caste are an inseparable part of him and define him as an individual. The Chinese view the family as an indissoluble organism, link the ancestors and their decendants into a living union and have a highly complex concept of the individual. For Marx the human subject necessarily requires specific material and social conditions, without which he remains indeterminate and abstract, and therefore he, *together with* these conditions, constitutes an individual. Liberal writers generally define the individual in austere and minimalist terms. For them the naturally given biological organism, neatly encapsulated in the body, is the individual.

The liberal conception of the individual is of relatively recent origin. The Classical Athenian believed that to render physical service to another in return for a monetary reward, even if it was for a short time, was a form of slavery and unworthy of a free man.

Almost right up to the end of the Middle Ages a craftsman's tools were believed to be inseparable from him. They constituted his 'inorganic body'; they were an integral part of his body as his hands and feet were. To deprive him of them was to mutilate him. With the rise of bourgeois society, almost everything became alienable, and men were free to sell their labour and their means of production. Therefore an individual had so to be defined that in selling his means of production and the capacities, skills and activities of which his labour consisted, he was not deemed to be selling himself. He had to be seen as somehow separate from, and only contingently related to, them so that *he* was deemed to remain free even when his activities and skills were no longer under his control.

Since almost everything about an individual was considered alienable, including his skills, capacities and activities, the crucial question arose of what was to be considered *essential* to him, such that *its* alienation was *his* alienation and his loss of control over it amounted to his loss of freedom. Bourgeois society by and large located his essential humanity in the interrelated capacities of choice and will. These represented man's *differentia specifica* and were the basis of human dignity. The individual was, above all, an agent. As long as he was not physically overpowered, hypnotised or otherwise deprived of his powers of choice and will, his actions were *uniquely* his and therefore his *sole* responsibility. It did not matter how painful his alternatives were, how much his character had been distorted by his background and upbringing or how much his capacities of choice and will were debilitated by his circumstances. As long as he was formally able to choose, his choices were his responsibility. The individual was abstracted from his social background and his circumstances, which therefore could not be considered co-agents of, or co-responsible for, his actions. He stood alone, all by himself, stripped of his social relations, circumstances and background, facing the world in sovereign isolation and, like God, exercising his unconditioned freedom of choice and will. Bourgeois society equated the individual with an abstract mental capacity, namely, the capacity to choose and will, and defined him in asocial terms. The fact that the concepts of will and choice should have acquired such unprecedented importance in the thought of the late medieval nominalists, Hobbes, Locke, Rousseau, Bentham, Kant, J. S. Mill and others should not surprise us.

When the individual is so austerely conceived, the question arises of how he is related to his alienable bodily and mental activities and powers. They cannot be conceived as his modes of being, the ways in which he expresses himself and exists for himself and others; they can be understood only as things he *has* rather than as part of him. Bourgeois writers appropriately defined them as his *properties*, which in legal language became his *possessions*. If 'he' referred to the totality of his being and not merely to his will or choice, his powers and activities could be seen as an integral part of him, as *constitutive* of him, and therefore not as his possessions, which he could dispose of 'at will'. He could not alienate them, any more than he could alienate his will or choice. And his so-called 'freedom' to sell his capacities and activities appeared not as freedom but as slavery. The lean and austere bourgeois definition of the individual had, of course, a very different implication.

Men can be inviduated then, in several different ways, the bourgeois mode of individuation being one of them. It is therefore not the *only* way in which to define the individual. What is more, since men can be individuated in different ways, the bourgeois mode of individuation must be shown to be better than others and not merely assumed to be self-evident and natural. Further, it is profoundly biased. If we were to individuate men differently, for example, in the manner of the Classical Athenians or Marx, we would have to recognize each individual's right to those conditions without which he cannot live, flourish and become an individual. By contrast, the austere and minimalist conception of the individual, which entitles him to nothing save the relatively unhindered exercise of his formal capacity for choice and will and allows him no claims upon others save forbearance, suits bourgeois society well. It enables it to blame and punish its members for their actions on the ground that they have freely chosen and are accountable for them. At the same time, it releases society from the obligation to increase their range of real alternatives and give them greater control over their lives. In other words, bourgeois society defines the individual within the limits of, and in a manner conducive to, its conditions of existence. Its definition is ideological.

Like is conception of the individual, bourgeois society's conceptions of liberty, equality, right, justice and so on are also ideological. If we defined the individual as constituting an organic unity with his conditions of existence, so that a man not abstracted from but taken *together with* them constituted an individual, we would have to define freedom as access to a share in the control over them and non-interference in his use of them. And, likewise, we would have to define equality as equal access to, and control over, these conditions as well as equal opportunity to develop one's abilities. Since bourgeois society defines the individual in minimalist terms, it defines liberty and equality too in extremely narrow terms. For it liberty is the absence of interference by the government; equality is the formal equality of rights; a right is the capacity to do what one likes with one's own; and justice is whatever is offered by the market.

Bourgeois society does not merely define the individual in a certain way; it embodies its minimalist conception of the individual in its legal, social, educational, moral, economic, political and other institutions. It sets up the minimally defined individual as the norm to which all its members are required to conform. They are told that they lack dignity and are subhuman unless they stand on their own feet, make no claims on society, accept full responsibility for the consequences of their actions, however painful and stark the alternatives, bear their social misfortunes with dignity and blame none but themselves for them. The moral and legal institutions and practices of bourgeois society ensure that its members live up to that norm. Bourgeois society made the isolated and abstract individual the basic unit of moral and political life and institutionalized him in such a way that he *appears* to be the sole moral and political reality. In other words, the socially created reality is turned into the ontological reality, and a socially generated fact is presented as a natural fact.

Most contemporary political philosophers continue to think about man within the narrow individualist framework of thought. Their ideas about the individual, choice, will, liberty and so on centre on the austerely defined individual embodied in the practices and institutions of modern society. Not many of them ask if men may not be individuated differently, if the conditions man needs in order to grow are not external but integral to and indivisible from him, and therefore he, together with them, constitutes an *individuum*. It would be crude and most misleading to suggest, as Marxists do, that they are all bourgeois writers or advocates of bourgeois society. Far from it. Rather, they do not probe deeply enough, do not ask really searching questions about the nature of the individual, and take for granted the socially institutionalized definition of the individual. As a result, their conceptions of man remain ideological. They illegitimately universalize contemporary man and present him as somehow 'natural'.

2

Another feature of twentieth-century political philosophy, which it shares with the entire tradition of political philosophy, is the degree to which it remains subordinated to the demands of philosophy.

Political philosophy is the philosophical exploration of political life. It is satisfactory only if it is both philosophical in its reflection and does full justice to the rich and complex texture of political life. Our tradition of political philosophy has, with a few notable exceptions, remained heavily dependent upon the tradition of general philosophy and has paid greater attention to its philosophical than to its political dimension. This has had several important consequences.

First, most political philosophers have assumed that philosophy is a homogeneous mode of inquiry that can be uniformly applied to whatever subject matter happens to interest the philosopher. And, accordingly, they have adopted the prevailing view of the nature of philosophy, borrowed its tools, modes of investigation and forms of reasoning, and applied them to the analysis of political phenomena. Thus they have assumed that there is a uniform technique of conceptual analysis which can be applied equally to the analysis of logical, scientific, mathematical and political concepts. It is at least arguable that political concepts are radically different from the other three and require a distinctive mode of analysis. Although we cannot argue the point here, it is not too difficult to show that political concepts are inescapably historical, culture-bound and value-impregnated in a way that the other types of concept are not. And although, like the other kinds of concept, they are 'essentially contested' in the sense that contestability pertains to their very essence, they are contested for very different reasons and in very different ways.

Second, many a political philosopher has assumed that, like philosophers in general, they should aim to develop a body of universally valid propositions. One may wonder it this is an appropriate and attainable objective in politics. Political life is inescapably historical and deals with men not in the abstract but as they have come to be in a given historical period. For example, the modern European state is a unique historical institution; some of its features have historical analogues, but in its totality it is without a parallel. And it has to contend with the modern European man, who has acquired desires, needs, aspirations and qualities of temperament and character not to be found among his Classical and medieval ancestors. This means that in order to understand the politics of the modern European state, we need a distinctive body of concepts.[7] To take an example, the concept of liberty, understood as non-interference, makes sense only in the modern European context, in which men have acquired the consciousness of being autonomous and distinct selves and a desire to make their choices themselves. The applicability of the concept is limited in the sense that the world of human relationships which it signifies and comprehends is unique to modern Europe. What is true of liberty is true also of the concepts of right, privacy, social equality, law, the Civil Service and so on.

Indeed, one may wonder if the modern European man is not significantly different from his predecessors and his counterparts in other parts of the world. No doubt he shares several general capacities with them. However, he has developed and related them differently. For example, although he shares the capacity of reason with others, his reason takes a particular form, operates in a particular way and occupies a particular place in his way of life, which are all different from those of others. One may wonder, therefore, if an abstract concept of reason designed to apply to all men everywhere is not too indeterminate to capture the specificity of his reason and to explain his form of life. One may push the argument to its logical conclusion and ask whether a general conception of man, which so many political philosophers have so freely invoked, has any explanatory power at all. In short, political philosophy needs to come to terms with the historicity of political institutions and concepts and to reconsider its traditional ambition to offer an universally valid body of knowledge. Aristotle remarked that one cannot expect the same degree of precision in human affairs as in mathematics. Following him, one may ask if philosophy can aim at the same degree of precision and the same type of knowledge in human affairs in general and politics in particular as it does in the other areas.

Third, since philosophy has been the dominant partner, the fortunes of political philosophy have remained tied to the recurrent crises and changing fashions of philosophy. Every crisis in philosophy has produced a corresponding crisis in political philosophy. We only have to think of the way in which logical positivism and linguistic philosophy paralysed political philosophy for several decades. Further, since political philosophy lacks a distinct and independent identity, it is entirely at the mercy of general philosophy, and lacks coherence and consensus. This is evident in the judgements political philosophers make about each other. For some Arendt is a high-level journalist but not a philosopher, since she does not analyse concepts or define terms and is primarily didactic. For others Berlin is not a political philospher but a man of letters because he has not developed a philosophical system. Similar judgements are freely made about Oakeshott, Macpherson, Popper and others. Each school of philosophy, and of political philosophy, has its own favourites. Again, the close connection with philosophy has been a source of both strength and weakness for political philosophy. Political philosophers have rightly remained sensitive to the relevant work done by philosophers in such areas as epistemology, metaphysics, methodology and logic and have used it to understand the nature of action, human conduct, ideology, political argument, rules, authority, law and so on. They have also, however, remained indifferent to, and ignorant of, relevant work done in the fields of social psychology, economics, social history, sociology and anthropology. To be sure, this is a relatively recent trend, for until a few decades ago philosophers, and also therefore political philosophers, took a keen interest in, engaged in controversies about and even wrote books about these and other areas. Once philosophy came to be defined in narrow terms, political philosophy followed suit. While a philosopher who is primarily interested in logic or epistemology may ignore the social sciences, it is difficult to see how a political philosopher can, for they have much to say that is relevant to the understanding of political life.

Fourth, since our tradition of political philosophy has remained heavily dependent upon the tradition of general philosophy, it has been widely and automatically assumed that the practice of political philosophy is deemed to require no further qualifications than the mastery of philosophical skills. It is enough if one is philosophically well versed; one need not possess intimate and detailed knowledge of political life itself. It has meant also that political philosophy has come to be dominated by philosophical rather than by political concerns. Political philosophers select and concetrated on problems because of their general philosophical rather than their specifically political-philosophical significance, that is, because they appear to them to raise interesting issues of larger philosophical significance rather than because their resolution is necessary to explain or illuminate a specific area of political life. Further, since our tradition puts considerable premium on philosphical skill and not enough on intimate knowledge of political history, institutions and political life in general, it is not uncommon to find highly sophisticated philosophical systems which have a rather poor political content and whose analyses of political life are naive and *simpliste*. When their philosophical subtleties are pared away, some of them seem to rest on nothing more elevated than unexamined prejudices shared with the 'masses'. As we have seen, Popper's theories of reason and criticism are innocent of consideration of the way in which modern society is constituted, and he has limited understanding of the social and economic factors contributing to the steady decline of the liberal society which he holds so dear. Rawls' elegant theory of justice has limited relevance to modern society. Marcuse's sociological analysis is abstract and does not connect with historical reality. Macpherson's accounts of the Third World and communist countries are unrecognizable and vitiate his discussion of democracy. Indeed, there is hardly a twentieth-century political philosopher who has made a systematic attempt to understand the nature and structure of modern society. As a result, their assumptions and analyses remain somewhat naive, and their thought does not connect with, or explain, the contemporary world.

Fifth, since our tradition of political philosophy is so heavily subordinated to the demands of philosophy that it is sometimes little more than philosophy applied to politics, it is not surprising that political philosophers are often judged by their philosophical subtlety rather than by their political insight. Thus Plato, Aquinas and Hobbes are awarded higher marks than Tocqueville, Locke, Montesquieu and Mill on the grounds that their systems of thought are coherent, comprehensive, rigorously analytical, conceptually tidy and so on. Obviously, these are all philosophical rather than political criteria of evaluation. It may be that Plato, for example, is a better philosopher than J. S. Mill, but that does not *in itself* make him a better *political* philosopher. If we are to argue that Plato, Aquinas and Hobbes are better political philosophers than Locke, Mill and Marx, we need to show not only that they are better philosophers but also that they offer more profound and perceptive analyses of *political* life. *Prima facie* this does not seem to be the case. It could be argued that although J. S. Mill may be philosophically inferior to Plato, his analysis of political life is more perceptive and illuminating, and that although philosophically Marx is much less satisfactory than Kant or Spinoza, he offers a more insightful analysis of political life than does either of the others.

Once we liberate political philosophy from the overbearing influence of philosophy and view it as an autonomous discipline rather than as a 'branch' of philosophy, we recognize the need to define philosophy not as a monolithic and homogeneous form of inquiry but as one that can adjust its objectives, tools and methods of investigation to suit its subject matter. Even as we define scientific inquiry broadly to take account of the fact that both economics and physics, although very different in their methods and tools of analysis, are still sciences, we need to define philosophy as a family of inquiries. Political, moral and social philosophy are not branches of so-called general philosophy, rather they are autonomous disciples sharing nothing more than a tendency to ask certain types of questions.

Political philosophy, as I have noted in the preface to this book, is a complex discipline. Philosophy is a theoretical activity; politics is a practical activity. Philosophy is concerned to understand and to explain; politics involves choosing between conflicting goals and values, assessing social practices and institutions in terms of their ability to satisfy human needs, and defending or exploring alternatives to them. A theory of a practical activity is therefore subject to two fundamental constraints. It must analyse and explain the practical activity concerned, otherwise it ceases to be theoretical. It must also evaluate human goals and values, provide principles for assessing social practices and institutions and in general guide and illuminate practical choices, as otherwise it distorts the practical nature of the activity concerned. Political philosophy is therefore necessarily both theoretical and practical, both explanatory and normative. It has a *dual* telos, and betrays its nature if it becomes wholly theoretical and formal, or wholly practical and didactic. The delicate integration of its two conflicting tendencies calls for considerable skill and self-discipline. Most writers fail to achieve it and become either didactic or highly formal.

Since political philosophy has a dual nature, it is hardly surprising that every political philosophy is informed by both theoretical and practical or intellectual and moral concerns. The theoretical impulse lacks vitality, direction and urgency unless grounded in a moral impulse; and the moral impulse lacks focus and detachment unless informed by the theoretical. Although it may begin in a desire to understand, often a political philosophy springs from a moral problem. A political philosopher is troubled and disquieted by the kind of life his fellow citizens live and which, since the state is a compulsory association, he is forced to share. He may feel that they live lives that are unworthy of men or lack depth, a sense of purpose or meaning. Or he may feel outraged by the inequality, injustice and hypocrisy of his society or by the lack of imagination and intelligence which may have brought the world to the brink of a global holocaust. Or he may feel that modern society compromises the freedom, integrity and moral autonomy of its members, requires them to do things they wholly disapprove of, treats them as children requiring paternal protection, and so on. Whatever the source of his moral outrage, the political philosopher wonders how his society or the world came to be in such a state, how it is sustained, whether anything can be done about it, whether there is an alternative and so on. These and other questions launch him on his philosophical inquiry. The philosophy he develops is judged both by the degree of its moral and sociological penetration and by the depth and subtlety of his philosophical analysis.

3

The third and final feature of contemporary political philosophy which we may briefly discuss is the considerable ambiguity of its subject matter. Until the end of the nineteenth century and even beyond, there was general agreement that political philosophy was concerned with the nature of collective life and the major institutions of which it was composed. There is hardly a major political philosopher who has not discussed the nature of the family, the system of property, the major social groups of his society, the structure and constitution of the state, the purposes of government, the nature of citizenship, relations between states, the nature of war and so on. Plato, Aristotle, Aquinas, Hobbes, Locke, Rousseau, Bentham, J. S. Mill, Kant, Hegel, *et al.* developed fairly articulate theories, or at least views, about each of these subjects. Twentieth-century political philosophy presents a very different picture. With a few exceptions, there is hardly a political philosopher who has developed a comprehensive philosophical system that embraces these subjects. Most have preferred to confine their attention to the structure of the state. It is hardly surprisingly that most of our discussions about property, citizenship, the relation between the government and the economy, social classes and even war continue to be dominated by the categories and assumptions inherited from our nineteenth-century forbears.

Even with respect to the structure of the state, to which most political philosophers have devoted their attention, there is a noticeable shrinkage of subject matter. For example, there is little discussion of forms of government, the subject to which earlier philosophers paid considerable attention. This cannot be because the twentieth century has not thown up novel forms of government. Indeed, unlike the eighteenth and nineteenth centuries, which introduced only one new form of government each, namely, the representative and the democratic, the twentieth century has thrown up several. The totalitarian form of government of Nazi Germany is the most obvious. However, there are others. The communist governments of the Soviet Union and the East European states are unique and cannot be described as despotic, tyrannical, dictatorial, autocratic or totalitarian. The quasi-democratic forms of government that are developing in parts of Asia and the tribally

constituted and one-party-dominated forms of government that
have emerged in parts of Africa are, again, all unique and cannot be
easily subsumed under any of the half-dozen forms of government
theorized by the political philosophers. None of these forms of
government has so far had its Montesquieu or Tocqueville. Even
within the liberal democratic states, the physiognomy of the state is
changing profoundly. Corporate powers have increasingly become
integrated into the structure of the state, and the conduct of public
affairs is becoming a 'partnership' between them and the government. However, the categories in terms of which most political
philosophers conceptualize the state are rooted in nineteenth-
century liberalism and are almost wholly inadequate. Hegel's
Philosophy of Right has more to say about the modern state than
does the work of many of our contemporaries.[8]

There are several important ways in which the subject matter of
political philosophy is undergoing profound change. We may
briefly mention two. First, political philosophy today is in a
situation similar to that of philosophy a few centuries ago. When
the different areas which had hitherto been the concerns of
philosophy broke away and developed independent disciplines of
their own, philosophy was left to deal with highly general and
formal issues and became increasingly metaphysical. A similar trend
is discernible in political philosophy today. Such separate areas as
international relations, ethnic studies, political anthropology, the
study of political institutions and of public administration are
becoming separate disciplines. Increasingly deprived of its subject
matter, political philosophy shows signs of becoming highly formal,
of concentrating upon the all too familiar metaphysical enterprise of
building abstract models and conceptual frameworks.

There is no reason why it should find itself in such a predicament.
The sub-disciplines within which the study of politics is breaking up
are constantly throwing up problems of philosophical interest. For
example, the comparative study of governments raises difficult
questions about the nature, purpose, units and methods of
comparison, the relation between form of government and so-called
political culture, the possibility of cross-cultural generalizations and
so on. Ethnic studies raise large questions about the nature of a way
of life, how it can be preserved, the nature of membership of a
political community, the ways in which different cultures can be
accommodated within a single community and so on. International
relations raise large questions about the nature of national interest,
war, the use of violence, the justification of external interference in
the affairs of a state, the ethics of foreign aid and so on. Although

some interesting and philosophically relevant work is going on in these and other areas, it lacks depth and sophistication. Political philosophy has an important contribution to make here. Unless it reclaims new territories and opens itself up to new problems, it will either become metaphysical or continue to feed on its past and become a *history* of political thought.

The second respect in which the subject matter of political philosophy is changing is a result of the profound changes taking place in the world at large. Interdependence between states is increasing in both scale and depth. Their economic interdependence is a well established fact. The spread of nuclear weapons among the small and unstable nations poses universal dangers, not to mention the stake which all states have in preventing a nuclear holocaust. Thanks to a changing attitude towards nature and the environment, there is a universal feeling that nature is mankind's common heritage and that concerted efforts must be made to preserve the ecological equibrium and the different species of animals. In short, mankind is no longer a mere biological species, not merely a regulative moral principle, but a distinct political entity and a locus of moral and political claims. The human *community* has common problems, and it is something to which one can belong and to which one can have obligations. Once we appreciate the full implications of this, the philosophical discussion of politics acquires a new dimension. Such questions as whether and what obligations one has to men struggling for survival, freedom or justice in other countries, how these relate to one's obligations to one's own community, how mankind's common stake in survival and freedom can be institutionally articulated, the nature of sovereignty and the character of global citizenship become central to political philosophy.[9] Political philosophy has hitherto been concerned with the *polis* and has devised its questions and concepts accordingly. It defies imagination to contemplate what change political (cosmopolitical?) philosophy will need to undergo when the cosmopolis replaces the *polis* as its primary framework of reference.

Notes

Chapter 1: HANNAH ARENDT

1. *Thinking* (Harcourt, Brace, Jovanovich, London, 1978), pp. 15, 54.
2. ibid., p. 113
3. ibid., pp. 57f., 122.
4. ibid., pp. 54f. See also *Human Condition* (University of Chicago Press, London, 1968), pp. 187f., and *Between Past and Future* (Faber & Faber, London, 1961), pp. 201ff. The two works are hereafter referred to as *HC* and *PF* respectively.
5. *Thinking*, pp. 14f., 164ff.
6. ibid., pp. 58, 62.
7. ibid., pp. 15, 54f., 57.
8. ibid., pp. 164f.
9. ibid., p. 57.
10. MSS, Box, 16, *Philosophy and Politics*, pp. 28ff.; and *HC*, pp. 5f.
11. *Thinking*, p. 5; *PF*, pp. 14, 15, 31, 42, 45, 69, 87, 91, 94, 106, 109. See also *On Revolution* (Viking Press, New York, 1963), pp. 156f., 222.
12. MSS, Box 16, *Philosophy and Politics*, pp. 40f.
13. *HC*, pp. 3f.
14. *Thinking*, pp. 170f.
15. MSS, Box 16, *Philosophy and Politics*, pp. 42, 44.
16. *HC*, pp. 8f., 179, 181f., 193. See also *The Origins of Totalitarianism* (Allen & Unwin, London, 1951), p. 20.
17. *HC*, pp. 136f., 141, 144, 168.
18. ibid., p. 87.
19. ibid., pp. 136f., 144.
20. ibid., pp. 190f., 233f., 243f.
21. ibid., p. 198.
22. *Crisis of the Republic* (Harcourt, Brace, Jovanovich, New York, 1972), pp. 216f.
23. *On Revolution*, pp. 239ff.
24. ibid., pp. 266ff.
25. Many of the points only briefly sketched in the chapter are discussed

at length in my *Hannah Arendt and the Search for a New Political Philosophy* (Macmillan, London, 1981).

Chapter 2: ISAIAH BERLIN

1. 'Does Political Theory still Exist?', in Peter Laslett and W. G. Runciman (eds.), *Philosophy, Politics and Society* (Basil Blackwell, Oxford, 1962), pp. 2f.
2. 'An Introduction to Philosophy', in Bryan Magee (ed.), *Men of Ideas* (BBC, London, 1978), p. 25.
3. ibid., pp. 38f.; *Philosophy, Politics and Society*, pp. 23f.
4. *Philosophy, Politics and Society*, pp. 18f.
5. *Men of Ideas*, p. 39.
6. *Philosophy, Politics and Society*, p. 26; see also *Four Essays on Liberty* (Oxford University Press, London, 1969), p.xxxii.
7. *Philosophy, Politics and Society*, p. 26.
8. ibid., p. 25.
9. *Four Essays*, p. 99.
10. *Against the Current* (Hogarth Press, London, 1979), p. 298.
11. *Philosophy, Politics and Society*, p. 28. Italics added.
12. ibid., pp. 24f.
13. ibid., p. 24.
14. *Men of Ideas*, pp. 31f.
15. *Philosophy, Politics and Society*, p. 30.
16. ibid., p. 31.
17. *Against the Current*, pp. 80f., 301; see also the useful introduction by Roger Hausheer.
18. *Four Essays*, pp. lvi, 145f.; see also *Russian Thinkers* (Hogarth Press, London, 1978) pp. 86f.
19. *Men of Ideas*, pp. 34f.
20. *Vico and Herder: Two Studies in the History of Ideas* (Hogarth Press, London, 1976), pp. xviff.
21. *Four Essays*, p. 145; *Concepts and Categories*, pp. 194f., 198.
22. *Four Essays*, p. 167.
23. *Russian Thinkers*, pp. 106f.
24. ibid., pp. 168f.
25. *Against the Current*, pp. 45f.
26. ibid., p. 58.
27. ibid., pp. 74f.; *Concepts and Categories*, pp. 194f.
28. *Against the Current*, p. 127.
29. ibid., pp. 120, 121, 128f.; *Vico and Herder*, pp. xxiiif., 153f., 204f.
30. *Vico and Herder*, p. 212; *Against the Current*, pp. 68, 76, 80, 129, 332; *Four Essays*, p. li.
31. *Philosophy, Politics and Society*, p. 9.
32. *Four Essays*, pp. 137, 178, 192; *Concepts and Categories*, p. 190.
33. *Four Essays*, p. 138.

34. ibid., p. xxiv.
35. ibid., p. 127.
36. ibid., p. 137.
37. ibid., pp. 40, 102; *Concepts and Categories*, p. 102.
38. *Concepts and Categories*, pp. 95, 96, 98, 100; *Against the Current*, p. 78.
39. *Four Essays*, pp. li, 102, 169,
40. ibid., pp. 1, 102.
41. ibid., p. 171.
42. ibid., p. 121.
43. For a careful analysis, see C. B. Macpherson, *Democratic Theory* (Clarendon Press, Oxford, 1973), pp. 104f.
44. *Four Essays*, pp. 131f.
45. ibid., p. 144.
46. ibid., pp. 132f., 153, 154.
47. ibid., pp. li, 168.
48. ibid., pp. 122f.
49. ibid., p. xxxix.
50. ibid., p. xlviii.
51. ibid., p. 122.
52. ibid., p. lvi.
53. ibid., p. 123.
54. p. 158; *Concepts and Categories*, pp. 190f.
55. ibid., pp. 191, 192. Professor Berlin has been kind enough to clarify that he regards these as conditions and not forms of freedom.
56. ibid., pp. lii, xli.
57. ibid., pp. 126, 165.
58. ibid., p. 124.
59. ibid., p. 126.
60. ibid., pp. 153, 162.
61. For two interesting critiques, see Macpherson, *Democratic Theory*, pp. 111f., and Bernard Williams, 'Conflicts of Values', in Alan Ryan (ed.), *The Idea of Freedom* (Oxford University Press, Oxford, 1979), pp. 222ff.
62. Professor Berlin has been kind enough to clarify that he does not subscribe to moral subjectivism.
63. For a good discussion, see Charles Taylor in *The Idea of Freedom*, pp. 175ff.
64. *Four Essays*, p. 126.
65. ibid., p. lvii.

Chapter 3: C. B. MACPHERSON

1. 'Do We Need a Theory of the State?', *European Journal of Sociology*, XVIII, 1977, pp. 223f.; see also *Democratic Theory*

(Clarendon Press, Oxford, 1979), pp. 195f. The article is hereafter referred to as *EJS* and the book as *DT*.

2. *DT*, p. 29.
3. ibid., p. 198.
4. ibid., p. 202.
5. *EJS*, p. 225.
6. *Political Theory of Possessive Individualism* (Clarendon Press, Oxford, 1962), p. 15. This work is hereafter referred to as *PI*.
7. *PI*, pp. 6f.
8. ibid., pp. 100, 104; *EJS*, p. 227.
9. *PI*, p. 275.
10. *Canadian Journal of Economic and Political Science*, XXIX, 1963, p. 566.
11. *PI*, p. 99.
12. ibid., p. 268.
13. 'The Economic Penetration of Political Theory', *Journal of the History of Ideas*, XXXIX, 1978, pp. 101ff.
14. *PI*, pp. 4ff.
15. *DT*, pp. 195ff.
16. *EJS*, p. 243.
17. *DT*, pp. 43, 51, 54, 56, 58.
18. ibid., p. 54. Also *The Real World of Democracy* (Oxford University Press, Oxford, 1975), p. 38. This book is hereafter referred to as *RW*.
19. *DT*, p. 55.
20. ibid.,m p. 53.
21. ibid., p. 236.
22. ibid., p. 51.
23. ibid., p. 58.
24. ibid., p. 53.
25. ibid., pp. 64, 65.
26. *Canadian Journal of Economic and Political Science*, XVI, 1950, p. 101.
27. *RW*, pp. 39, 41.
28. *EJS*, p. 242.
29. 'Human Rights as Property Rights' in *Dissent*, 1977, pp. 72ff; C. B. Macpherson (ed.), *Property: Mainstream and Critical Positions* (Basil Blackwell, Oxford, 1978), ch. 1.
30. *RW*, pp. 6f.
31. *PI*, pp. 262f.
32. *DT*, pp. 26f.
33. ibid., pp. 25, 173, 234; *PI*, p. 262; *RW*, pp. 1, 3, 6; *Life and Times of Liberal Democracy* (Oxford University Press, Oxford, 1980), pp. 1, 2, 20, 21, 114, 115. This work is hereafter referred to as *LD*.
34. *RW*, p. 11.
35. *LD*, pp. 23ff.

36. ibid., pp. 44f.
37. ibid., pp. 77f.
38. ibid., pp. 93f.
39. *RW*, p. 3.
40. ibid., pp. 18, 22.
41. ibid., pp. 28, 32f.
42. ibid., p. 35.
43. 'Individualist Socialism?', *Canadian Journal of Philosophy*, VI, 1976, pp. 195f. For a good discussion of this aspect of Macpherson's thought, see D. F. B. Tucker, *Marxism and Individualism* (Basil Blackwell, Oxford, 1980), pp. 95ff.
44. *DT*, p. 38.
45. ibid., p. 34.
46. *PI*, p. 18.
47. Steven Lukes makes the point well in 'The Real and Ideal Worlds of Democracy', in Alkis Kontos, (ed.), *Powers, Possessions and Freedom* (University of Toronto Press, Toronto, 1979), pp. 145f.
48. *DT*, pp. 108f.

Chapter 4: HERBERT MARCUSE

1. *Negations: Essays in Critical Theory* (Penguin Books, Harmondsworth, 1972), pp. 45f.
2. ibid., p. 85; *One Dimensional Man* (Sphere Books, London, 1969), p. 112. This book is hereafter referred to as *OM*.
3. *OM*, p. 113. Marcuse observes, 'nobody really thinks who does not abstract from that which is given, who does not relate the facts to the factors which have made them, who does not in his mind undo the facts. Abstractness is the very life of thought, the token of its authenticity.'
4. ibid., p. 46.
5. ibid., p. 45.
6. ibid., p. 136; *Studies in Critical Philosophy* (Beacon Press, Boston, 1973), pp. 90f. This work is hereafter referred to as *Studies*.
7. *Negations*, pp. 68f., 141.
8. ibid., p. 150.
9. ibid., pp. 143f.; see also ibid., p. 142, where Marcuse observes, 'There is no philosophy alongside and outside this theory.'
10. *OM*, p. 10.
11. *Negations*, p. 153; *Counter-Revolution and Revolt* (Beacon Press, Boston, 1972), p. 34.
12. *Negations*, p. 74.
13. ibid., pp. 72f.
14. *OM*, pp. 112, 148; *Negations*, pp. 83f.
15. *OM*, p. 175.
16. *Negations*, pp. 134f.

17. *OM*, pp. 9, 10. Italics added.
18. *Negations*, p. 152. Marcuse observes, 'Happiness presupposes freedom: at root it is freedom. Conceptual analysis reveals them to be ultimately identical', ibid., p. 180.
19. *OM*, pp. 21f.; *The Aesthetic Dimension* (Macmillan, London, 1979), pp. 16f.
20. *Studies*, p. 223. Marcuse here observes that in modern society, 'the "given" liberties militate against freedom, that is, self-determination.'
21. *OM*, pp. 4f.
22. *Studies*, pp. 51ff.
23. ibid., pp. 72f., 91f.
24. *Eros and Civilization* (Beacon Press, Boston, 1969), pp. 180f. This work is hereafter referred to as *Eros*.
25. *Negations*, pp. 159ff.
26. *Eros*, p. 25.
27. ibid., p. 170.
28. *An Essay on Liberation* (Allen Lane, London, 1969), pp. 89f.; *Dialectics of Liberation* (Allen Lane, London, 1969), pp. 185f. The first book is hereafter referred to as *Essay*.
29. *Negations*, pp. 152, 161.
30. ibid., pp. 170f., 186f.
31. *OM*, pp. 122, 128, 130.
32. *Negations*, pp. 154f.; *Counter-Revolution*, pp. 63f.
33. *Essay*, pp. 21f., 29f., 59f., 92.
34. *Eros*, p. 186.
35. *Negations*, pp. 39f.
36. ibid., p. 14.
37. *Essay*, pp. 80f.
38. For Marcuse, 'the end of government is not only the greatest possible freedom but also the greatest possible happiness of man.' See 'Ethics and Revolution', in Richard T. De George (ed.), *Ethics and Society* (Macmillan, London, 1968), p. 134.
39. *Essay*, pp. 73f.
40. *Ethics and Society*, pp. 136f.; *Counter-Revolution*, pp. 53f.
41. *Negations*, p. 74.
42. This point is fully discussed in my 'Utopianism and Manicheism: A Critique of Marcuse's Theory of Revolution', *Social Research*, 39, 1972, pp. 643f.
43. *Reason and Revolution* (Routledge & Kegan Paul, London, 1954), p. 25.

Chapter 5: MICHAEL OAKESHOTT

1. *Experience and its Modes* (Cambridge University Press,

Cambridge, 1933), p. 60. This work is hereafter referred to as *EM*.

2. ibid., p. 58.
3. ibid., pp. 4, 82, 347, 349, 350.
4. ibid., p. 151.
5. ibid., pp. 73f., 77f., 329, 345f.
6. *On Human Conduct* (Clarendon Press, Oxford, 1975), p. 30. This work is hereafter referred to as *HC*.
7. ibid., p. 3.
8. ibid., p. 57.
9. ibid., pp. 3, 17, 19. Sometimes Oakeshott equates theorems and postulates; on other occasions he distinguishes them. This is also the case with his distinction between features and postulates. On several occasions a characteristic is presented both as a feature and a postulate; for example, pp. 109, and 111, where law and justice are presented as both features and postulates.
10. ibid., p. 10; see also *EM*, p. 347.
11. *HC*, pp. 25, 33.
12. ibid., pp. 59, 86, 112.
13. ibid., p. 55.
14. ibid., pp. 56, 58, 86, 120.
15. ibid., p. 79.
16. ibid., pp. 55, 63. Arendt generally prefers verbs, Marcuse nouns, and Rawls adjectives. The differences spring from their different ontologies.
17. ibid., pp. 60, 62
18. ibid., pp. 114, 116, 117.
19. ibid., p. 121.
20. ibid., pp. 119, 242, 314, 316, 317, 319; see also 'On Misunderstanding Human Conduct', *Political Theory*, IV, 1976, pp. 356, 366.
21. 'The Vocabulary of a Modern European State', *Political Studies*, XXIII, 1975, p. 340.
22. *HC*, p. 119.
23. ibid., pp. 242, 313.
24. *Political Theory*, p. 367; *HC*, pp. 158, 168.
25. *HC*, p. 122.
26. ibid., pp. 128f., 138.
27. ibid., p. 149.
28. ibid., pp. 142, 143. Although judges and the police are engaged in ruling, they are not rulers. The 'civil rulers' rule by means of them. Oakeshott seems to think that although all *cives* are subjects, only those are *ruled* who have had anything to do with the courts and the police. In other words, only the delinquent are ruled. But for them, civil association would not need ruling. This would suggest that Oakeshott does not really need the concept of a civil ruler.

29. ibid., p. 158.
30. ibid., p. 168.
31. ibid., p. 154.
32. ibid., p. 156.
33. For Oakeshott revolutions and civil wars are not politics, for they signify dissent from the authority of *respublica*; see *HC*, p. 164,
34. For Oakeshott there is 'no place in civil association for so-called "distributive justice"'. A distribution of substantive benefits or advantages 'requires a rule of distribution and a distributor in possession of what is to be distributed, but *lex* cannot be a rule of distribution of this sort, and civil rulers have nothing to distribute'.
35. *HC*, p. 180; see also *Rationalism in Politics* (Methuen, London, 1962), p. 124.
36. *HC*, p. 314.
37. 'The Vocabulary of a Modern European State', pp. 320f.
38. ibid., pp. 321, 335, 421f.
39. *HC*, p. 323.

Chapter 6: KARL POPPER

1. *The Logic of Scientific Discovery* (Hutchinson, London, 1962), p. 15. This work is hereafter referred to as *LSD*.
2. *Conjectures and Refutations* (Routledge & Kegan Paul, London, 1963), p. 256. This work is hereafter referred to as *CR*. For a brief and useful statement of Popper's philosophy, see Bryan Magee, *Popper* (Fontana, London, 1973).
3. ibid., p. 257.
4. ibid., pp. 80f.
5. ibid., p. 80.
6. ibid., p. 94.
7. ibid., pp. 193, 194.
8. ibid., p. 82.
9. *LSD*, p. 19.
10. ibid., pp. 15, 19, 22; *CR*, p. 216.
11. *CR*, p. 215.
12. *LSD*, pp. 18, 19, 53; *CR*, p. 31.
13. Paul Arthur Schilpp, *The Philosophy of Karl Popper* (Open Court, La Salle, Illinois, 1974), p. 1036. This work is hereafter referred to as Schilpp. Popper recommends the tradition of rational and critical discussion on the ground that it is 'the only practical way of expanding our knowledge', *CR*, p. 51.
14. ibid., p. 62. See *Open Society and its Enemies* (Routledge &

Kegan Paul, London, 1962), vol. II, p. 371, where Popper uses the terms epistemology and methodology interchangeably. This work is hereafter referred to as *OS*.

15. *OS*, II, pp. 373f.
16. ibid., p. 391; *CR*, pp. 9, 25.
17. *OS*, II, pp. 375, 377.
18. *CR*, pp. 5ff.
19. *OS*, II, p. 260.
20. 'The Logic of Social Sciences', in Theodor Adorno *et al.*, *The Positivist Dispute in Sociology* (Heinemann, London, 1976), p. 104.
21. ibid., p. 90.
22. Schilpp, pp. 199, 114.
23. *OS*, II, pp. 369f., 396.
24. *CR*, p. 197.
25. *LSD*, p. 50.
26. *CR*, p. 199.
27. *OS*, II, p. 376.
28. ibid., p. 221; *Positivist Dispute*, pp. 88f., 95, 293.
29. *OS*, II, pp. 224f.
30. Schilpp, pp. 1090, 1091, 1152, 1154.
31. ibid., p. 1089; *CR*, p. 362.
32. *Positivist Dispute*, pp. 102f.
33. Schilpp, p. 718; *CR*, pp. 198, 199.
34. Schilpp, p. 53.
35. ibid., pp. 1065, 1071f., 1078.
36. ibid., pp. 1147, 1078.
37. ibid., p. 1148.
38. ibid., p. 1112.
39. ibid., p. 1065.
40. Schilpp, pp. 149f. For a good discussion, see Anthony O'Hear, *Karl Popper* (Routledge & Kegan Paul, London, 1980), pp. 171f.
41. *OS*, I, p. 24.
42. ibid., pp. 23, 110.
43. ibid., p. 114.
44. ibid., p. 109; *OS*, II, p. 162.
45. *OS*, II, p. 237.
46. *CR*, p. 346.
47. *OS*, I, pp. 284f.; *OS*, II, p. 304; *CR*, p. 361.
48. *OS*, I, p. 285; *CR*, p. 361.
49. *OS*, I, pp. 157f., 167f.; *OS*, II, pp. 333f.; *Poverty of Historicism* (Routledge & Kegan Paul, London, 1969), pp. 158f. This work is hereafter referred to as *Poverty*. For a good discussion, see John Gray, 'The Liberalism of Karl Popper', *Government and Opposition*, XI, 1976, pp. 342f.
50. *OS*, II, p. 334; *Poverty*, p. 68.
51. *Poverty*, pp. 46, 69, 83ff.

52. *OS*, I, pp. 158, 161, 163, 281, 291.
53. ibid., p. 285. Popper observes, 'if there could be such a thing as socialism combined with individual liberty, I would be a socialist still', Schilpp, p. 27.
54. *OS*, I, pp. 158, 167.
55. ibid., pp. 158, 159.
56. *OS*, II, p. 222; Schilpp, p. 1025.
57. *OS*, I, pp. 163, 167, 285.
58. *OS*, II, p. 206; *Poverty*, p. 75.
59. *OS*, I, p. 111.
60. *OS*, I, pp. 172f., 202; *CR*, p. 132.
61. *OS*, II, p. 242.
62. *OS*, I, p. 294.
63. *OS*, I, pp. 144.
64. ibid., pp. 124f.; *OS*, II, p. 151.
65. *OS*, I, p. 265.
66. OS, II, p. 151.
67. *OS*, I, p. 265.
68. *OS*, II, pp. 124f., 335, 338.
69. ibid., p. 130.
70. ibid., pp. 132, 331.
71. ibid., pp. 238, 357.
72. ibid., p. 369.
73. Schilpp, p. 91, where Popper observes that the theory of knowledge is 'decisive' for our attitudes to ourselves and political life; see also ibid., p. 1053, where he says that his 'emphasis on criticism' represents the 'unity' of his theoretical and practical writings.
74. For different views on the unity of Popper's work, see Gray; 'The Liberalism of Karl Popper'.
75. *Positivist Dispute*, p. 291.
76. *CR*, p. 132.
77. Schilpp, p. 855.
78. ibid., pp. 119, 598.
79. ibid., pp. 1151f.
80. *OS*, I, p. 125; *OS*, II, p. 385.
81. *CR*, p. 356.

Chapter 7: JOHN RAWLS

1. *A Theory of Justice* (Clarendon Press, Oxford, 1972), pp. 46f., 577f.
2. ibid., p. 47.
3. ibid., p. 48.
4. ibid., p. 20. For Rawls principles of justice are to cohere with our 'considered judgements duly pruned and adjusted', ibid.
5. ibid., p. 49.

6. ibid., p. 52.
7. ibid., p. 50.
8. ibid., pp. 19, 20, 364.
9. ibid., p. 391.
10. ibid., pp. 581f.
11. ibid., p. 5.
12. ibid., p. 10.
13. ibid., p. 7.
14. See his essay in P. Laslett and J. Fishkin (eds.), *Philosophy, Politics and Society*, 5th Series (Basil Blackwell, Oxford, 1979), pp. 10f.
15. ibid., pp. 51, 175, 581.
16. ibid., pp. 130f.
17. ibid., pp. 19, 252, 253, 255. Following Kant, Rawls calls this 'negative freedom'.
18. ibid., p. 92.
19. ibid., p. 584.
20. ibid., pp. 147, 255, 256.
21. ibid., p. 136.
22. ibid., pp. 175f.
23. ibid., p. 6.
24. ibid., p. 512.
25. ibid., p. 303.
26. ibid., p. 302.
27. ibid., p. 61. *Philosophy, Politics and Society*, p. 12.
28. *A Theory of Justice*, p. 204.
29. ibid., pp. 152, 542, 543. It is interesting that Rawls equates level of civilization with the satisfaction of basic wants.
30. ibid., p. 73.
31. ibid., p. 84.
32. ibid., p. 199.
33. ibid., p. 200.
34. ibid., p. 223.
35. ibid., p. 356.
36. ibid., p. 275f.
37. ibid., p. 331f.
38. ibid., p. 112f.
39. ibid., p. 114.
40. ibid., p. 337.
41. ibid., p. 114f.
42. ibid., pp. 114, 335f.
43. ibid., p. 116; see also p. 376, where Rawls says that 'only the more favoured members of society are likely to have a clear political obligation as opposed to a political duty.'
44. ibid., p. 335.
45. ibid., p. 363.
46. ibid., p. 391.

47. ibid., pp. 371f.
48. ibid., p. 373.
49. ibid., pp. 374, 375.
50. ibid., p. 366.
51. ibid., pp. 381, 382.
52. ibid., p. 19. Rawls frequently uses the terms 'natural' and 'reasonable' as well as such expressions as 'We can affirm', 'We think', 'We are confident' and 'I assume that there is a broad measure of agreement.' It would be useful to examine each of these in order to identify the group on whose behalf he speaks. This point is well illustrated by Brian Barry, *The Liberal Theory of Justice* (Clarendon Press, Oxford, 1973).
53. ibid., pp. 14, 15.
54. ibid., p. 182, where Rawls gives a weak defence of his position against the charge of utilitarianism. He does not notice that it is not so much the motive for adopting the principles of justice as his defence of them that is utilitarian. For him the original position exemplifies the moral way of thinking and is recaptured every time we think morally. Hence utilitarianism characterizes his view of moral thinking.
55. ibid., p. viii.
56. Italics added.
57. *A Theory of Justice*, p. 159.
58. ibid., pp. 72, 73, 74, 311, 312.
59. ibid., p. 15.
60. ibid., p. 178.
61. ibid., pp. 16, 17.
62. For a useful discussion, see Benjamin Barber's 'Justifying Justice' in Norman Daniels (ed.), *Reading Rawls* (Basil Blackwell, Oxford, 1975), pp. 283f.
63. *A Theory of Justice*, p. 363.

Chapter 8: SOME REFLECTIONS

1. I have discussed it at length in my *Marx's Theory of Ideology* (Croom Helm, London, 1981).
2. For a perceptive discussion, see Larry Siedentop, 'Two Liberal Traditions', in A. Ryan (ed.), *The Idea of Freedom: Essays in Honour of Isaiah Berlin* (Oxford University Press, Oxford, 1979), pp. 153ff.
3. Berlin himself says that his idea of liberty is that of 'the classical English philosophers', *Four Essays on Liberty* (Oxford University Press, London, 1969), p. 123.
4. There are, of course, some exceptions. The British idealists take a positive view of liberty. However, this is because they are taken to be under Hegelian influence. There are also some French philosophers

who subscribe to negative liberty, but they are very few and largely exceptions to the rule. Berlin's list of the champions of positive liberty includes Spinoza, Rousseau, Kant, Fichte, Hegel, Marx, Comte and Montesquieu.

5. *On Human Conduct* (Clarendon Press, Oxford, 1975), pp. 301,302, 321.

6. See my *Hannah Arendt and the Search for a New Political Philosophy* (Macmillan, London, 1981), ch. 3.

7. See Oakeshott's excellent last essay in *On Human Conduct*, and Quentin Skinner, *Foundations of Modern Political Thought* (Cambridge University Press, Cambridge, 1979).

8. For a good discussion, see John Dunn, *Western Political Theory in the Face of the Future* (Cambridge University Press, Cambridge, 1979).

9. See Peter Singer's perceptive essay, 'Famine, Affluence and Morality', in P. Laslett and J. Fishkin (eds.), *Philosophy, Politics and Society* (Basil Blackwell, Oxford, 1979), pp. 21ff.

Bibliography

The major works by the philosophers discussed in this book are cited in the Notes. The following *Festschriften* or collections contain exhaustive bibliographies for their respective subjects.

Daniels, Norman   *Reading Rawls* (Basil Blackwell, Oxford, 1975).

King, Preston, and Parekh, B. C.   *Politics and Experience: Essays in Honour of Michael Oakeshott* (Cambridge University Press, Cambridge, 1968). Bibliography updated by J. L. Auspitz in *Political Theory*, 4, 1976.

Kontos, Alkis   *Powers, Possessions and Freedom: Essays in Honour of C. B. Macpherson* (University of Toronto Press, Toronto, 1979).

Ryan, Alan (ed.)   *The Idea of Freedom: Essays in Honour of Isaiah Berlin* (Oxford University Press, Oxford, 1979).

Schilpp, Paul Arthur   *The Philosophy of Karl Popper*, vols. I and II (Open Court, La Salle, Illinois, 1974).

Index